Minuit

Steven D. Spalding

MINUIT

DALKEY ARCHIVE PRESS
Dallas / Dublin

First Dalkey Archive edition, 2023

Library of Congress Catalog-in-Publication Data: Available.

Isbn Paperback: 978-1-62897-399-0
Isbn Ebook: 978-1-62897-420-1

Interior design by Anuj Mathur
Cover design by Kit Schluter

www.dalkeyarchive.com
Dallas / Dublin

Printed on permanent/durable acid-free paper.

TABLE OF CONTENTS

ACKNOWLEDGMENTS

I owe a deep debt of gratitude to a number of people who have given generously of their time, encouragement, and support over the years. Looming large at the origins of this project are Ross Chambers, whose thoughtful and wise guidance was always a pure act of intellectual generosity, and Anne Simonin, whose work revealed so much about the fascinating wartime origins of the publishing firm whose story is examined here. Her assistance at this book's beginnings helped spark my fascination with that firm's unique destiny and my passion for exploring *la suite*. Marie-Claire Ropars-Wuilleumier, whose remarkable lines of thought—perhaps better termed as incarnating a unique kind of line of flight—I have never ceased to admire. Her kind and inspiring role at the origins of this project cannot go unacknowledged. Helping me variously in the trenches thereafter have been many dear friends and colleagues, including Todd Reeser, Arnaud Buchs, Ben Fraser, Grace An, Elizabeth Knutson, and Thomas Wagener—to name just a few. I thank the institutions, colleagues and students that have shaped my perhaps highly irregular though immensely rewarding path through academia: Université de Paris VIII Vincennes-Saint-Denis, University of Michigan, Université de Lausanne, University of Utah, Oberlin College, Christopher

Newport University, and the United States Naval Academy.

Most of all I thank my three angels, Karine, Eva, and Emery.

Minuit

INTRODUCTION: TOWARD A SOCIOLOGY OF LITERARY VALUE

How does a novel accrue value? How do certain new and unknown authors and their works make their way from obscurity into the pantheon of the greats, or—at least—the firmament of the stars? What does studying the trajectory of certain authors or works teach us about the structure of culture, and the role of literature in it? These are the basic questions to which this book seeks to establish the elements of an answer.

My work stems from the supposition that the value of literature has always and *a priori* hinged on an historically defined set of discourses. Few would contest the assertion that how many Americans think about literature has changed dramatically over the last two or three decades. From the canon debates and political correctness of the 1980s and 1990s, to the rise of Cultural Studies as a relatively or at least somewhat partially institutionalized discipline, and the advent of technologies impacting how and what we read in the 1990s, 2000s and beyond, significant portions of American society have engaged, in one way or another, in a reconsideration of the notion of literary value. Similar forces have altered the place, role, and prestige of literature and literary culture in France, including new technologies of leisure and changes in its education system. More so than in the United States, which seems to have far fewer qualms with—and much less at stake in—a decline of the literary, French culture has traditionally defined itself and its exceptionalism *through* its literary culture: one only has to witness the routine—even annual—hand-wringing in the French press over the reading habits of the younger generations. Although the reasons for this do fall beyond the purview of this book, *how* it is so that at certain moments in French cultural history, literature—and widely considered "difficult" literature at that—enjoyed a certain national role, is indeed within the scope of the present work. Through its tight focus on the fortunes of one small literary publisher, my work sets out to develop a history of the valuation of literature in France at particular key cultural moments, and to examine both the historical agents and nature of certain discourses of literary value.

The purposes for doing so are two-fold. First, I am interested in articulating literary history with broader cultural history, in an effort to combat the tradition of approaching literature and discourses of literary value as purely self-defined, self-confined, or even self-sufficient phenomena. Literature has always stood in a position of only very relative autonomy with respect to political, economic, and cultural forces. And so my second purpose has been to examine the specific cultural and historical factors that mediate the autonomy of the literary field at given points in the history of twentieth-century France.

In what follows, I introduce the two main components of this undertaking: the sociologist whose thinking on the structure of literary culture provides many of the theoretical underpinnings of my work, and the publishing house whose extraordinary trajectory across French cultural history allows us to peer into the workings of French publishing and literary culture. I then briefly describe the steps each chapter takes toward situating that publisher, Editions de Minuit, within the competing discourses of value organizing the literary field.

During the sixty years that followed its inception as a clandestine press in Nazi-occupied France, Editions de Minuit succeeded in creating and sustaining a significant place for itself in the French cultural landscape, often against difficult odds. One sign of its success is the preponderant space given many of its authors in most literary studies covering the period of Editions de Minuit's existence so far; it is clear that most, if not all scholars and readers of twentieth-century French literature would be able to recognize the publisher's enduring imprint. Much of what is considered canonical French literature from the latter half of the century originally bore the Minuit stamp, from the major works of Samuel Beckett, Claude Simon, and Marguerite Duras, to those of Alain Robbe-Grillet. This book asks where Minuit found itself in French literary culture at the end-of-century, on the eve of the age of digital and internet media, and how it secured that position. To do so, I tell parts of the publisher's history, with the aim that broader changes in the system of cultural production can be discovered through the story of Minuit. While others have written parts of Minuit's history, my intention is to contribute new elements to the writing of that history. I focus on discrete moments in the history of Minuit in order to bring to the surface elements of a sociological analysis of literary value. My work is an attempt at cultural history, and at re-situating literature—specifically novels—within the very processes of dissemination and reception that imbue them with significance. To this end, I not only present important moments in Minuit's history, but also describe the principal components of the French literary culture during each time period.

The setting for each study is essentially the same—the Parisian literary world and the domains with which it overlaps—but the structural conditions governing that world changed considerably from one time period to the next. By measuring these changes and detecting their impact on cultural production and its valuation, I intend for the case of Editions de Minuit to contribute to how students and scholars of French culture understand the nexus of literary and cultural discourses that bears upon the value of literature.

In his 1996 essay *On Television*, Pierre Bourdieu delivers a critical assessment of television and its impact on cultural production, describing what he considers the intellectually impoverishing effects of television journalism.[1] While the specific grounds and aim of his critique are not of immediate concern to my project, in his essay Bourdieu accomplishes something of great interest: by reintroducing several of the most important sociological concepts from his work since the 60s into the specifically contemporary conjuncture of the late 1990s, Bourdieu is effectively updating those terms, and re-casting his vision of French culture in the light of the new subject of television. His essay can be read as a classic Bourdieusian approach, deploying his signature terms in a simplified form for the non-academic audience he is addressing,[2] but such a reading would overlook the way in which *On Television* functions as a supplement to his more extensive academic works, especially *The Rules of Art*, revealing a set of conditions that challenges the system described by his theory of culture.[3] *On Television* thus lends itself well as a key for certain concepts from Bourdieu's work that I put to use throughout this book; as a passkey, *On Television* will also lead us toward earlier works by Bourdieu, which furnish the basic conceptual tools for the sociology of literary value I pursue.

On Television echoes most directly *The Rules of Art* and

provides glosses of much of the analytic of culture established therein. Instead of the "literary field" of *The Rules of Art*, however, Bourdieu writes about the field of journalism.[4] What is a "field," and what are its limits? What is the relationship between a field and agents within it? What guides the relationships among agents in fields, and among fields? Bourdieu's thinking supplies an eminently practical grasp of the structural relations governing cultural agency:

> Un champ est un espace social structuré, un champ de forces—il y a des dominants et des dominés, il y a des rapports constants, permanents, d'inégalité qui s'exercent à l'intérieur de cet espace—qui est aussi un champ de luttes pour transformer ou conserver ce champ de forces. Chacun, à l'intérieur de cet univers, engage dans sa concurrence avec les autres la force (relative) qu'il détient et qui définit sa position dans le champ et, en conséquence, ses stratégies.
>
> ~
>
> A field is a structured social space, a field of forces, a force field. It contains people who dominate and others who are dominated. Constant, permanent relationships of inequality operate inside this space, which at the same time becomes a space in which the various actors struggle for the transformation or preservation of the field. All the individuals in this universe bring to the competition all the (relative) power at their disposal.[5]

Fields are marked by an internal logic of competitive contest among the particular exertions of force, or power, by each agent within each field. Agents struggle to change or sustain the overall structure of domination that holds each of them in balance at any given moment, and determines the relative strength of their position within the field. The differential measure of strength from agent to agent embodies the *objective relations of force* that constitute the field and pre-determine the strategies employed by each agent.[6]

One may be led to ask, how useful is it to speak of fields? The term is a common metaphor for the contexts in which people work; Bourdieu's use of the term conveys a compelling image of the complexity of cultural systems that resonates with the—also common—perception that the realm of productive activity is constantly ramifying. Bourdieu's elaboration of the concept of fields gives it specificity and transparency, making it a valuable historical tool for designating a system with an internal relational structure as well as an external one. Fields are both structural and permeable.

Minuit's publishing history and strategies form a lens with which to re-construct different states of the literary field in France, and the first axiom of this project is the synchronic analysis of relational positionality: that is, taking snapshots of positions among key figures (agents for Bourdieu) at specific points in time. Yet this supposition requires nuancing. The emphasis on relationality among agents grounds Bourdieu's sociology in an especially *readerly* mode of cultural criticism—something perhaps more akin to recent kinds of cultural studies than to traditional sociology.[7] I say *readerly*, since his theory invokes a practice of critical reading that translates such signifiers as "field," "agent," and "objective relations of force" into an historical analysis of individuals and organizations operating within a given context at a given time. The discourses structuring agents' activities—which Bourdieu's sociology ultimately seeks to critique—can be decoded from within the positions described in the above citation. The analytic of fields requires two important nuances: first, there is the fundamental importance of factors external to the field itself, which invites the need to account for the overlap among certain fields. This point is never fully heard in Bourdieu's work, but can be deduced from the comparison of specific examples of his texts (I pursue this comparison presently). External factors can impact upon and provoke profound transformations to the very terms of relational positionality among constituents of a field. Secondly, the notion of field as Bourdieu defined it above places all the constituents of a field in some form of concrete relationship; in contrast, I suggest that each position in a field offers its own specific discourse of *its* field, and that relational positionality can sometimes articulate itself in exclusive terms. In such a case, one constituent would claim to belong to a different field than another, but this does not justify redrawing the limits of the field; instead, I construct the French literary field to encompass all those parties that venture into the "field of struggle"—to take Bourdieu's term—in which the definition of proper, or legitimate, literature is at stake. It is a field on which much ink is spilt to theorize, claim, or deny the status of literature, in the modes of conservation or transformation.

That is not to suggest that Bourdieu focuses only on the internal structures of fields: rather, his sociology seeks to reveal the implicit, hidden, true *distinctions* that order the social. "Field" is a sign for categorizing sets of orders that together make up the cultural sphere. We have seen how Bourdieu seeks to pinpoint the internal structure of fields, designating their structural hierarchies; what, now, of this larger encompassing structural order? *On Television* further defines fields, again in the context of the field of journalism, this time viewed from "above":

> Le monde du journalisme est un microcosme qui a ses lois propres et qui est défini par sa position dans

> le monde global, et par les attractions, les répulsions qu'il subit de la part des autres microcosmes. Dire qu'il est autonome, qu'il a sa propre loi, c'est dire que *ce qui s'y passe ne peut pas être compris de manière directe à partir de facteurs extérieurs.*

> Journalism is a microcosm with its own laws, defined both by its position in the world at large and by the attractions and repulsions to which it is subject from other such microcosms. To say that it is independent or autonomous, that it has its own laws, is to say that *what happens in it cannot be understood by looking only at external factors.*[8]

Bourdieu's terminology borrows from chemistry: autonomous fields are buffeted by one another like atoms, yet their internal positive and negative forces are more determinant of their makeup than external ones. They are defined by a differential relational structure similar to the spectrum of positions within each field; as microcosms, the hierarchical structures governing each of the fields are homologous to the structure of the overall system of fields. Yet the matter of autonomy in the second part of the quote is problematical—are all fields autonomous in the same way, and is autonomy merely an elision of the *indirect* external factors that *do* in fact determine the hierarchies of the fields? Taken together, the concepts of autonomy and field seem antithetical: in this regard a comparison of *The Rules of Art* and *On Television* is instructive: one text describes the gaining of intellectual freedom that is portrayed as greatly imperiled in the other.

The apparent contradiction only resolves itself, in my view, by granting that autonomy is a rare and unusual condition of fields, and that in each field autonomy is distributed unevenly.

The problem of autonomy is central to the narrative of *The Rules of Art*. Much like that text, *On Television* traces the appearance of a new configuration of certain cultural fields, with the enormous difference that this new configuration effects a loss of autonomy. In the former text, the new literary and artistic aesthetic appearing in the late nineteenth century is a major achievement for art and literature, against bourgeois commercialism. In the latter text, commercialism is the driving force working behind television to damage the autonomy of certain fields. One would want the second text to speak to the first: what of the autonomy of the literary field, in the age of television? The answer, I suggest, has to do with the difficult difference between internal and external factors of change to the field in question.

For Bourdieu's system, the proposition that external factors—such as the logic determining which fields are culturally dominant, for instance—are held in check by laws internal to each field creates the possibility of escape from the structural determinism weighing heavily on the agents of any given field. There is tension, in *The Rules of Art*, between the critical task of accounting for the structural parameters conditioning—threatening even to (over-)determine—individual agency, and the desire to identify a privileged domain of intellectual freedom somewhere in the fields of culture. Yet ultimately art and literature are set within the contexts of their respective fields, subject to mediation by the conditions of each; in the television essay, television is an uncontained force that imposes its own law on the field of journalism, and potentially on all the others. This law, which Bourdieu names after the term for television's audience ratings system ("*audimat*"), expresses the logic of viewer-appeal, and is in essence the law of the market: already limited by a self-reinforcing framework of consensus, journalism is being led, for the sake of commercialism and market share, to produce a non-democratic homogeneity of public discourse. What prevents the "*lectorat*"—a term generally referring to the reading public, though here Bourdieu means the tastes and preferences of the reading public—from performing the same function as that of the *audimat* and disrupting the intellectual autonomy of the literary field? How well does the literary field manage to negotiate the powerful law of commercialism? This question leads us to consider the third complement and last of conceptual categories I borrow from Bourdieu, after those of "fields" and "autonomy," that of *value*.

Part of the interest of Bourdieu's work for literature scholars lies in its contextualization of what is sometimes attributed as inherent to literary works: their value. Traditionally imputed to the works themselves as an intrinsic, and—to the cultivated reader—evident, durable aspect of great literature, in Bourdieu's analysis, value acquires a double social dimension: articulated both in response to, and through, structures of social relations. The study of Flaubert in *The Rules of Art* illustrates the first of these aspects by exploring the social *address* of his aesthetic project[9]—the theory of "art for art's sake" is also a literary aesthetic that invests value in a particular way, aimed at re-orienting a given configuration of the then-nascently autonomous literary field. The second social dimension manifests itself via the structures of reception that preside over short-term and long-term assignations of value to works and their authors. Before further addressing matters of value specific to the literary field, a brief detour to Bourdieu's earlier work, *Distinction: A Social Critique of the Judgement of Taste*[10] can provide some important considerations adjacent to—although curiously underplayed in—the lexicon of value in *The Rules of Art*.

Distinction analyzes cultural habits of consumption as produced by a system of taste, which is in turn determined by a rigid, class-based system of education. The educational system produces belief in the literal "value" of knowledge, presented as hierarchical. The hierarchies of class and taste, reproduced in and by the schools, are reflected in the social order of "lifestyles," a spectrum opposing legitimate, aristocratic practices from all others.[11] The amount of educational training one has amounts to their sum of *educational capital*. The grid of values asserted by the social structure is also inscribed in cultural objects[12]: they betoken investments in certain practices, lifestyles, political positions, and tastes, and the conditions that make such investments possible. In the context of the social realm of meaning, the term "value" acquires a willfully economic meaning: social distinction and taste are grounded in the material conditions of the uneven capitalist distribution of wealth. This provides an initial hypothesis in response to the question I raised above as to the law of commercialism in the literary field: *Distinction* leads us to suspect that commercialism is both subject to and attenuated by the competing discourses of taste, which are informed by class and educational capital. Thus, consumer demand is differenciated and allows a spectrum of autonomous literary aesthetics to flourish, each with their corresponding partisans among the reading public.

Pursuing the economic metaphor further, taste in *Distinction* equates to a logic of investments of value: the return on the investment in any given object is *symbolic capital*. An intangible commodity, symbolic capital represents all the rewards borne by social prestige and respectability; although only implied in *Distinction*, foremost among the benefits of symbolic capital is admittance into the "aristocracy of culture" and into the concomitant processes devoted to the reproduction of legitimate culture, such as the body of knowledge sanctioned by the system of education.

Distinction presents an economics of culture that discerns the economic and political valences of cultural goods. Bourdieu's argument has its strengths and weaknesses: on the one hand, it is clear that the crucial importance he gives to the role of the educational system in disseminating a structure of taste needs to be retained for an analysis of literary culture. I extend this role to the immediate tastemakers of the literary field as well, including publishers and journalists (I will return to this shortly). On the other hand, his analysis of the correlation between educational capital and cultural capital assumes a high correlation between class, education, and taste. Overestimating the exchange value between educational capital and cultural capital, Bourdieu excludes the possibility for the educational field—and its system of values—to become further and further divorced from the values of the social field, and thereby cede its authority over taste to other quarters. Similarly, his conception of the social field has powerful potential for linking discourses which may at first appear disparate, as the space in which economics, politics, and the literary/artistic fields negotiate the actual configuration of culture is perforce many-sided. However, Bourdieu overvalues the elite dominance of taste, and underestimates the impact of processes of democratization on the different systems of capital—cultural, educational, and symbolic. By stressing the "aristocracy of culture," he creates a blind-spot with respect to the changing configurations of value in late-capitalist, globalizing economies. We now turn to *The Rules of Art*, to a chapter focused specifically on literary goods that elaborates the theory of cultural objects begun in *Distinction*.

Of Bourdieu's work, "The Market for Symbolic Goods" provides his fullest account of the specific economy of the literary field. Throughout the text, Minuit appears as an example of one pole of his spectrum of types of cultural producers, and there are several other elements to retain for our purposes. Foremost among them is the placing of symbolic capital in contradistinction to economic capital:

> "Economic" capital cannot guarantee the specific profits offered by the field—and by the same token the "economic" profits that they will often bring in time—unless it is reconverted into symbolic capital. The only legitimate accumulation, for the author as for the critic, for the art dealer as for the publisher or theater director, consists in making a name for oneself, a name that is known and recognized, *the capital of consecration*—implying a power to consecrate objects [. . .] or people [. . .] and hence of giving them value, and of making profits from this operation.[13]

Bourdieu is describing the ideal functioning of what I call the structure of reception. The "specific profits offered by the field" are a fundamental part of the field's autonomy: value, in the literary field, is created by transfers of symbolic capital within a heavily coded system of positions, each of which correspond to a relative amount of power to consecrate. Sustaining the belief that these positions are autonomous with respect to the law of commercialism is a key part of their discourse. Paradoxically, in the economic metaphor the term "position" becomes the sign of possession of symbolic *capital*: the fields of art and literature are imitative in their refusal of commercialism. It should be clear from this model how coterminous the aims, and destinies, of author and publisher are, and the importance of the strategies of the latter to the consecration of the former. On the one hand, as Bourdieu reports from one of his sources, "a publisher [. . .] is his catalogue," but so, too, is the success of the authors dependant upon the ability of the publisher to accumulate and maintain a maximum of symbolic capital.[14]

That symbolic capital resides in the belief in certain authorities and in the value of the end results of their exertions; this belief is produced either in the social field by the orders of taste (class, education), according to *Distinction*, or now, alternatively in the literary field by publishers, authors, and critics. In its description of the structure of the literary field, *The Rules of Art* reduces the importance of class, education, and even political valences in understanding the orientations of the cultural producers—these factors are not considered directly relevant to the literary field. The education system, for instance, only plays a role "post mortem, and after a long process," even though its long-term role is definitive, as it creates "a converted public."[15] Both of these assertions are contradicted by the example of Minuit, which highlights the educational field's capability of imparting symbolic capital in the literary field on the one hand, and on the other its inability to produce a reading public for the field's products.

By extending Bourdieu's model, we can say that the *patterns of circulation* of symbolic capital give the literary field shape, and reveal the emergence of newly consecrated positions and/or the resurgence of established ones. Bourdieu terms the stakes of what I'm calling patterns of circulation as a "struggle" for the power to define what is legitimate.[16] This is close to the struggle described in *Distinction* over dominant taste. Bourdieu seems clearly to have the New Novel in mind when he characterizes the essence of the struggle as temporal, between

> those who have already left their mark and are trying to endure, and those who cannot make their own

> marks in their turn without consigning to the past those who have an interest in stopping time, in eternalizing the present state; between the dominants whose strategy is tied to continuity, identity, and reproduction, and the dominated, the new entrants whose interest is in discontinuity, rupture, difference and revolution. *Faire date* is at once to make a new position exist beyond established positions, ahead of those positions, en avant-garde, and in introducing difference, to produce time itself.[17]

The contest for symbolic capital, then, is always generational, and the literary field a living history in perpetual revolution. Again, the example of Minuit provides conflicting evidence for this model. In one instance, the story of Minuit's achievement of a position rich in symbolic capital via the New Novel, Bourdieu's assertions have an obvious literal relevance; in the other, Minuit's second phase, the structure of the field has evolved in such a way as to make Bourdieu's dialectical model appear outdated.

The texts by Pierre Bourdieu that I have discussed have helped to generate the contours of a hermeneutic tailored to the questions guiding this book involving the changing value of literature in France. Positionality, the makeup of and structural relations among the cultural zones of production classed into fields, the orders of taste in the cultural aristocracy, the laws of consecration and succession particular to the literary field, the circulation of—or struggle for—symbolic capital: these are the conceptual tools used to construct the historical analyses of this book.

I begin that historical analysis in Chapter I with a look at Editions de Minuit's failure to convert the high prestige of its clandestine activity into capital success in the immediate postwar period. How could the publisher's greatest strength, that of incarnating resistant France during Vichy and the Occupation, turn into its greatest liability? Bourdieu's positionality points us toward understanding the complex dynamics at work at the time. I explore the contrast between Sartre's rise as France's foremost writer-intellectual and Minuit's decline; a paradoxical turn of events, since each defined literature in strikingly similar ways.

The departure of its publisher, Vercors, from Minuit in 1948 signaled Vecors's defeat in the chase for cultural capital engaged in by the new intellectual milieu formed at Liberation. The best solution for Minuit's difficulties, it appeared to its new publisher, Jérôme Lindon, was to depart from Vercors's publishing vision entirely. By examining the set of associations and alliances Lindon initiated in the early 1950s, I discuss in Chapter II how Bataille's journal *Critique*, the publication of Samuel Beckett, and the arrival of Robbe-Grillet each contributed differently to the re-invention of Editions de Minuit as a serious literary publisher. I examine Lindon's careful crafting of a particular image for the Minuit imprint, and the development of an editorial collaboration with Robbe-Grillet that had, from the beginning, certain modernist inclinations. The critical support lent by Barthes upon the publication of Robbe-Grillet's first two novels reinforced Lindon's and Robbe-Grillet's burgeoning editorial line and endowed it with a critical vocabulary that emphasized its newness and vitality. Barthes's theme of newness galvanized Lindon's reinvention of Minuit as an outsider with claims on high literature.

Chapter III focuses on the initial period of the New Novel: the creation of the name, and the shaping of Minuit's editorial line to capitalize on the name. I look at Minuit's role in producing the New Novel, as well as the New Novel's place in Minuit's publishing. By accompanying its publications with various strategies of promotion, Minuit provided both an enigmatic publishing product and a discourse of legitimization for that product. Indeed, Minuit's marketing techniques are important artifacts that reveal much about the creation of value. The Minuit catalog, I argue, needs to be viewed as a claim on a total vision of literary and intellectual French culture. In it, the New Novel appeared alongside Lindon's agressively committed stance against the Algerian War, showing not only the separation of literature from political engagement but also how *both* taken together represented the modern readership to which Lindon's Minuit sought to appeal.

After the Algerian War, Minuit's claims on value and cultural capital changed as Lindon turned to new publishing and marketing practices. Chapter IV examines the New Novel's international dimension as well as the usefulness of its performance abroad in making the argument for the New Novel's modernity, an argument whose success I read as dependent on the close association between the New Critical approaches to literature developing in the early 1960s and the New Novel as an exemplary text for those approaches. The New Novel's success is also illustrated in Minuit's literary publishing: Minuit all but stopped publishing new authors in the 60s and centered on publishing the New Novel authors. The New Novel was becoming, as Lindon would fear, an institution. At the same time, Lindon expanded Minuit's publishing in the humanities and social sciences, further strengthening the association between the ongoing New Novel and the newest generation of academics, critics, and intellectuals. The 60s saw a gradual migration of Minuit authors traditionally outside the consecrated institutions of culture into those same institutions, becoming by the latter 60s and early 70s a core part of how French education represented contemporary French culture.

Chapter V examines the post-1968 era of Minuit publishing

through the prism of its in-house literary journal, *Minuit*, published between 1972 and 1982. As a tool for trying out new work by mostly young, unpublished authors, *Minuit* was clearly intended to supply the publisher with new talent. Judging by the journal's inability to establish a new generation of authors in the Minuit catalog, however, *Minuit* seems to have mostly been a failure. A successor for the New Novel only becomes possible at Editions de Minuit in the 80s with the publication of the "young authors." Chapter V examines the conjunction in the closing decades of the twentieth century and the beginning of the 00s of the New Novel's final act and the rapid consecration of the young authors as a kind of rebellious break from the New Novel's long shadow. Their success in the changing arena of mainstream media on the eve of the digital age illustrates how Jérôme Lindon's efforts to reinvent Minuit once again and lay claim to literary value paid off.

CHAPTER I

Minuit's Failed Venture in Committed Literature

I take up the history of Editions de Minuit at a time when everything seemed to be going to the publishing house's advantage. Minuit was on the side of the victors in 1944. As France's political left emerged from clandestinity with new strength and legitimacy, so too did the cultural left—comprised mainly of those who participated in the literary Resistance. The formerly underground organization was now an important sign of the enduring spirit of the nation. Riding into legitimacy with the prevailing political movement and affiliated with most of its members, Minuit ought to have experienced an easy and successful reconversion. Instead, from the moment it ceased to be an outlawed organization, Minuit began to decline. The attempt to make the clandestine organ of resistance into a strong participant in the field of French letters, alongside the older and established houses, was a failure. Tied closely to the re-ordering of the literary field in the immediate postwar period, Minuit's failure signified the end of its venture in committed literature, precipitated the crisis in which it lost its founder and figurehead, Vercors, and established the conditions for a new start, beginning in late 1948, under the direction of Jérôme Lindon. This chapter seeks to understand Minuit's failure through the divisions within the literary Resistance under occupation, and traces the fate of different wings of that cultural bloc in the immediate postwar.

In part one, I report information that brings to attention how it was that Minuit found itself on the verge of financial collapse as early as 1948. Its cultural capital was bound up with that of Vercors, its publisher since its inception and an important member of the Comité National des Ecrivains (CNE).[1] Minuit's fortune in the immediate postwar years is a remarkable demonstration of the complex adjustments that constituted France's return to political stability and equilibrium. Those adjustments initially had to do with the bitter political climate—as well as the overall failings—of Libération and épuration, and took different, even contradictory forms.[2]

Many of the contradictions of the postwar literary field are bound up in France's embrace of Sartre, whose rising star contrasts sharply with that of Vercors's Editions de Minuit. Sartre's theorization of committed literature made him better suited for the status of France's leading intellectual than his peer Vercors. I argue that they were two sides of one coin: the divestment of capital from Minuit-style writing that foregrounded the memory of Vichy and Occupation went hand in hand with its investment in a Sartrean concept of literature that pushed those memories away. Sartre's success earned capital initially enjoyed by the literary Resistance at Liberation, and appropriated for Gallimard the cultural limelight initially held by Vercors's Minuit. Thus, Minuit's failure under Vercors's direction can be ascribed in large part to Sartre's impact on literary life, giving rise to the unusual conjuncture of demand that placed a high value on Sartre and his theory of literary commitment, while at the same time spurning the committed publications of Minuit and most of the other new producers who, less ambiguously than Sartre, came out of the Resistance.

Still more contradictions crop up in the shifting alliances of the immediate postwar years: by following the literary and political activities of Jean Paulhan up to and after Liberation, I discuss ways in which positions of capital in the *prewar* literary field effected their return, and in so doing helped to close the parenthesis of the war and of the arrival of new post-Resistance producers in the field. A prominent participant in creating the literary Resistance, after Liberation Jean Paulhan turned against the movement and fought hard to undermine and discredit the postwar institutions of the literary Resistance, publishing caustic pamphlets and articles at Gallimard and stinging articles at *La Table ronde*. The 1952 publication of Paulhan's *Lettre aux Directeurs de l'épuration* at Editions de Minuit was an even stronger statement than his earlier texts, since it announced that Minuit was no longer allied with postwar Resistance culture. That shift hinged on the takeover of the publishing house by Jérôme Lindon in 1948. As his tenure as head of Editions de Minuit developed, Lindon departed from Vercors's editorial model and drew inspiration from Paulhan's Gallimard.

Why it was that Vercors's editorial strategy failed to generate new financial or symbolic capital is best understood in terms of the broader tensions and contradictions of the literary field at the time. Sartre and Paulhan are vital to understanding the dynamics of that field and serve to situate Minuit's trajectory from triumphant to moribund as a product of those complex dynamics. Approached via the prism of these three very different positions, Minuit comes across as a victim of its own success: because it was demarcated in uncompromising political terms, its early postwar position became an impediment to its ability to maneuver in the rapidly changing climate of the cultural marketplace.

1. Minuit and the Literary Resistance

Nazi occupation and Vichy were the catalysts of an extraordinary coalition of Resistance writers who rallied around the goal of reclaiming legitimate cultural production for the salvation of the French nation. Despite the origins of Vichy in Third Republic culture, the wartime literary field was a peculiar and lopsided one: many publishing houses and right-wing literary personalities collaborated with the occupying power as part of a concerted effort—along with such institutions as the French Academy—to produce continuity and sustain the French in their belief in the structures of their culture (although the effort no doubt deceived no one).[3] The terrible political and economic realities of life under fascism and economic penury skewed the usual modes of field-production: those realities included the persecution of radicals and specific target-groups—including figures designated as dangerous intellectuals—the Otto List (a list of books banned by the Germans) and censorship by Vichy officials, the increasing material constraints on production such as limits on paper and a limited market for the sale of books and journals. The field of legitimate cultural production thus artificially constituted was—it comes as no surprise—a spectrum of right-wing positions, from ultranationalist, bourgeois, and Catholic Vichyites to pro-European fascist collaborators. In Appendix A, I provide a grid that shows the sanctioned and clandestine positions of the wartime field.

The connections between literature and nation are probably never so important as when nations are diminished by deep political division or serious military threat. Under Nazi Occupation and collaborationist Vichy rule, literary culture was an important instrument of ideological domination and control, further deepening the fractures of a defeated and divided society. A number of recent historical studies have provided extensive accounts of the cultural policies of the Vichy government, of the collaboration by the right-wing literary elite in the occupied zone, and of the strategies and struggles undertaken by a minority to form and sustain an oppositional cultural discourse.[4] It comes as no surprise, then, that the discourse of literary Resistance before and after Liberation promoted its writers as the guardians of true French culture. At war's end, the triumph of the literary left over the right provoked a redistribution of the literary field that was anything but a return to normal—normal understood as something resembling pre-war conditions. Instead, mirroring the exclusionary politics of the Fascist regime, the CNE sought to enforce a ban on writers and publishers tainted by collaboration. Made up principally of writers associated with *Les Lettres Françaises*, which shared writers with Editions de Minuit, the CNE represented the core group of the Parisian literary Resistance. In becoming the publisher of the CNE[5] by early 1943, author and Minuit co-founder Vercors guaranteed a prominent role for himself in that organization.

Many wartime Resistance writers went on to contend for national prestige in the immediate postwar period, expecting to parlay their Resistance credentials into the more substantial cultural capital of what Patricia Ferguson has called the public writer (the *écrivain* as opposed to the *auteur*). Though on very unequal footing in 1944—Vercors enjoyed certain advantages over Sartre—Sartre and Vercors were two of the strongest rivals to become national literary figures. Both represented a kind of committed literature [*littérature engagée*]; and the success of one kind and the failure of the other have much to do with their differences and the different models of engagement to which each subscribed. The kind of figure of cultural authority these writers sought to become was not new to French culture and cultural history. It belongs to a tradition extending as far back, arguably, as Pascal. In her book *Literary France: The Making of a Culture*, Priscilla Ferguson discusses a series of writers—including Voltaire, Rousseau, Hugo and Zola—each of whom incarnated, by her analysis, a certain uniquely French "public writer" position.[6] Her work identifies the kind of national role that literary figures sometimes came to fulfill. At specific moments of crisis, literature, or at least specific literary figures of the hour, provided strong national leadership in the absence of effective political cohesion. Dovetailing with Bourdieu's focus on the changing configurations of the literary field, Ferguson's analysis reminds us of the particularly national role some writers can come to play in offering a heroic image for public consumption. In the example of Vercors and Sartre, the rise of one and fall of the other reflected the expression of readers' choices among opposing cultural priorities.

In 1944, drawing strength from Minuit's reputation and from the success of his own wartime novels, Vercors was a better candidate for becoming a premier public writer than Sartre, despite being an outsider to the established literary field. His activities in the immediate postwar were an extension of the model of literary engagement shaped during the war by the most active members of the literary Resistance, many of whom, initially grouped around *Les Lettres Françaises* and the CNE, continued to constitute the core of Resistance culture in the postwar period. That model predates the influential theory of literary engagement Sartre first articulated in 1945, and corresponds more closely with the kind of engagement exemplified by Mauriac—which I discuss presently—than by Sartre. Before looking at Sartre's theory of commitment and his rise in cultural capital I turn first, then, to the models of literary engagement—very different notions of writer, literature, and nation—that coexisted within the wartime literary

Resistance and informed Vercors's direction of Minuit. It is the image of the openly engaged public writer—the writer as public figure, or celebrity—as opposed to the mysterious and unknown author of *Le Silence de la Mer*—that comes to fit Vercors at Liberation. His own writing from 1945 on primarily took the form of the political essay—*Souffrance de mon pays* (1945), *Le Sable du temps* (1945), and his chapter of *L'Heure du choix* (1946-1947) are some examples—as did many of the texts he selected for publication at Editions de Minuit. Fashioning himself after Mauriac's example (without imitating Mauriac's catholicism), Vercors presented himself as the political conscience of postwar Resistance culture. To do so, he had the benefit of the success of his two wartime novels, as well as the notoriety that came from being co-director of the CNE.[7] A look at Mauriac's style of personal, public writerly engagement shows the type of punditry that inspired Vercors's postwar activities.

By wartime, François Mauriac was a firmly entrenched fixture of the French literary landscape with a substantial body of writing behind him, and he enjoyed the cultural prestige of being a member of the Académie Française. A Catholic anti-Communist, Mauriac's wartime commitment amounted to contributing an important essay, *Le Cahier noir*, to Vercors's Editions de Minuit, and participating in the meetings of the CNE and *Les Lettres Françaises*. His establishment credentials made his adherence to the literary Resistance all the more striking: as the sole member of the sharply right-leaning Académie Française to join the literary opposition, Mauriac brought the legitimacy of that elevated, privileged status to the risky clandestine enterprises. It involved his own reconversion from a more traditionally guaranteed, comfortable position—and the capital it represented—to joining ideological adversaries. Still, as one discovers in many of his early wartime letters, Mauriac was already a favorite object of abuse in the collaborationist press, and he must have felt—as his letters of complaint addressed to Drieu la Rochelle and others suggest—cut off from many of the elements of the literary field likely to share his religious beliefs.[8] Resistance was the only acceptable moral choice. As Mauriac points out in a letter from 1943 addressed to an unidentified member of the clergy, France "benefits" from the "privilege" of having "the most timid episcopate in the world"; further on he rails that the church has failed to face "these heinous years" and give examples of heroism to the younger generations.[9] The second terrible consequence of this dereliction—in addition to discrediting the Catholic Church—is to allow active, motivated young people to fall under the influence of the Communists, thereby producing a further "dechristianization" of France.[10]

For Mauriac, the religious and the political overlap to such an extent that the crisis in Vichy/Occupied France excludes all possibility of producing literature, and—in theory at least—evacuates the question of literary value. In one letter, Mauriac mentions the difficulty he has concentrating his thoughts on "subjects worthy of attention" and looks forward to a time when "there will only be personal miseries, and where we will rediscover the right to be writers and to have a private life."[11] His first piece for *Lettres Françaises* comes in mid-1944, quite late in the war, even though he had been involved for over a year; more striking though are his private comments upon reading a review of Sartre's *Les Mouches* in the *Lettres Françaises* in 1943. Furious, he writes in a letter to Jean Blanzat: "I am seething with indignation after reading L. F. [. . .] The paper put to waste, the risks run to shove that huge panegyric to Sartre's rubbish down the throats of the poor readers! At such a moment! When there is *everything* to be said! Such literary posturing makes me wretch. I intend to inform them of my resignation."[12] While this is an early sign of the hostility toward Sartre that will involve much spilled ink in the late 40s and 50s, Mauriac's more pressing point is clear: the *Lettres Françaises* should not waste precious paper on useless praise for worthless literature—in this case, Sartre's "rubbish"—when there are more pressing and urgent matters worth writing about. Literature in the sense of literary fictions must be put aside for a public, national rumination over the country's political division and the moral problems of that schism. Mauriac sets the example in his *Le Cahier noir* of the same year.

Le Cahier noir exhibits Mauriac the public writer as amply as any of his contributions to *Lettres Françaises.* The text stages a first-person narrator—presumably Mauriac himself—grappling with contempt for his compatriots and fear of the evil around him in an effort to restore his spiritual strength and integrity. At stake in doing so is nothing less than the survival of his country. The "conscience examining itself" in the text is the moral conscience of a nation that has succumbed to cowardice: "so many French are driven by an elemental passion: fear!"[13] The narrator reviews the cowardice of his countrymen, the divisions among them, and determines, surprisingly, that "the working class alone was faithful to profaned France"—a sentence of note, because in later correspondence Mauriac regrets the line, the only mark of class-consciousness in his text, and wished to have it removed.[14] Hence in Mauriac's wartime commitment lies a theoretically pure sense of engagement that privileges the intellectual guidance of his country over literature in the sense of "belles-lettres." Mauriac himself put aside novels for eleven years (from *La Pharisienne* in 1939-1940 until publication of *Le Sagouin* in 1951) in preference for the kind of essay-writing on display in *Le Cahier noir.* Invested in powerful established field-positions—as a columnist for *Le Figaro* and, after its inception in 1953, weekly contributor to

L'Express—Mauriac was a major figure in mainstream culture after Liberation, weighing in on virtually all of the political crises of the Fourth and Fifth Republics.

At Liberation, Vercors assumed a similar image of the engaged public writer, having abandoned allegorical fiction. Turning to the literary engagements of Minuit and the literary Resistance, I discuss the hardening of Vercors's public writerly commitments into Minuit's postwar editorial line. In stressing historical accounts and political essays over novels, Vercors set dangerous limits on the range of Minuit publishing and lost his grip on the genre that had made him famous.

During 1943 and 1944, Minuit published texts that were valued as illustrations of the political argument of the Resistance and thought to exemplify true French literary genius and tradition. As Jacques Debû-Bridel writes in 1944: "we expect literature to be exemplary."[15] This role, sealed by the success of Vercors's *Le Silence de la mer*, was primarily assigned to fiction. Debû-Bridel's review of Vercors's novel in *Lettres Françaises* succinctly expresses the order of political and literary priorities of both the journal and the literary Resistance movement. He emphasizes the text's literary quality at a time of hardship that might have excused imperfections and flaws: "Vercors manages to express and present himself in a form that, in normal times, would have pleased the most sensitive of bibliophiles" The novel's embodiment of quality is its first area of victory; its second—only—is to have achieved "the free expression of French thought." The novel's triumph is its grasp of French nature and character: "Vercors's inspiration was happily to have made silence the essential theme of his brilliant narrative. Knowing how to convey the mute, stubborn opposition of the French people to the enemy's advances, this is the secret of *Le Silence de la Mer*'s emotional power."[17] This volume and Jacques Maritain's *Chroniques Interdites* are held up as evidence that "the silence has been broken." At the center of it all stands Editions de Minuit: "[F]or Editions de Minuit it was a matter of proving that French Thought still lived on, independent, free, and rich. We have that proof."[18] In a later issue of *Lettres Françaises*, Debû-Bridel refers to a letter from an Englishman who declares that, because of Editions de Minuit and its publications, "France, alone among all the occupied countries, continues to produce works of great art." This international approval serves as validation of both the journal and the publisher and confirms them in their respective roles as producer and guardian of the true French national cultural identity.

By autumn 1944, Minuit had published more than two dozen titles by a mix of new and experienced writers. Included among the latter were Jean Cassou, Louis Aragon, Jean Guéhenno, Pierre Bost, Jean Paulhan, François Mauriac, and Paul Eluard. Aside from Vercors himself, the new names included Elsa Triolet, Claude Aveline, Claude Morgan (director of *Lettres Françaises*), Jacques Debû-Bridel, and Yves Farge. Whether as writers or editors, all of these individuals became participants in the field of the immediate postwar and beyond. Such affiliations made Minuit part of the cultural enterprise of the Resistance and tied its capital to that undertaking. Appendix A lists many of the new journals, newspapers, and publishers that began legitimate activity in 1945. These ventures range from wartime literary journals from both the occupied and unoccupied zones to newspapers and magazines started after Liberation in Paris and other cities, as well as new publishing ventures. For this group of cultural agents—what I call the culture of the Resistance—to create a lasting structural reconfiguration of the literary field after Liberation, it needed to effectively discredit the traditional holders of cultural capital, such as the major pre-war cultural producers, and create its own capital. But both operations proved problematic.

It was primarily the CNE that took on the first of these goals: the triumphant site of credibility and authority at Liberation, the CNE also needed to find ways of securing its position in the postwar field. What role would the CNE play in rebuilding French letters? How would it wield its symbolic capital in the literary field? In an issue from November of 1943, the writers of *Lettres Françaises* put forward a very specific notion of what the CNE's role in shaping postwar France should be, calling for the CNE's involvement in deciding the future punishment of collaborators. They made their case in the lead, front-page article:

> Le Comité national des Ecrivains, [. . .] s'adresse au Gouvernement de la France et lui demande d'être habilité à constituer à l'image du Comité de la presse une commission assistée d'un Conseil de juristes qui sera chargée d'examiner du point de vue professionnel et sans préjudice des actions judiciaires qui pourraient d'autre part être engagées contre les personnes, la conduite des écrivains depuis juin 1940 afin d'éclairer l'action de la justice et de préparer les libres conditions de l'exercice de la profession dans l'avenir.
>
> ~
>
> The National Committee of Writers [. . .] addresses the Government of France in calling for authorization to constitute a Council of Jurists modeled on the Press Committee and to be put in charge of examining the conduct of writers since June 1940, from a professional point of view and without bias concerning legal actions that may be forthcoming

> against individuals, so as to inform the administration of justice and to prepare conditions for the free exercise of the profession in the future.

The text suggests that the CNE's role would be non-ideological, objective, even technical: for the good of justice and for the future of the literary field, the CNE has a specialized "professional point of view" to contribute. Nonetheless, ambiguity slips into the quote's final clause, which is the only part of the piece where it is suggested that there is more involved than the punishment of individual conduct. The preparation of the conditions of the exercise of the literary profession seems to imply that the return to a state of "free" activity in literary affairs was predicated on the carrying out of such punishment. The CNE would continue to exist well after the épuration trials had ended, and its mission statement would later change; still, the predication of the return to "free exercise" upon justice being dispensed sheds light on the problems that would begin to surface less than a year later: what form would that justice take? How unbiased would—could—it be?

The CNE's first obstacle—acquisition of official, legal sanction from the interim government—proved to be insurmountable. As Gisèle Sapiro relates, the CNE's influence on officially sanctioned measures of épuration was consequently fairly minor.[20] The legal structures of épuration were being formed just as the CNE repeated its demand for involvement a year later in the first non-clandestine issue of *Lettres Françaises*. A committee designated by the Ministry of Education Nationale was in charge of directing the review and reprimand of collaborationist writers and publishers, and was to include four members drawn from each of six different, new official organizations of writers and artists: the CNE, the Société des gens de lettres, the Société des compositeurs dramatiques, the Société des auteurs et compositeurs de musique, the Société des orateurs conférenciers, and the Association des écrivains combattants. The CNE would not, in and of itself, constitute a legally empowered body. As a result, its policies and their enforcement were always a priori political in nature rather than juridical. Still, the CNE did have its four votes on the *Commission de l'épuration de l'Edition*, including that of Vercors.

In the long run, its lack of legal status turned out to be a major blow to the CNE's credibility as an authority in the literary field, robbing its initiatives of the force of law and making the achievement of its mission ever more difficult. In 1945, however, the CNE found its own blacklisting to be an effective means of preventing targeted writers from getting published. The CNE's blacklists committed its members to never be published alongside any of the listed writers, or with any journal or collection that published them.[21] The CNE ban could only work for as long as the CNE membership represented a fairly broad spectrum of writers with enough importance and standing for their adherence to the CNE policy to matter. In this way, the CNE hung much of its authority—its power to define what is legitimate and illegitimate literature—on the prestige commanded by its authors. Once the CNE started to lose influential members and began to be perceived as purely partisan—indeed, with its vocal directors Aragon and Triolet, too Communist—its ability to exercise authority in the literary field began to slip. Meanwhile, like other new publishers to emerge in 1945, Editions de Minuit was working on the second of the major goals of Resistance culture, that of developing cultural capital. A look at the fortunes of Minuit's author list and booklist in the period 1945-1949 sheds some light on Minuit's state of virtual bankruptcy in 1949.

In late 1944 and 1945, Vercors, now *Président Directeur-Général* of Minuit, was the darling of the Parisian literary world. One journalist described his stardom in radiant, though perhaps somewhat exaggerated, terms: "Vercors, who is spoken of the world over. Vercors, that all of literate France knows henceforth, and with her London, New York, Melbourne [. . .]. Vercors, translated in every language, welcomed from the beginning as a peer among the greats, from Gide to Charles Morgan."[22] His *Le Silence de la mer* would be translated into sixteen languages and become one of the best-selling books of the first half of the century.[23] In an issue of *Lettres Françaises* in the fall of 1944, Vercors expressed the hard-line politics of exclusion that he, in his capacity as influential member of the CNE and representative to the committee on épuration, espoused:

> C'est tellement commode d'oublier! [. . .] C'est tellement beau le pardon, n'est-ce pas, tellement élevé et noble [. . .]. Ce serment je l'ai fait il y a un an. Je l'ai fait après qu'un homme échappé du bagne SS d'Oranienburg m'eût [sic] raconté avec simplicité ce qu'il y avait vu [. . .] Et ce serment était: "N'oublie jamais!"
>
> ~
>
> It's so convenient to forget! [. . .] Forgiveness is so beautiful, isn't it? So noble, and lofty [. . .]. I made an oath a year ago. I made it after a fellow who escaped from the SS prison in Oranienburg told me in the simplest of terms what he saw there [. . .]. My oath was this: "Never forget!"[24]

There is to be no forgetting and no forgiveness: "publishing a text is an act," one for which authors can be brought to justice.[25] Anne Simonin—author of the most extensive history of Editions de Minuit in wartime and the immediate postwar years—argues that Vercors's public pronouncements gave the appearance that he was the "official representative of the CNE's 'hard line'" because other members who were of the same opinion kept their views to themselves.[26] Her point suggests that Vercors came to occupy the position almost by naive accident: because no one else wanted it, as if his lack of experience in the literary field and the kinds of accommodations it requires prompted him to pursue the uncompromising politics that he did.

This understanding emphasizes the difference between those experienced members of the culture of the Resistance who, because they had been participants in the pre-war literary field, knew best how to protect themselves for the long-term, and those uninitiated ones who unknowingly set themselves up for a fall. Perhaps the veteran *littéraires* suspected or knew to be inevitable what Vercors did not: the failure or impossibility of retribution. It is a difficult point to confirm; what is clear from statements like those quoted above is that Vercors *did* believe in the necessity and possibility of épuration. Vercors's stance made him a valuable public figure in that he represented a position of purity in a field tainted by collaboration. When the need for such a figure began to diminish, Vercors's cultural capital began to decline, and as opinion turned against épuration, his identification with it would become a liability.

Even at its height, Vercors's notoriety was not selling Minuit publications. Though short-lived, the symbolic value of its clandestine titles allowed Minuit to enter the literary market in a position of strength. The first year of postwar reprints of its wartime publications brought in considerable revenues. In fact, profits from reprints obscured what was a pattern of net losses mounting in each annual report. Anne Simonin cites an internal annual report indicating that, without the profits from reprints, "it was not earnings of 502,000 francs that would have been recorded on May 31, 1946, but rather a loss on the order of 2.5 million."[27] None of Minuit's new titles that year earned back their cost. The report for the following fiscal year indicated a loss of one million francs—corresponding to both inadequate sales of the year's new publications and—most interestingly—a substantial drop in demand for its wartime titles. In each year of the 1945-1948 period, Minuit's costs exceeded revenues; meanwhile, over the same period, its total sales figures were cut in half. Shrinking gross profits meant a sizable reduction in Minuit's ability to produce new titles, which of course in turn foreclosed the opportunity to hit upon a successful title. As it happened, none of Minuit's new titles from this era sold well: more than half of Minuit's sales figures represented sales of Vercors's two wartime publications. Moreover, by 1950, just two years after Jérôme Lindon took control of Minuit from Vercors, few of those titles could still be found in the Minuit catalog. In taking over, Lindon inherited responsibility for company debt, which had climbed to twelve million francs by 1949. Why did the triumphant publisher of the Resistance fall so far, so fast?

The speed with which demand for Minuit's booklist disappeared suggests a dramatic change in perspective among readers, and the content of that list may suggest some answers. Of the fifty-seven titles published between 1945 and 1948, approximately thirty-nine dealt with the war and its aftermath, in essay or narrative form (six of them by Vercors himself). The tight focus of Minuit's material indicates an editorial direction informed virtually exclusively by Vercors's political commitment. The 1946 collection of essays he published under the title *L'Heure du choix* provides a glimpse into his objectives. Composed of texts by Vercors and four other CNE activists, *L'Heure du choix* analyzes ethical and political issues relating to "rational reconstruction" and "societal renewal." The authors describe themselves as neither politicians nor members of any party, rather as "fellow fighters" ["*compagnons de lutte*"]. The pun mocks "fellow travelers" ["*compagnons de route*"] to imply a more serious commitment to the cause, and the provocative nature of their theses resonates with their desire to appear as such. They present themselves as the thinkers and architects of "future society."[28] Pioneers of a new socialist revolution, Vercors and his authors were attaching their bids for cultural capital to the appeal of their political vision. Part of their job, therefore, was to frame socialist ideas so as to make them more welcome. The following quote from the preface asserts their commitment to intellectual activism in just such terms:

> [. . .] la tâche essentielle, que nous n'avons pas la prétention d'accomplir ici, est de faire ressurgir—rénové, vivant et, autant que possible dans la société actuelle, vécu—l'humanisme qui est au cœur même du socialisme et de ses luttes.[29]
>
> ~
>
> [. . .] the essential task—which we do not claim to accomplish here—is to rekindle the humanism that is at the very heart of socialism and its struggles, one that is renewed, living, and as much as possible in the society of today, lived.

In and of itself, this mission statement is not a radical departure from Sartre's "compagnonnage"; indeed, written and published shortly after Sartre wrote *L'Existentialisme est un humanism*, it sought to borrow something of his rhetorical strategy. But unlike Sartre, they present concrete prescriptions for building "future society" and their commitment to cultural revolution is a direct and practical deliberation on how to go about it. By contrast, Sartrean commitment, as I argue presently, understands literature as enjoying an important degree of distance or even separation—articulated as intellectual autonomy—from the hands-on process of crafting political outcomes. This distance was an essential part of his fellow-travelership. It permitted Sartre to espouse the cultural revolution from afar, and draw from its popularity while restricting his concept of commitment to a much more philosophical form of activism at the same time. Part of his skill lay, then, in eschewing the pragmatic strategies of commitment espoused by Vercors and Aveline.

Claude Aveline's essay in *L'Heure du choix*, titled "Les Eglises et l'homme," compares communism and capitalism to established religions and then weighs their respective chances of enduring in the future society. The Catholic Church in France would not have "an important role," since in order to do so, the Church would—as its wisest members point out—need to recover its "original purity," yet "such a total reversal is inconceivable."[30] The hope for "universal socialism" lies in a communism that never forgets that "the cause to defend is not just that of the collectivity, but that of man as well."[31] In his article on revolution, Jean Cassou develops the Marxist theme of revolution as the sole means of true social progress. His article asserts that revolution is an inherent element of French culture: "Revolutions follow upon one another like so many instances of consciousness regained by the French people."[32] Revolution is thus a constitutive part of the nation: "France, the French homeland, the French nation, the French state can only be this: a permanent celebration of federation."[33] Both Resistance writers and, equally importantly, prominent figures in the postwar Resistance "establishment," Aveline and Cassou are advocates of a total cultural politics that hinges on sweeping away entrenched institutions in favor of new ones—an engagement manifest in their publication by Editions de Minuit.

Vercors and another contributor, André Chamson, each make explicit the writer's role in social renewal, and emphasize the traditional posture of the writer as an alienated figure as inadequate. Vercors advanced himself in the role of political activist, and his editorial career was a complement to that role. The opening lines of Vercors's contribution to *L'Heure du choix* suggest the kind of connection he saw between them:

> Nous ne sommes pas des rêveurs. Nous savons très bien que la politique n'est pas une affaire de saints ni de poètes. Ceux-ci (les saints, les poètes) peuvent montrer la route, une route idéale, immaculée comme celle d'une carte Michelin. Mais il ne suffit pas qu'elle soit portée sur la carte: il faut la réaliser [. . .].
>
> ~
>
> We are not dreamers. We know full well that politics is no affair for saints or poets. These last may indicate the path, an ideal path, immaculate like one on a Michelin map. It is not enough to trace it on a map: it must be carried out [. . .].[34]

Chamson describes the same sense of commitment, but goes a little further by endowing all forms of creativity with the power exemplified by literature and art—the power to guarantee France's place "at the center of History."[35] Chamson inscribes the literary Resistance within Communist doctrine. The artist, the writer, and the worker all have their role to play in creating a new, increasingly classless nation, one returned to its rightful place of prominence despite its having lost "control of events." The preservation of permanent human values—the task fully accomplished by the literary Resistance in the face of "Hitler's savagery"—was an example of the engagement with

History inherent to every creative act. There is an "close alliance" between creativity and "the movements of life," such that creativity gives rise to "new realities." In this way, Chamson articulates the vision of an historical continuity between the wartime literary Resistance and its postwar commitment that many of its members hoped to see realized.

Accounts of the major episodes from the war (such as *Toulon* [1943, 1945] and *L'Armistice* [1944, 1945]), essays on the war or the contemporary postwar political situation (like *L'Heure du choix, La Patrie se fait tous les jours* [1947]), political allegories (including all of Vercors's fiction): through texts such as these Vercors's Minuit attempted to document much of France's wartime history. The firm's Communist leaning is hardly surprising, given Minuit's origins and the massively left-wing nature of the CNE. But Vercors's initial popularity and Minuit's position solidly in line with the national mood at Liberation were not enough to sell his endeavors (with the exception of his two wartime novels) to the reading public. Nor, in a further major setback, could they prevent the flight of symbolic capital from Minuit, as Vercors's authors returned to their original publishers or defected to new ones. Much of the reason for these failures lies in the difference between "compagnon de route" and "compagnon de lute." Turning now to the literary commitments of Jean Paulhan and Jean-Paul Sartre, therefore, I look at two alternative cultural reworkings of the wartime literary Resistance that were to win out over Vercors's Minuit.

2. Paulhan, Doyen of the literary Resistance

For Jean Paulhan, one kind of literary engagement preempted all others: a commitment to the uninterrupted history of great French literature. Known as "l'éminence grise" of French letters, Paulhan occupied a prominent position in the culture industry long before and long after the war, as both editor of *La Nouvelle Revue Française* (*NRF*) and as Gaston Gallimard's right-hand man. While at first glance they may appear surprising or incongruous, both his wartime and postwar allegiances make sense in light of his chief, overriding commitment to literature, and to the network of authors he believed best served its interests. His long-term ties with Editions de Minuit underscore how, at different times, Minuit was useful to his agenda. An important supporter of Editions de Minuit during the Occupation, Paulhan would renew that association after Vercors's departure, becoming a crucial source of contacts and support to Lindon, who was in return—as I discuss in the next chapter—of service to Paulhan's Gallimard.

As director of the prestigious literary journal the *Nouvelle Revue Française* (*NRF*) from 1925 until its publication was suspended in 1940, Jean Paulhan exerted significant influence on the literary field via his specific editorial choices in cementing the position of the *NRF* and through his role in the publishing decisions at Gallimard. Critics have consistently characterized both Gallimard and the *NRF* as having been particularly able to attract, promote, and advance young authors into becoming writers of long-term importance and value, at a time when other journals could not.[36] Particularly striking in this regard is Paulhan's recruitment of Sartre, Leiris, Queneau, Bataille, Ponge, and Blanchot (among others) into Gallimard's list in the two years before and during the war. In several instances, this was accomplished through publication in the *NRF*. Even after Drieu La Rochelle took over direction of the *NRF* in 1941, Paulhan—who was offered the position of co-director, which he refused—remained behind the scenes. One index of his continued importance even under the Nazi regime is his quick release from German custody in 1941 at Drieu La Rochelle's request.[37] In this respect, Paulhan's first allegiance throughout the wartime period was to preserving and sustaining the network of authors associated with the journal and the publishing house, and who consequently formed the very structure of his own cultural capital. The enormous body of correspondence between Paulhan and his network is that has been published is rivaled only by an equally extensive unpublished collection, both show his ties to both older important literary figures (such as André Gide, Jean Schlumberger, François Mauriac) as well as new.[38] In that way, Paulhan is an index of two branches of the literary field that formed around the structural divide of officially sanctioned vs. clandestine during the war. The official branch was made up of old and new positions of cultural capital (such as the Académie Française on one hand and the younger collaborationist presses on the other) and the clandestine group was mainly composed of newly developing authors and unknowns, along with their publishing outlets.

Louis Parrot, in *L'Intelligence en guerre*, describes Paulhan as the "hub" of the clandestine group, and as instrumental in forming what became the literary Resistance. As such, Paulhan was able to bring his own prestige to bear on launching and supporting clandestine modes of cultural production in three significant areas: first, the literary journal, second, the literary press, and third, the single organ of unity among the resistant intelligentsia, the CNE. In 1941 and 1942 Paulhan encountered more new authors as he became involved in these clandestine projects, thus continuing his pre-war *NRF* role of cultural impresario and arbiter of legitimate value. First there was *Messages*, a literary journal intended by its founder Jean Lescure to be the anti-*NRF*,[39] and published in the occupied zone, which featured contributions by many of the Gallimard authors, recruited for the purpose by Paulhan. Second, he became involved in the editorial direction of a new publishing house with Vercors and Yvonne Paraf-Desvignes: Les Editions de Minuit. As a conduit for texts and guidance, Paulhan brought his insider's knowledge to a group of newcomers to the literary field. As Anne Simonin argues: "Paulhan himself and his relations, literary or otherwise, represented a decisive contribution to Editions de Minuit."[40] Lastly, along with François Mauriac, Paulhan became the senior figure of the CNE, which was composed primarily of relatively unknown young authors. By bringing authors like Sartre, Leiris, and Queneau into the CNE, Paulhan was responsible for their participation in the literary Resistance. This affiliation put Paulhan not only at the core of an organization that was to take center stage at Liberation but also in a position of influence over the clandestine cultural bulletin, *Les Lettres Françaises*, produced by the executive committee of the CNE. This is how Sartre, whom Paulhan had seen publish *La Nausée* at Gallimard, came to be accepted into the CNE and to contribute to the *Lettres Françaises*.

Even at that time, when the German and Vichy regimes were taking aim at undesirable books and their authors, Paulhan placed great emphasis on the quality of writing that sought to take a stand against the regime. Gisèle Sapiro documents the anxieties of the director of *Lettres Françaises*, Claude Morgan, over Paulhan's reception of the early issues of the journal.[41] He was worried that Paulhan would not like the issues for their poor literary quality, and then perhaps withdraw his willingness to get involved: by all indications, he was right on the first count.[42] The anecdote raises the entire question of target readership and purpose: in retrospect, to the uninitiated it may seem odd for a pamphlet of first four, and then eight, pages in length published under circumstances of extreme political repression to be overwrought about matters of literary professionalism. The urgency of the message it had to deliver may be thought to outweigh stylistic considerations. However, they knew Paulhan, and they knew they needed to win his approval: their supposition that Paulhan might have not contributed because of qualms over quality attests to the primacy of his commitment to literature as belles-lettres. The manifesto of *Lettres Françaises*—page one of number one, 1942—can aid in understanding just how much is at stake in this question of quality. First, it announces the formation of the *Front National,* which is the early form of the CNE, and explains that it is the expression of an "immense resistance movement"; furthermore, it is "from this moment on a decisive force in the fight to liberate the country."[43] It identifies Hitler's plan to subjugate France and its culture, reducing it to a "minor role" in Europe by assassinating "French intelligence." The French writer is to do his part in the Resistance by defending French letters, by saving their "joy" and making "our French air unbreathable for these scribes from Germany." Together, representing a broad coalition of France's outlawed political and religious affiliations—"gaullists, communists, democrats, catholics, protestants"—they will defend "the values that made our civilization glorious." Unlike some of the local, (non-political) literary reviews produced in the unoccupied zone—e.g. *Confluences, Fontaine*—*Lettres Françaises* must of course be anonymous; its literary value is its only claim to legitimacy, made all the more vital by the tenor of its claims to embody the best of French culture: aesthetics and politics must match up.

One of the first articles to appear in the journal may have

contributed to Paulhan's initial distaste. An article titled "Feue la N.R.F." by Claude Morgan picks a target of attack that for Paulhan must have been a sensitive one, and in so doing communicates more about the aspirations of the editors. Other collaborationist newspapers and journals will not be named over the two years of issues. Morgan employs indelicate terms to describe the *NRF*: "ever since she fell into the hands of Drieu La Rochelle and Ramon Fernandez she is nothing more than a cadaver—a stinking one."[44] Yet Morgan establishes here what was to be a consistent pattern in *Lettres Françaises* of naming individual collaborators, responding to articles printed in the collaborationist press, attempting to discredit them in their own terms—often those terms involve the appropriation by collaborators of some national literary figure—and issuing threats against the authors. All of the infamous literary personalities are named, including Brasillach, Chateaubriant, Jouhandeau, Rebatet, Chardonne, Thérive, Daniel Rops, and Paul Morand. This naming could have been a further aggravation to Paulhan and be taken as an implied judgment on his particular position: many of these authors were not only Gallimard authors, but also Paulhan's friends and correspondents.

Paulhan's letters provide a privileged window into Paulhan's intellectual *habitus*—one which, by virtue of its private, discrete, and personal nature defines his stance as very different from that of the public writer. His correspondence reveals a very varied set of positions expressed to his interlocutors. One position does, however, remain constant: regardless of the nature of his addressee, from collaborator to resistant, Paulhan very scrupulously separates their political agreements or disagreements from an ongoing debate over or discussion of literary matters. The two sides are almost never, for Paulhan, of the same coin—only rarely in the wartime correspondence was he obliged to connect the two, and in those instances the connection is very limited. A 1944 letter to Marcel Jouhandeau demonstrates the clear separation Paulhan maintained between politics and literature. Jouhandeau had collaborated with Drieu La Rochelle on the *NRF*, and thereby enjoyed protection from German harassment. In one moment Paulhan severely upbraids his addressee for the emptiness of his references to individual courage in light of the internment of Jews or the accidental shooting of their countrymen, and then in the next moment turns to matters of typography. The contrast is a stark one, at a time when the generic difference between politics and literature must, according to others in the literary Resistance, be suspended:

> Bien cher Marcel, de ton courage personne (ni surtout moi) ne doute. Mais en ce moment, je te prie, n'en parle pas. Ouvre les yeux. [. . .] Ce n'est pas toi qui viens de mourir en prison, c'est Max Jacob. Ce n'est pas toi qui as été tué par des soldats ivres, c'est Saint-Pol Roux. [. . .] Dans un temps où nous avons tous à montrer du courage, tu es le seul (peu s'en faut) qui ne soit pas menacé [. . .].
>
> Je relis l'essai, aussi bouleversé que la première fois. De ce que je corrige peu de choses à te dire. Ta dactylo, ton imprimeur ont la rage des circonflexes [. . .] J'espère n'en pas oublier.

> My dear Marcel, no one (nor do I especially) doubts your courage. But at this moment, I beg of you, do not speak of it. Open your eyes. [. . .] It is not you who just died in prison, it's Max Jacob. It is not you who was killed by drunk soldiers, it was Saint-Pol Roux. [. . .] At a time when we must all show

> courage, you are the only one (just about) who is not under threat [. . .].
>
> I'm re-reading the essay, just as overwhelmed as the first time. As for corrections there is little to report. Your typist, your printer, they have a thing for circonflex accent marks [. . .] I hope I don't miss any.[45]

The political divide that separates the safe Jouhandeau from the hunted Paulhan—in several letters he evokes in passing his having needed to relocate due to "an incident"—and that Paulhan expressly exaggerates ("you alone are not under threat") has nothing to do with the realm of literary communication in which the two could not be closer in matters of taste, education, and value.

A letter to Armand Petitjean in 1943 illustrates one of the ways Paulhan expressed the relationship between politics and literature. Petitjean was a collaborator who apparently sought, as did many of the collaborationist intelligentsia (among others), to place blame for the defeat in 1940 on the intellectual elite. The editors of Paulhan's letters quote Petitjean explaining the very loaded question he had written to Paulhan, asking him if he felt that the *NRF* had "prepared [. . .] the French for the trial of June, 1940."[46] Like the example above, Paulhan's reply is surprising: "Dear Armand, is it really loyal to ask people questions that cannot be answered unless one cultivates an inordinate amount of pride in oneself?"[47] In one gesture, Paulhan undercuts the arrogance of Petitjean's question and rejects the presumption that the *NRF* might be somehow responsible for military defeat. As he continues his response, it becomes clearer that for him, the role of the prewar *NRF* and his own role as its director do not entail accountability with respect to the actions of others. He cites Confucius who, when asked what his first move would be if he were asked to reestablish order in a China on the verge of ruin, replied: "The thing is self-evident, [. . .] it would be enough to watch over words and the proper understanding of language."[48] Paulhan goes on to explain his citation: "He meant that there is no disorder without an error of language at its origin."[49] Compared to the detailed political approaches later taken by his Resistance partners, Paulhan's was a guarded, reserved understanding of the relationships between literature and politics. It was one that, ultimately, would not echo the Resistance's belief in the responsibility or accountability of writers who sided or sympathized with Vichy.

What Paulhan's response does not do is defend a defensible record: in the years leading up to the war, Paulhan's *NRF* showed strong commitment in adopting a nationalistic stance toward events,[50] a defense, furthermore, that could be directed toward attacks from either the right or the left. Paulhan declines any discussion of the writer's public responsibility, in preservation of a notion of literature and of literary praxis as practices that exist at a remove from social and political realms. The letters convey a sense of Paulhan's wartime commitment—one that, perhaps more by accident than out of a sense of moral duty, was so central to strengthening the unity and productivity of the resistance writers' efforts. They also reflect Paulhan's long-term investment in sustaining the literary field and his guiding or steering role in it. As an editor of writers from both sides of a deeply divided literary field, he had much to lose in alienating either faction. His agile strategy of accommodating his network of writers on the right through the separation of literature and political position, while coordinating, encouraging, and networking the writers on a left of all stripes (catholic, communist, existentialist) must be understood in terms of his position in the literary field. The advantage of such a strategy is that, in terms of cultural capital, Paulhan loses nothing of his prestige among important allies on the entrenched right, and stands to gain much from the left.

In a short text written in December 1944, a piece to honor those who lost their lives during the Occupation, Paulhan summed up the previous four years:

> Ce n'est pas que notre vie ait tellement changé, pendant ces quatre ans. Nous avons continué à travailler comme avant (parfois un peu moins, c'était agréable; souvent à des entreprises défendues, qui nous amusaient). Nous avons continué à manger. [. . .] L'amour, les amitiés, les livres allaient à peu près comme avant (même, on avait plus de temps pour lire). Somme toute, nous étions au courant; nous maintenions tous les contacts.
>
> ~
>
> It is not that our lives changed so much during these past four years. We carried on working as before (sometimes less, which was nice, sometimes at undertakings that were forbidden, which amused us. We carried on eating. [. . .] Love, friendships, books went on just about as much before (we even had more time to read). All in all, we kept current, we kept up with all our contacts.[51]

Naturally, it made sense for Paulhan to minimize his wartime experience in order to honor the dead; no other sacrifice or suffering compares to theirs. Still, his astonishing encapsulation of literary life under the Occupation expresses more than just appropriate humility. Unlike virtually all of the literary Resistance—indeed, it is hard to imagine a Vercors, Chamson, or Aveline describing their war in this way—Paulhan favored the literary field's return to "normal," and in little time turned against the literary Resistance's efforts to establish itself in the postwar field. He became opposed to the CNE's efforts to blacklist writers in 1944 and 1945, and, after a long period of absence from the CNE in 1945, finally withdrew formally in 1946. That same year, Paulhan began to publish articles and interviews attacking the CNE and its directors and defending authors they had blacklisted—a project that grew in size and significance each year.

Notable among them was Paulhan's "Réponse à l'enquête 'Approuvez-vous ou non cette forme de sanction qu'est l'interdiction de publier des écrits?'" in *Le Figaro littéraire*, a newspaper that was the principal forum for another important former member of the literary Resistance, François Mauriac.[52] For Mauriac, articulating his progressive Catholic Gaullism meant near-constant denunciations of Sartre, the CNE, and the PCF. At odds in most respects, Paulhan and Mauriac were thus united during wartime in favor of the literary Resistance, and then united once again to fight against it. In 1947, articles in *Les Cahiers de la Pléiade* and a series of tracts called "Letter to the Members of the CNE" intensified Paulhan's offensive. A number of these texts were collected and published at Gallimard in 1948 as *De la Paille et du grain*. That year, he rejoined Mauriac by becoming a board member of *La Table ronde* and publishing articles in it regularly. *La Table ronde*, as I discuss below, was the right-wing answer to *Les Temps modernes*, and is taken by most historians to have sounded the end of the exclusion of right-wing authors from the literary field. In three years Paulhan went from the editorial board of Sartre's *Les Temps modernes*[53] to that of *La Table ronde*: the political significance of his trajectory is matched in degree by the polemical rhetoric of many of his later articles.

Paulhan's objections to épuration were initially rather uncontroversial. In "Quelques raisons de nous réjouir" ["A Few Reasons for Delight"] he worries about the impact of discriminating among writers on the strength of their politics, and his concern seems somewhat pedestrian:

> Nos écrivains résistants vont être assaillis de tous côtés. Journaux et revues leur arracheront des poèmes, des contes, des essais qu'ils écriront à la va-vite. Les voilà perdus pour la littérature. [. . .] Pendant ce temps, les écrivains collaborateurs, bien tranquilles, travailleront à l'écart. Après cinq ou dix ans, ils rentreront en force avec des œuvres mûries. Nous ne pourrons pas tenir le coup.
>
> ~
>
> Our resistance writers will be attacked from all sides. Newspapers and journals will extract poems, short stories and essays from them that they will have to rush out. And just like that they will be lost to literature. [. . .] During this time, the collaborationist writers, left alone, will work on the sidelines. In five or ten years, they will come back in force with fully mature works. We will never hold up.[54]

The patriotic treatises and narratives are at best "simply boring," and at worst they move readers to flock to the other camp: "they give one a violent desire to say the opposite."[55] In *De la Paille et du grain*, his attacks become more frank, direct, and even shocking. He takes aim at the CNE, Vercors, Aragon, Cassou, Morgan, and *Les Lettres Françaises* with very scornful statements: "Between us, I am not very proud, seeing what they have become, to have founded *Lettres Françaises*."[56] Paulhan is disgusted by the Resistance's notion of justice—"the fury of their denouncements, their hatred"—and asserts the writer's right to err. Pointing to "lies, errors and contradictions"[57] in statements made by the leaders of the CNE, he muses whether making mistakes is not inherent in literature itself: "It's enough to make one wonder if it is not to the author's advantage to be guilty, if it is not part of literature, if we should not want to quickly become guilty, and if we should not just invite the writer into the realm of error and madness once and for all."[58] He goes to extraordinary lengths in his desire to thwart and confound the efforts of "the famous writers," even to the point of trampling the limits of taste:

> Ah! Je voudrais être juif, pour dire—avec plus d'autorité que je n'en puis avoir—que j'ai pardonné à la France, une fois pour toutes, son impuissance à me défendre. Je voudrais être juif pour travailler—avec plus de force que je n'en ai—à rendre à la France toutes ses voix, toute sa voix. Je voudrais être juif pour devenir le meilleur des Français.
>
> ~
>
> Ah! I would like to be Jewish, so as to say—with more authority than I can have—that I forgive France, once and for all, her powerlessness to defend me. I would like to be Jewish in order to work—with more strength than I have—to give back to Franch all of her voices, all of its voice. I would like to be Jewish to become the best of the French.[59]

Was this an illustration of an "error of language"? This offensive polemical ploy suggests that the blacklisted authors were the scapegoats of misplaced Holocaust guilt, and seems more like another tactic to undermine the authority of his foes rather than his sincere analysis of the reasons behind the épuration.

Regardless, it is a hypothesis that doubtlessly pleased members of the right, both moderate and radical, in that it brushed aside the question of real guilt for real crimes.

Ultimately, Paulhan's literary views led him from the core of the Resistance to that of the resurgent right, resulting in a significant shift of political balance in the literary field. The return of Gallimard to publishing activity after its owner Gaston Gallimard's scrutiny and release by the épuration meant that Paulhan's vision of literary production could once again assert itself. In addition, Paulhan's polemics greatly helped sap the momentum and capital of the literary Resistance as a cultural force. As more and more of the writers and editors scrutinized by the épuration were released with minimal punishment—including both Gallimard and Grasset, publishers of Paulhan and Mauriac—the agenda of the CNE became easier and easier to discredit. Seemingly ironically, because it was based entirely upon its claims of moral strength, the literary Resistance found itself caught up in a crisis of moral authority that it was unable to contain.[60] The damage done, however, did not fall equally on everyone: for various reasons that I now explore, Sartre's popularity and influence were not casualties of the return of the right. Rather, Sartre's doctrine of literary engagement combined aspects of both Vercors's and Paulhan's postwar stances in order to serve a cultural demand for both an image of national heroism and the idea of a pure, independent literary tradition. Ironically, while Editions de Minuit was best suited to reflect that tradition, Gallimard would take the upper hand.

3. Sartre and the Vichy Syndrome

The most remarkable figure of the late 1940s was Jean-Paul Sartre. His rise to prominence did not only diminish the chances for new producers such as Minuit to meet the demands of readers; I argue that the success of Sartre's theoretical position of commitment went hand in hand with a neglect of the Resistance literature that Minuit published. Rather than invest in Minuit's project to document and analyze the war, readers chose to turn to Sartre and the circle of intellectuals grouped around him at *Les Temps modernes*. To grasp what that choice meant requires a look at Sartre's manifesto of postwar literary culture, "Introducing *Les Temps modernes*" ["Présentation des Temps modernes"]. Underlying its theorization of literature and literary commitment was the description of a heroic intellectual posture whose appeal would link the figure of Sartre to "committed literature" for several decades. In fashioning such a pure, heroic posture, Sartre presented French culture with a screen memory that veiled France's collaborationist past. In so doing, Sartre contributed to the post-Vichy myth of a pure "Eternal France" initiated by Charles De Gaulle. That myth has best been described by Henry Rousso, who termed it the Vichy Syndrome. Rousso's theory, which I return to below, helps us understand the unusual conjuncture of demand that placed a high value on Sartre and his theory of literary commitment while at the same time spurning the committed publications of Minuit.

Before turning to Sartre's text, it is important to return to some of what Patricia Ferguson has written about the public writer. Ferguson proposes to "attempt to define and analyze *the specific sense of culture* that gives direction to the whole configuration of writers, readers, and literary institutions."[62] This "sense of culture" is an ideology of nationalism, according to which culture is homogeneous: the sense of culture is "specific" and uniform, and therefore subject to representation in simplified terms. Many writers have enjoyed a level of intellectual prestige in France that writers in other literatures have not. This is because writers have often had the opportunity to serve a public and national purpose: "where politics divides so bitterly, literature can offer a vital source of union."[63] The various modes by which writers became identified with a national identity that she reviews—Voltaire for instance is termed "the writer as philosophe and the philosophe as *littérateur*," Hugo is the "writer-prophet"—all involve a moment when the writer begins to play a socially committed role, thus suturing "the world of private belief"—his or her writing, in other words—with the "world of country"—the realm of collective history and memory.[64] Those writers who succeed in becoming public writers in these ways see their lives become identified with the life of the nation, their senses of French culture adopted into the nation's imagery of itself. Compelling signs of this canonization include the entombment of some writers in the Pantheon and the official state burials granted to figures like Hugo. In Vercors's pun that we saw above on "compagnon de route" and "compagnon de lutte," the half-rhymed words "route" and "lutte" mark the immense difference between the actively committed and the armchair revolutionaries. In Sartre's case, it appears that it was precisely the kind of remove from the politics of épuration and its backlash that crystallized his appeal as a source of union for a culture predominantly left-leaning in the postwar but leery of divisive polemics from either the extreme left or extreme right. In other words, Sartre's appeal came from his idealization of Resistance values, rather than his practice of them.

By 1945, Sartre had accumulated many of the honors of an elite education and an impressive literary career; they make up an important component of why his personal history lent itself to blending with national history. Of bourgeois background and a former student at the Ecole Normale Supérieure, Sartre first gained recognition through his philosophical works, *L'Imagination* (1936) and *L'Etre et le Néant* (1943). Also, *La Nausée* (1938) earned him very significant notoriety in the literary field prior to World War II. During the war, he wrote two of what have become his most famous plays (*Les Mouches* and *Huis Clos*[65]), two volumes of *Les Chemins de la Liberté*, and, in the only direct expression of his anti-Vichy stance, contributed a small number of articles to the clandestine *Lettres Françaises*. War's end in France marked the beginning of an intense period of activity—ending in 1953, which is perhaps significant, as I shall discuss in Chapter II—that stands out as one of the most prolific of his career: in just the first two years, he published two novels written during the war, two plays, and five essays of considerable length.[66] By wartime Sartre had garnered enough cultural capital to be published at Paulhan's behest by Gallimard, the publisher of Gide, Céline, Jean Paulhan and many others of the literary elite, and in the pre-war *Nouvelle Revue Française* (the articles reprinted in *Situations*), the most important literary journal of the time and primary authority over literary matters.[67] Hence, his prewar writings can be considered his ticket of admission into a privileged intellectual and literary elite, and a logical conclusion of his advantaged education and class background. In this sense, then, the Sartrean identity that emerges in the postwar benefits in part from the profile of someone who had garnered legitimacy and cultural capital in the prewar configuration of the literary field.

The text with which Sartre launched *Les Temps modernes*—it appeared as the first article in the first issue—situates the journal's intellectual and cultural agenda within a logic of social change. "Introducing *Les Temps modernes*" displays a double strategy that is visible in other examples of Sartre's writings. This strategy simultaneously deploys two positions of authority: the first literary, and the second philosophical. As a literary critic whose credentials include numerous critical articles in major literary journals, Sartre announces a crucial break with the French literary tradition concerning what it means to be an author, and how literature is to be valued. This is the rupture that was probably meant to be signaled by his choice of title, *Les Temps modernes.* That break, in turn, is anchored in the almost sociological turn he takes in theorizing authorship before and after Occupation. He then pursues his argument as philosopher, and attaches his view of the author to a fundamental definition of man and human freedom. At the same time, the argument functions as a personal apologia: firstly, the alliance of literature and philosophy that Sartre's text emphasizes is one that only someone with his credentials could undertake. Secondly, his line of reasoning is underscored by an anxiety over class: Sartre's philosophical argument rescues him from difficult questions of social class implied in his initial literary argument. At stake in the question of class is Sartre's own role in bringing about social change or revolution—the role his text sets out to define. Let's look at how these issues are played out in the text.

From the very first lines, Sartre begins to develop a notion of the social function of literature and of writers. Sartre's tone is sharply critical, and bespeaks an impending, necessary change of values: "All writers of middle-class origin have known the temptation of irresponsibility. For a century now, it has been a traditional part of the literary career."[68] The Realists, Flaubert, followers of "Art for Art's Sake": all gave into the class "temptation" of social irresponsibility. They ascribed aesthetic value to literature that is "gratuitous" and "bereft of roots."[69] Their choice was the wrong solution to the dilemma posed by their social existence "at the margins of society": "[t]he truth is that unsure of his social position, too fearful to stand up to the bourgeoisie from whom he draws his pay, and too lucid to accept it without reservations, [the Realist] has chosen to pass judgment on his century and has thereby convinced himself that he remains outside it, just as an experimenter remains outside the system of his experiment."[70] In trying to think their way outside of the class system, they abdicated their responsibility to commitment and acquiesced before social injustice. While on the one hand, one cannot miss the antecedent of Bourdieu's (much later) concerns with the autonomy of literature, and the interest in the same period of literary history, the difference in conclusions is equally unmistakable: where Bourdieu identifies the emergence of a literary field self-defined as newly autonomous with respect to political and economic constraints, Sartre sees individual bad faith, hypocrisy and self-delusion. Indeed, in Sartre's view there is no autonomous space outside the social realm. He insists that, paradoxically, to believe oneself outside society is to reinforce the split in values between the social classes. That is why the "man of letters" is ill at ease at mentioning his career title in public,[71] and goes from experiencing pride one day to shame the next:

> [. . .] un jour, il en est fier, il se sent clerc et gardien des valeurs idéales; le lendemain il en a honte [. . .]. Auprès des bourgeois qui le lisent, il a conscience de sa dignité; mais en face des ouvriers, qui ne le lisent pas, il souffre d'un complexe d'infériorité [. . .].
>
> ~
>
> [. . .] one day he is quite proud of it, he feels himself to be a cleric and guardian of ideal values; the following day, he's ashamed [. . .]. In relation to the middle-class people who read him, he is aware of his

> dignity; but confronted with workers, who don't, he suffers from an inferiority complex [. . .].[72]

The author experiences this class alienation because he is not creating something useful—what Sartre calls "an act."[73] The author's shame results from an awareness of not belonging to the productive working-class.

Sartre wants to redefine the social standing of authors and to rehabilitate their historical role in terms other than the useless "ideal values" of the bourgeoisie; his solution is to articulate writing as a highly productive activity meant to align the writer more closely with the working-class. Authorial alienation is a result of bourgeois values, which constitute a uniform, illusory worldview: "In fact, though, one *constitutes* oneself bourgeois by choosing, once and for all, a certain analytic perspective on the world which one attempts to foist on all men and which excludes the perception of collective realities."[74] His example in this instance is Proust: "Proust *chose himself* to be a bourgeois. He made himself into an accomplice of bourgeois propaganda, since his wrok contributes to the dissemination of the myth of human nature."[75] Sartre casts his own position as new, progressive, legitimate, and revolutionary. At stake in "Introducing *Les Temps modernes*"—as in the creation of the journal—is the assertion, via a critique of bourgeois writers as a class, of a viable social role for Sartre himself. Clearly, the class-anxiety of Sartre's "homme de lettres" is his own. In situating the new man of letters within a logic of social utility, Sartre seeks to satisfy that anxiety.

The wartime lesson of social responsibility—"[t]he Occupation taught us [our responsibility as writers]"[76]—is a fundamental point of departure for Sartre's critical project. But it was the épuration—the postwar purge of collaborators— he asserts, that finally brought this value hierarchy home to the irresponsible writers who still subscribed to the old bourgeois values. Authors under fire for collaborating make the painful realization that their writings have a social signification that they had ignored. Sartre's characterization of them is derisive: "'What do you mean?' They ask. 'Does the stuff someone writes actually commit them?'"[77] However, those writers who did not directly collaborate also share in guilt.

To equate the publication of "a book that was merely useless" with full collaboration may seem extreme, but it reiterates an ethical imperative born of Vichy France that informs the direction of Sartre's argument.[78] His comments on Flaubert reveal two very different aspects of his use of this axiom in his argument. On one hand, Sartre makes the observation that there is always a material side to theoretical claims of autonomy or social independence: "Flaubert [. . .] believed he had withdrawn outside the social machine [. . .] does not his meticulous art presuppose the comfort of Croisset, the solicitude of a mother or a niece, an orderly regimen, a prosperous commercial endeavor, dividends received on schedule?"[79] This is the beginning of a sociological approach to literature that Sartre does not pursue further in "Introducing *Les Temps modernes*"[80] because, on the other hand, he is seeking to create a positive criterion of literary value as social and political usefulness. To do so, he universalizes the ethical imperative of the purge and judges Flaubert in its terms: "I hold Flaubert and Goncourt responsible for the repression that followed the Commune because they didn't write a line to prevent it."[81] In the aftermath of World War II, these comments were likely perceived as a forceful historical reevaluation of cultural authority and significance. It may be that only later does his argument appear conspicuously self-serving. Sartre's attack amounts to scapegoating: in setting himself apart from Flaubert and Goncourt, he is constructing himself as a useful, and internally consistent, figure of ethical authority endowed with considerable political power. In the context of a literary field undergoing épuration, the pure "act" of denouncing Flaubert produces Sartre's commitment as the alternative to bourgeois writerly irresponsibility and implies the effectiveness of such commitment. His conception of the committed writer's power to effect change is what rings somewhat false: Sartre was no more capable of bringing Vichy to an end than Flaubert and Goncourt could likely have prevented the post-Commune repression.

Much of "Introducing *Les Temps modernes*" deals with literature and aesthetics, and presents an image of Sartre as a literary figure as opposed to a philosophical one; it is the latter pages that constitute an attempt on Sartre's part to incorporate—perhaps gently—philosophical discourse into the literary context. He pursues a series of philosophical assertions about man and human freedom in which he must attempt to reconcile class revolution with individual liberty, and balance his focus between the set of choices and circumstances that make up a "situation" and a defense of the free spirit that animates that situation and can transform it. Yet, as fundamental as his philosophical points are, given the generic constraints of "Introducing *Les Temps modernes*," Sartre does not indulge in an elaborate development of a philosophical argument in this piece. Instead, he casts the text as a manifesto, and as such privileges assertions over explanation. He even rejects the appellation of philosopher itself while at the same time wielding weighty notions like "analytic cast of mind" and "synthetic" one[82]—"What remains is to explain it—but this is the philosopher's business, not ours."[83] A term provided by Anna Boschetti in reference to a different context seems particularly appropriate for describing the threadbare alliance of socialism and individualism deployed by Sartre in these pages: "Sartrean prophetism."[84] It is also an apt expression for capturing the political fantasy Sartre expresses here. He holds out the promise that his activity as an intellectual, and more generally the work of *Les Temps modernes*, will liberate proletarian man—whom he describes deferentially:

> [. . .] un homme n'existe pas à la manière de l'arbre ou du caillou: il faut qu'il *se fasse* ouvrier. Totalement conditionné par sa classe, son salaire, la nature de son travail, conditionné jusqu'à ses sentiments, jusqu'à ses pensées, c'est lui qui décide du sens de sa condition [. . .] [et qui] donne au prolétariat un avenir d'humiliation sans trêve ou de conquête et de victoire [. . .]. Tel est l'homme que nous concevons: homme total. Totalement engagé et totalement libre. C'est pourtant cet homme qu'il faut *délivrer*, en élargissant ses possibilités de choix.
>
> [. . .] a man does not exist in the same way that a tree or a pebble does: he must *make himself* a worker. Though he is completely conditioned by his class, his salary, the nature of his work, conditioned even in his feelings and his thoughts, it is nevertheless up to him to decide on the meaning of his condition [. . .] [and] to give the proletariat a future of constant humiliation or one of conquest and triumph [. . .]. Such is man as we conceive him: integral man. Totally committed and totally free. And yet it is the free man who must be *delivered*, by enlarging his possibilities of choice.[85]

Writing in a simple and direct style, perhaps as part of his own injunction to appear practical, Sartre here becomes prophet, advocate, and guide of the working class. Sartre so vividly portrays the social inscription of his program that little is left to the imagination: the narrative here is one of heroic agency—to be read, once again, against the backdrop of the culture of the purge, one that is obsessed with a narrative of betrayal. Whereas the purge offers a negative view of the bourgeois writer as traitor, Sartre offers the positive alternative of the writer as intellectual who can work with the proletariat. At the same time, Sartre echoes the discourse of the purge in condemning the theory of literary "gratuitousness." The worker is the hero of his own "conquest" and "victory," while the intelligentsia assist as mindful, responsible stewards, somehow external to the system of class that binds the worker, in the way prophets have always been in some part otherworldly.

Sartre's postwar cultural frame of reference is more explicit elsewhere than in the citation above. The philosophical line of reasoning he provides for his conception of man and freedom privileges the worker as the basic unit of social change—"[w]ithout its future, society is no more than an accumulation of raw data."[86] The image of the worker-hero here seems to have been derived from none other than the Communist promotion of the French Resistance fighter as provider of a victorious future. From a left-wing perspective, Sartre is contributing to a postwar myth about the nations occupied by the Nazis that was simultaneously being promoted by De Gaulle: "If, in occupied countries, the entire working class rose up against the invader, it was undoubtedly because it felt wounded in its revolutionary aspirations [. . .]."[87] His aim is not to set the historical record straight, but to universalize the socialist narrative; it also conveniently serves the purposes of the "maquis d'après-guerre," those who, after the war, falsely claimed to have been part of the Resistance. His judgments on the intellectual class, as we have seen, are much more astringent: in his capacity as philosopher of human choice, Sartre is also competent to expose the mistakes of the past while outling a more responsible future.

What, then, of literature? In this light, Sartre's earlier critique of men of letters appears to have derived from a reading of literature as the inevitable expression of choices made in the social realm. Is literature essentially a form of (auto) biography? The concluding pages of "Introducing *Les Temps modernes*" provide some broad remarks on literature and its place in the Sartrean project. They are surprisingly frank and reflect a new set of priorities. Literature, in *Les Temps modernes*, is to satisfy a didactic role. The "social function" that Sartre seeks to rescue for it—"[. . .] we will simply congratulate ourselves for [. . .] literature's having become again—at least for us—what it should never have stopped being: a social function"[88]—is a subordination of style, quality, and technique to social address and instructive utility. Literature presents a set of tools from which the critics are to make selections according to their capacity to express commitment: "[. . .] our critical essays will attempt to define in their broad lines the—new or ancient—literary techniques best suited to our designs."[89] Each genre may serve to advance the journal's project in a unique way: "[. . .] we will draw from every literary genre in order to familiarize the reader with our conceptions; a poem or a novel, if inspired by them, may well create a more favorable climate for their development."[90] Hence Sartre assembles both the theory and practice of engagement. It is only in the next-to-last line of the piece that Sartre evokes an undefined notion of purely literary merit, when he asserts that all submissions must not only cohere with the concerns of the editorship but must present "in addition, literary merit."[91]

Sartre offers literature as an instrument for communicating an agenda of change grounded in the idea of the working-class figure he evokes throughout the article. Sartre's program had to earn the approval of a field and a culture emerging from Nazi Occupation. His significance with respect to the field and the broader realm of French culture, as well as that of *Les Temps modernes*, depended in part on the force of that vision, and its ability to address socially perceived needs. The combination of strategies I have parsed here helps us to guess what those needs may have included—and to understand how Sartre brought together several different claims on cultural capital and authority. On the one hand, he is a sign of continuity with respect to France's fundamental, elite cultural institutions, such as the Ecole Normale. Also, he could count on being known as an unsullied figure within the context of France's purge, one whose wartime engagements represent an ethical continuity with the past. Furthermore, the designation of a "committed literature" puts a name, and a mode of intellectual activity, upon his wartime record, while offering an attractive alternative to the image of the bourgeois writer as irresponsible that emerged from the condemnatory activities of the *épuration*. The very pursuit of commitment as the dominant criterion of value becomes a way of converting the fact of his wartime activities—as relatively private and limited as they were—into capital in the postwar period. On the other hand, Sartre's social critique of elder figures of literary and intellectual authority asserts a rhetorical break with the past; the espousal of a new class consciousness positions him in the irreproachable role of guide and prophet to that engine of social revolution, the working class. It was the attractive nature of this figure and the appeal of his discourse that made for the success of his claims and turned Sartre into a key icon of the French postwar. Sartre's message and its "medium" satisfied a cultural demand.

Part of Sartre's "medium" was *Les Temps modernes*. His journal was an assertion of cultural capital, because of the major difference it bore with respect to previous journals: namely, the cultural figure of Sartre himself, on his way to becoming an icon, stood out in a way the figures associated with other journals did not. Part of this assertion can be read in the journal's name, which asserts that difference boldly: the Sartrean position is "modern" and all others are out of date. As founder and director, Sartre made the journal an extension and platform for his own set of priorities.[92] Its success or failure was tied to Sartre's ability to develop his position of authority in the field, while at the same time serving as one means of doing just that.

Another way was to create the appearance of a group or school. As the announcement of a cultural program, "Introducing *Les Temps modernes*" works alongside another strategy important to the development of Sartre's cultural capital, the presentation of a group. Complementary to the manifesto-style rhetoric of "Introducing *Les Temps modernes*" was the actual presentation of an editorial committee whose members would become readily identified with Sartre. Thus, if—as Anna Boschetti has recommended—we take *Les Temps modernes* as a mouthpiece for Sartre and a Sartrean habitus, a very important component of his cultural capital stems from the appearance of a group. The list of members of the editorial board printed in the first issues of the journal includes an impressive array of prestigious figures, including Merleau-Ponty, Beauvoir, Leiris, Aron, and Jean Paulhan. Each of them—on the strength of very different individual credentials—represents additional cultural capital that added to the strength of Sartre's position and to the momentum of his rise. Fairly well in keeping with an established pattern for French literary movements, groups, and schools, the subsequent departures of the figures listed above from *Les Temps modernes* (with the exception of Beauvoir) marked their need to differentiate themselves from Sartre, and are in part further evidence of Sartre's success.[93] Like his seminars on Existentialism in

1946—which met with an enormous public response, adding to his fame as philosopher—"Introducing *Les Temps modernes*" and other texts of this period served the function of rounding out the image of Sartre as a dominant public intellectual.

Henry Rousso, in *The Vichy Syndrome: History and Memory in France since 1944*, describes the development of a national crisis of memory around France's experience of Occupation and Collaboration.[94] The "Vichy Syndrome," France's long silence about—and in more recent times, obsession with—the Vichy period owes much, in Rousso's analysis, to General Charles De Gaulle's 1944 inauguration of a foundational, post-Vichy myth that all but erases French collaboration. Rousso considers De Gaulle's statements in 1944 and 1945 as having legitimized the first retrospective visions of the Occupation.[95] The De Gaulle myth is of an abstracted, whole "eternal France," that freed itself of Nazi control, and that neither suffers nor has suffered any internal divisions. De Gaulle went so far as to turn the real and often brutal experiences of the resistance fighters into an abstract condition that applied to all French, resistance fighters and collaborators alike:

> Cette vision cohérente et relativement fermée sur elle-même [. . .] se définit moins comme une glorification de la Résistance (et certainement pas des résistants), que comme la célébration d'un peuple *en résistance* que symbolise l'homme du 18 juin [. . .] Elle tente de se superposer à la réalité autrement plus complexe et composite de l'Occupation. Son objectif inavoué était d'interpréter le passé en fonction des urgences du présent.[96]

~

> This coherent and relatively closed vision [. . .] is defined less as a glorification of the Resistance (and

> certainly not of the resistants), than as the celebration of a people in resistance symbolized by the man of June 18 [. . .]. It tries to superimpose itself on the far more complex and composite reality of the Occupation. Its hidden objective was to interpret the past according to the urgencies of the present.

Politically expedient because of the need to rally the nation, De Gaulle's vision raises a national image above any individual factional sign, to the detriment of the literary Resistance's themes of accountability and responsibility. It overlays the jagged, partisan landscape of France's cultural life with the illusion of unity and an equal share for all in the glory of a triumphant France.

According to Rousso's analysis, De Gaulle's myth-making vision of the Occupation unfolded in four more subsequent manifestations.[97] I make mention of this initial phase to suggest that aspects of the positionality I have examined in "Introducing *Les Temps modernes*" are compatible with the kind of historical revision of which De Gaulle's comments were symptomatic. So many elements of Sartre's profile match with those of Vercors and other members of the literary Resistance—indeed, their political agendas are strikingly similar, drawing as they do from the same sources—that one would expect the activism of each to benefit the others. And yet, Vercors and many of his colleagues were fated to relative obscurity in the long shadow of Sartre's literary engagement. My hypothesis helps understand Sartre's dominance in the literary field as owing in large part to his playing a political role as both a symbol of unity and a moral alibi in the post-Vichy myth.

One important advantage of Sartre's model over that of Vercors was its emphasis on the use of literature: it is reasonable to expect that a culture eager to cast its recent past in heroic terms would choose to see that narrative replayed in the regular installments of *Les Temps modernes*, over the detailed accounts grounded in historical fact that Minuit offered. The choice was of fictional narrative over historical narrative. In addition, Sartre's project of developing a literary political pedagogy comes across as much less disruptive, divisive—and ultimately altogether less engaged—than the very specific and sweeping raft of cultural reforms proposed, for instance, in *L'Heure du choix*. Instead of Vercors's "Never forget!" the French chose the re-membering of the past in Sartre's more accommodating terms. Moreover, that degree of accommodation extended as far as Sartre's becoming considered a key element of the survival of the fragile Fourth Republic. Sartre's appropriation of the Resistance narrative effectively robbed the more radical left of its agenda and the moral authority to pursue it.

The compatibility of Sartrean engagement with France's Vichy Syndrome was also of benefit to those participants in the literary field tainted by their wartime collaboration. By being absent during the peak moments of controversy surrounding the purge hearings—he was traveling in America at the time—Sartre avoided having to weigh in on individual cases. The voices of the CNE authors became easier to discredit as strident and radical against Sartre's silence. Foremost among those to benefit was Sartre's publisher, Gallimard, whose case was dismissed fairly quickly, despite the gravity of many of the charges against him.[98] As his publisher, Gallimard had an easier time returning to normal operations—including selling books by authors blacklisted by the CNE—because of the large sales of Sartre's publications. Thus, in a very real way, Sartre's prestige was a support for the position of Paulhan, who continued to reign as the literary "grey eminence" from the heights of his office at Gallimard.

In a very brief period of time, many of the authors published by Minuit in wartime, or who got their start at Minuit, left for the greater stability and prestige Gaston Gallimard could offer.[99] This literary equivalent of what economists call "capital flight" left Vercors's Minuit with even fewer opportunities to convert talent into financial strength. However, the capital flight may have turned out, in the long run, to be a blessing in disguise for Editions de Minuit. When Jérôme Lindon took control in March 1948—following a complicated series of family loans to the firm that culminated in something of a leveraged buyout—he had the advantage of being able to rebuild the house from scratch. Doing so successfully is another question altogether, and in the next chapter I look at Minuit's new publisher and the editorial changes he made in the early 1950s to redefine Minuit's bid for cultural capital.

CHAPTER II

Lindon, Robbe-Grillet, and The Critics: 1950-1955

1. Lindon's New Minuit

This chapter focuses on the figure of Jerôme Lindon and the growing association of important figures with Lindon and his authors in the first half of the 1950s. During this period, Lindon laid the groundwork for later triumphs, and assembled the important early elements of Minuit's reputation as a serious literary publishing house. These were years in which Lindon began to develop an editorial direction meant to signify Edition de Minuit's vital difference, later to be incarnated in the New Novel. The difference of the New Novel, its rethinking of the novel genre, was anticipated by many of Lindon's earlier publishing activities, many of which were defined and presented along similar lines of rethinking genre.

I first offer evidence that suggests why it was possible for Lindon to undertake the projects and create the associations that he did *when* he did. In the previous chapter, I described a uniquely limited postwar literary field, in which Sartre and his circle seemed able to issue orthodoxy; even when oppositional forces resurfaced they were compelled to address their opposition in Sartrean terms. The unusual failure of Vercors's (non-oppositional) Editions de Minuit in these circumstances held little promise for a young literary outsider intent on turning the house around. How did circumstances eventually change in Lindon's favor? I then depict the particular role of *littérateur* that Lindon played in his communications with me in recent years, and the significant statements they make about literature, criticism, and academic research. I portray the privileged status accorded by Lindon to one researcher in particular as part of a strategy to preserve those assertions. These relationships anticipate how I interpret the strategies employed by Lindon to develop Minuit's capital in the 1950s. By creating alliances—real or suggested—that were able, for reasons I discuss, to valorize one another through their association with the Minuit label, Lindon prepared the way for Minuit to become the focal point of the New Novel phenomenon and the consequent reconfiguration of the literary field.

Many of the literary figures of the immediate postwar continued to exert considerable influence throughout much of the 1950s. Sartre, the members of his group, and *Les Temps Modernes* still represented an important intellectual bloc that articulated Sartrean political views and cultural critique. However, the relatively straightforward and dichotomous picture of the literary field I discussed in Chapter I began to fragment. The emergence of new positions in the first half of the 1950s provided alternatives to the dominant voices on the left, as well as to the recently re-galvanized right. More importantly still, these positions were able to endure, and thus point to the development of demand for such alternatives. Lindon's efforts to define himself as a publisher and redefine the Minuit label participated in the same movement. His activities reinforced and were reinforced by other of the new positions: for instance, Lindon had an ally in the person of Maurice Nadeau—publisher and editor of *Les Lettres Nouvelles*, founded in 1953. In that first year of the journal's existence, an unprecedented amount of attention was given to Samuel Beckett—including an original text of his, reviews, and a lengthy article by Nadeau. The timing was apt and skillful on Nadeau's part: the first staging of *Waiting for Godot* began in January 1953 and its steadily mounting success throughout that year was undoubtedly beneficial to Nadeau's journal. Nadeau was among the first influential readers of Beckett, having written one of the earliest published reviews of his work for *Combat* in 1951. *Les Lettres Nouvelles* was to be a constant champion of Beckett, and Nadeau faithfully promoted his work in the journal and elsewhere. Nadeau's statements on his support for Beckett in his autobiographical essays are borne out in the publishing record: "*Les Lettres Nouvelles* is entirely devoted to Beckett. From the first issues on." Furthermore, with each new play or novel, Beckett "gives pre-release excerpts to *Lettres Nouvelles*."[1]

For as much as these endorsements of Beckett served Lindon's purposes, they also served Nadeau's journal in its drive to represent the defense of literature against ideological cooptation. "From the first issues on," Lindon's Beckett was assimilated to Nadeau's anti-political mission, outlined in his journal's first issue: "Crushed under the weight of ideology and bias, used as an escape or a weapon of propaganda, [. . .] literature is nonetheless something other than a concern only for aesthetes, more than a more or less refined form of distraction, or an unholy means of getting to ruinous ends."[2] Shortly, I will discuss further reasons why Nadeau's new position was of particular strategic importance to Lindon's Minuit, yet firstly, it is important to identify a number of the other significant new appearances shaking up the literary field in the early 50s, some of which had direct ties to Minuit and others that would in coming years.

If the case can be made that *Les Lettres Nouvelles* promoted a de-politicized, "art for art's sake" theory of literary production, then it makes sense to expect to find affinities and connections between *Les Lettres Nouvelles* and Jean Paulhan's *La Nouvelle NRF*. By dint of its long and powerful history—its long-accumulated capital—the return of Gallimard's flagship literary journal to print in 1953 was richer in symbolic valences than the upstart *Lettres Nouvelles*. The end of the ban on the journal—accepted under condition of the name change—dealt yet another blow to the fantasy of renewal in the immediate postwar. Its reappearance completed the return of the powerhouse Gallimard, once discredited for having collaborated with the enemy. In the same way that Gallimard's dynamic and large-scale production capabilities threatened to crowd out the smaller publishing houses like Minuit and Juilliard, the scale and capital of Paulhan's journal was a threat to smaller and less-secure journals attempting to carve out a niche in the field. Furthermore, the return of Paulhan's editorial direction was a stark re-assertion of anti-engagement values, summed up for many scholars by the motto "art for art's sake" and expressed in Paulhan's literary preferences. After several years "underground"—writing articles under pseudonyms, publishing through Editions de Minuit—the "éminence grise" held court once again.[3] Mauriac's comments on the reincarnation of the *NRF* are instructive as to who it was thought its readership would be. Mauriac realized that *La Nouvelle NRF* posed a specific threat to *La Table ronde*, which he hoped could preserve its mandate as "defender of literary value." In other words, he was concerned that the readers of the conservative, anti-existentialist, and anti-communist *La Table ronde* would switch to *La Nouvelle NRF*.

For Editions de Minuit, meanwhile, the return of Gallimard's journal meant the further dissemination of writings by certain authors that Lindon shared with his publishing rival. The most striking example is Blanchot, who, in addition to his contributions to *Critique*, kept a column in *La Nouvelle NRF*. Furthermore, Paulhan's affinity for Lindon's Minuit translated into attention and praise for Minuit authors before it had become in some sense necessary to attend to or praise them; before, for instance, Robbe-Grillet's *Le Voyeur* won the Prix des Critiques—which, as members of the jury, both Paulhan and Blanchot voted for. Editions de Minuit survived the lean years of the early 1950s due in part to the support of figures like Nadeau and Paulhan and their respective journals. In turn, their critical recognition provided encouragement—if not abundant financial reward—in Lindon's search for a productive editorial direction.

The emergence of these and other new positions in the field are not to be viewed as causes for Sartre's decline in prominence and cultural capital. Instead, they are symptoms of broader shifts in political sentiment and mood. The relaxation of Cold War tensions, the internal political tribulations of the Fourth Republic, the pacifying cultural effects of burgeoning prosperity, and the coming of new crises to the foreground—these are the kinds of forces that diminished Sartre's—or any single intellectual's—appeal and ability to set the terms of literary debate. Sartre's powerful watchword, literary engagement, was still on the lips of critics and commentators in the early 50s, but in just a few years had all but fallen off the agendas of critics other than those writing in predictably engaged publications. Even Mauriac, for whom Sartre and his engaged atheistic existentialism were highly motivating reasons to write, finally suspended his campaign. When Mauriac became a chronicler for *L'Express*—another fascinating and telling new field position[4]—his priorities and attention shifted from Sartre to international politics and French foreign policy. Finally, Sartre lost even more sway in the fallout from the Soviet Union's incursion and suppression of the Hungarian uprising of 1956. French intellectuals left the Parti Communiste Français in large numbers, including its most famous *compagnon de route*—Sartre—and as a result his sphere of influence was further diminished.

While Minuit's publisher never assumed the kind of iconic cultural status of Jean-Paul Sartre—remaining instead all but unknown to the reading public throughout this period and beyond—I argue that Jerôme Lindon represents a new alternative style of intellectual figure to that of Sartre. Lindon's publishing would be effective in helping to displace Sartre and his aesthetic from the fore of elite literary culture. my comparison of these figures—heroic çhampion of Resistance culture and self-effacing cultural producer—may seem an unlikely one, yet each was responsible for the literary moment and catchphrases of their day, and each came to embody the standards of value that articulated the spectrum of difference across the field of literature.

The many differences between Lindon and Sartre reveal a number of considerations about the kind of literary intellectual it was possible to be in the changing historical conjuncture. Lindon's style echoes that of Jean Paulhan, as discussed in Chapter I: as a publisher, and hence as a professional literary authority, Lindon subtly and without any overtly stated program, changed the categories by which texts were classified and ultimately recognized. The reconfiguration of value in the literary field occasioned by the New Novel phenomenon was to hinge in part on a project of rethinking genre that Lindon began to articulate as early as 1950. The literary "revolution" of the New Novel cannot be viewed separately from Minuit's other, earlier strategies of self-promotion: the assertion of the renewal of the novel genre is one component of a new systematization of literary genres first exemplified by Minuit's publications and the various modes of their presentation.

A number of researchers in publishing history and editorial theory have posited the literary editor as a figure who both prepares texts for publication and engineers their reception—and thus encompasses two very different roles, although each entails some form of mediation.[5] Such mediation can include modifying texts to match certain notions of what it is, or is not, appropriate to publish. It can also include using various tools to construct a text's readership: documentation such as flap copy and other promotional materials are ways of establishing a context for reading that should generate interest. However, in the case of contemporary French publishing in general and Les Editions de Minuit specifically, gaining access to correspondence and other archival documentation of those roles has, in my experience, proven very difficult. In order to begin to grasp something of the figure of Jerôme Lindon, one is obliged to proceed from one's own dealings with him, the sparse body of his writing and interviews, and what a number of his intimates have indicated about him. Other researchers have spoken of a "law of silence" in the French publishing world, one broken only rarely by insiders courageous enough to risk their own expulsion. One of the rare exceptions to that law is *Le Comité*, in which Michel Deguy, a reader for Gallimard for many years, gives a damning account of a flawed and arbitrary editorial process. Other available inquiries into publishing are much more reassuring about that process, even to the point of sounding like industry advertising. Witness, for instance, Laurence

Santantonios's "survey" entitled *Auteur/Editeur: Création sous influence.*[6] Her conclusion seeks to silence critics of the closed world of French publishing, by insisting at once on the material challenges faced by editors and on the conscientious efforts by both parties to preserve authorial freedom. The difficulties my own efforts have met are in their own right meaningful, and reveal much about Lindon's own use of silence to affirm a certain, long-standing set of notions about publishing and his role at Minuit—the very notions I presently seek to elucidate by drawing upon my experiences in conjunction with documents available in archives and in the literature.

Jérôme Lindon crops up from time to time as a discreet figure in the background of literary criticism on the New Novel. His generosity toward researchers is documented in references to him in many forewords, acknowledgements, and prefaces, which suggests a little-mentioned but vital role in shaping critical perspectives on his publications. Interactions between publishers and critics can engender the literary equivalent of brand loyalty; Lindon's influence, by encouraging connections between the imprint and its authors, has been an essential part of the mythology of Minuit and the New Novel. His success in this is beyond question: upon his death in spring 2001, the mythic figure—and a basic version of Minuit history—was eulogized in the French and international presses.

Some of these traits appeared in our exchanges: those of a polite, obliging, and astonishingly modest individual, who, despite his exceptional career, would refer to himself as no more than a mere novice reader. These traits stand in complete opposition to the negative reputation he had in certain quarters, according to which he was shrewd, parsimonious, severe, and more inclined to exert control than relinquish it.[7] In his dealings with me, Lindon alternated carefully between hands-on and very hands-off approaches to my questions, at times hinting at his ideas about his authors and at others withdrawing from explanation or interpretation under the claim of incompetence to do so. We exchanged correspondence on several occasions; the first, in 1995, culminated in a phone interview, during which he cordially listened to my questions and guardedly offered some comments. These primarily concerned the newer generation of Minuit authors, the "young authors" (see Chapter V). With respect to some of those authors, Lindon repeated information I recognized from previous interviews he had given, and which he clearly considered important details in their stories of literary success. For instance, he spoke of how Jean Echenoz's first publications originally sold a mere several hundred copies, whereas his novels currently sell very, very well. In 1995 I was working on a research project that posited the "young authors" as a kind of posterity, in certain formal literary terms, to the New Novel. Mine was a hypothesis that he was eager to discount—for reasons I discuss in the Chapter V—and citing Echenoz's very successful record of sales seemed to represent, for him, proof of a definitive break—even though the New Novel had, in fact, eventually also sold very well.

He decided that an interview in person with me would not be worthwhile, because, aside from the "very rough" "drafts of responses" he had provided, he was sure he could not be of more use. He insisted, furthermore, that his answers were mere "rough drafts" and were not—under any circumstances—to be quoted.[8] Indeed, most of our conversation to that point had been—at least it seemed at the time—unrevealing: one of the points he insisted upon was that he "merely" publishes what he likes, and that he leaves it to the critics to determine what they will from those texts.

Our second exchange in the summer of 2000 cast new light on the previous one, and reminded me of the figure that Lindon presented of himself in his writing, interviews, and elsewhere. This time, I had written him to set up an interview in advance of travel to Paris. As before, he responded immediately in a welcoming and gracious manner, agreeing to meet with me. In my second letter, this time from Paris, I included the following three groups of—perhaps overzealous?—questions that I hoped to put to him during our upcoming meeting:

> 1) When you became head of Editions de Minuit, did you have an idea of what you wanted Minuit's place or role to be? Were there sources of inspiration guiding your choices in the early years of the publishing house?
>
> 2) How was the editorial team made up in the 1950s and early 1960s? How were publishing decisions arrived at? Was there an apportioning of specialties?
>
> 3) Were there titles in the Minuit booklist—at any moment of the 1950s—that defined more than others the special character of Editions de Minuit? Which titles began to give the Editions de Minuit catalog its definitive shape?[9]

His reply to this second letter was short and to the point: it was no longer possible for us to meet, and in any case, his memory of the period in question had become so covered over by what had been written about it since that he had nothing new or interesting to say whatsoever. His curt message ended with one brief remark evoking the shock he had felt upon reading Beckett for the first time.

On reading his reply, it occurred to me that, in several essential ways, it was a repetition of our 1995 phone conversation. First, in each instance there was the same refusal to examine or offer statements about his own role and activities as publisher. Instead, he consistently abdicated authority over those activities and how they should be understood. Moreover, once again he seemed unwilling to acknowledge the interest of such questions. As any foreign student in France might wonder upon encountering resistance to their inquiries, I suspected that I was not "playing the game" properly. After all, I had discovered press interviews and profiles of Lindon from the mid-1960s on in which he had been more expressive. The same apparently holds true in the cases of numerous scholars of the New Novel who cite his extreme helpfulness in offering guidance in their research. What had I done wrong?

A possible answer may lie in the one major difference between the subject of our phone interview in 1995, and that of our correspondence in 2000—after all, on the earlier occasion he had at least been willing to speak with me on the phone. In 1995, I was working on the more recent generation of Minuit authors, those published since 1980. In his comments to me, Lindon sought to underscore that each member of the young authors was, in his view, very different with respect to the others. I could sense that he was gently urging me away from developing modes of comparison among them and toward reading them as distinct.[10] In my more recent contact, the subject was no longer strictly literary: I was now approaching Lindon, not for guidance among titles and authors in his booklist, but for information on the ideas, events, and strategies behind the construction of that booklist. The difference must have been substantial to a publisher whose first priority is to promote his new authors—a process in which I may, at first, have been seen to have some potential role, however small. My more recent research into the editorial strategy of Minuit in the 1950s could presumably play no part in any such process, as that generation of authors had already long since been canonized. There seems, therefore, to be an instrumentalization implicit in Lindon's relationship with critics and scholars—one that meant that, since my work could not be a part of it, I would be denied access to the inner reaches of the realm, the Minuit archives.

A second way in which our two interactions were similar relates to Lindon's stated deference to other authorities: in the first instance, he leaves it to critics and academics ("*les universitaires*") to interpret the works he chooses to publish, implying that choice reflects no consciously formed, intellectual decision-making. His position is a fascinatingly contradictory one, since in the same breath he both acknowledges his role in the editorial process, and disavows it: he makes a choice, but that choice is only casually motivated. The text in question, therefore, remains a pure, whole object, fully accessible on its own. On the one hand, spontaneous choice represents a certain guarantee of consistency of literary quality—as we shall see presently, this view corresponds to other texts and statements made by Lindon. On the other, the impossible removal of himself from the process is a myth meant to guarantee both the autonomy of the author, and the status of her book as unmediated text. The pure, unmediated text is the idealized object of consumer culture, as well as of certain brands of literary criticism. Furthermore, at the time of our conversation, I took his expressed deference to *universitaires* as flattering: myself a *universitaire* in training, I was being invited to occupy the space of discursive authority he was leaving for "us." In this light, his stance comes across as a brilliant positioning: cutting fairly clean lines between himself, the texts, and me as critical reader, Lindon at once affirmed the interest, importance, and viability of reading his authors and my capacity to conduct such readings. Naturally, that affirmation extended only to my use of his publications.

Yet there may also be another way of understanding his posture of deference to academic authority in the early- to mid-90s, a posture that imagines texts as eminently available for critical analysis, but also detached or separate from that analysis. In discounting the significance of his own relationship to his publications, Lindon seeks to preclude an over-determining interpretation—one that would diminish any text's potential to captivate as many different sources of legitimating authority for as long a term as possible. Thus, texts must be constants against the variety of interpretations that can be made of them, at once solicitous of intellectual endorsement and free-standing from it. His strategy makes sense in the particular context of Minuit's publishing in the 1990s, since, as I discuss in Chapter V, it is aimed at avoiding the kind of close relationship with academic criticism that helped identify Minuit as publisher of the New Novel, an interpretive role vital to Minuit's and Lindon's fortunes.

By comparison, in our more recent exchange, his deference to other authorities—those who have already studied Les Editions de Minuit in the 1950s—is a much more direct dismissal of my research questions. The implication being that what has already been written about such matters is sufficient, and that there is no merit in considering them further. While, as before, no reference is made to just who the authorities evoked may be, it seems clear that Lindon had one particular scholar in mind: Anne Simonin.

My exchanges with Jerôme Lindon revealed a set of postures

and tactics that speak to how Lindon related to critics; within that relation—or in my case, a contrasting non-relation—certain *a priori* assumptions appear with regard to how he hoped his own role would be understood vis-à-vis his publications, and how he intended for them to be received. My attempt to press further into the workings of Minuit prompted Lindon to take an equally revelatory stand. His unwillingness to either acknowledge my questions or make it possible for me to conduct research in the Minuit archives stemmed from a desire to undermine my inquiry as a whole: as guardian of Minuit's long-standing reputation for quality, Lindon had no intention of delivering the care of that legacy into the hands of an unknown outsider. In this light, it is very pertinent to consider the unique and privileged relationship Lindon accorded to Anne Simonin, by all measures the authorized custodian of Minuit's both literal and figural historical memory.[11]

The only substantive history of Minuit in existence is Anne Simonin's volume covering the period from 1941 to 1953. Published in 1994 by the Institut de la Mémoire de l'Edition Contemporaine (IMEC), her book is one in a series of IMEC publications focusing on publishing history that has been issued over the past ten years. As an initiative of the French publishers' union, a body presided over by Jerôme Lindon for many years, the IMEC enjoys a considerable degree of respect as curator of publishing culture. Simonin's text draws its authority from its publisher, on the one hand, and from Simonin's status in the university on the other.

To produce her work—originally a doctoral thesis directed, very significantly, by Pierre Bourdieu[12]—Simonin had unprecedented access to the Minuit archives. In the course of informal interviews with Simonin in 2000, it became clear that not only did she continue to have that access for a substantial period of time, but, in her capacity as custodian of the Minuit archives, she was able to stand as intercessor between researchers like myself—unsanctioned outsiders—and the archives, thus guaranteeing "editorial control," as it were, for Lindon, and providing negotiated access for researchers. Furthermore, through her extensive knowledge of both the literature on Minuit and the archival materials housed there, she functions to steer researchers—as she sought, in our conversations, to do with me—to areas of inquiry that are, in her view, gaps in the scholarship. In this way, she was in a position to lend her capital to the legitimization of research on Les Editions de Minuit, and, by extension, to stand in as a professional academic counterpart, and to some extent as an alibi, to Jerôme Lindon. Simonin represents an academic, disciplinary complement to Lindon's—on the one hand—personal stance of autonomy and the rather anti-disciplinary perspective he revealed to me on the other. Her role as alibi is to accredit the continued importance of the history of Les Editions de Minuit that Lindon de-emphasizes, if not always dismisses.

This relationship—one through which Lindon is able to orchestrate divergent positions relating to Minuit and the conservation of its image—is an example that prefigures a number of the strategies Lindon deployed in his continuous efforts to maintain and develop Minuit's capital in variable cultural contexts. The example I have been discussing involved the status of Lindon's "young Minuit authors" ["jeunes auteurs de Minuit"] as authors whose consecration was still at stake, and the issue of control over the cultural memory of Les Editions de Minuit. I now turn to the very different context of the early 50s to analyze some of the important early steps Lindon took and the strategies he used in constructing the Minuit of the New Novel era.

2. Publisher of Beckett

When the New Novel had begun to shake up the literary field in the last years of the 1950s, many rightly or wrongly began to identify Editions de Minuit, Jérôme Lindon, and Samuel Beckett with it. The right reasons for doing so form the subject of the coming chapters; but first, a striking instance of mistaken identification is instructive of just how strong those identifications would later become. In her biography of Simone de Beauvoir, Dierdre Bair[13] writes of Beauvoir's 1946 decision not to publish part of a text Beckett submitted to *Les Temps Modernes*.[14] Years later, in conversation with her biographer, Beauvoir confided that her decision not to publish Beckett's second piece was more than a run-of-the-mill rejection on "mere" grounds of unsuitability. In fact, in her view there was animosity between Beckett and Sartre: "[he] deliberately tricked me because he never liked Sartre and thought we were both out of touch with modern literature. It gave him pleasure to extend his dislike to me."[15] That there would have been any animosity between the two at even this early stage of their careers would seem surprising, especially since Beckett submitted his story to Sartre's journal with good hopes of its being accepted by this former acquaintance from the Ecole Normale Supérieure.[16] Bair's report of the conversation continues:

> Basically, she was "suspicious of that crowd that had started to gather around [Jerôme] Lindon and his press [Les Editions de Minuit]." As she sat in cafés, journalists and critics frequently teased her that "this New Novel" was all her and Sartre's fault, claiming that the new techniques in fiction were a logical reaction against their literature of commitment."[17]

Yet Bair does not point out that Beauvoir is conflating events separated by over a decade, as if the difference of position that would be common enough currency for critics to tease her about it in the late 50s—when the term "New Novel" and the authors that constituted its "crowd" began to circulate—already existed in these early days of the postwar formation of the literary field. Beckett's submissions pre-date his first encounters with Lindon by four years—years during which, moreover, Beckett unsuccessfully pitched texts to other publishers. Beauvoir's confusion of chronology underscores how Beckett would be assimilated to the modernist "crowd" gathering at Minuit seven and eight years after Lindon first published Beckett. The difference that Beckett could have represented in the literary field in 1946—indeed, the one acknowledged, to some extent, by the assertion of his unsuitability for *Les Temps Modernes*—would take some time to be produced.

When, in his letter, Lindon cited the moment of "shock" at reading Samuel Beckett for the first time, he was not revealing something new to Minuit lore. At once evoking the almost romantic narrative of literary discovery that Lindon recounted elsewhere—Beckett is the author of primary reference in every instance in which Lindon reflects on his career and on Minuit's history—Lindon's citation of Beckett in his letter to me also echoes the same strategy of presentation that made of Samuel Beckett the main symbol of Minuit's literary direction up until the New Novel. I argue that the mythologization of their relationship suggests that there was a desire for identification between Beckett the author and Lindon the publisher, and that there are compelling reasons involving Minuit's struggling position in the field for why Lindon sought such an identification. These are reasons that exceed the ostensibly "pure" convictions about literary quality that are constantly foregrounded in Lindon's references to Beckett.

One of the instances of Lindon's mythologization of his discovery of Beckett can be found in a three-page text entitled "La première rencontre," ["The First Encounter"] published in an issue of *Cahiers de l'Herne* dedicated to Samuel Beckett.[18] Lindon writes of the day he found three manuscripts of novels by Beckett on his desk; he began by reading *Molloy*.

> C'est de ce jour que j'ai su que je serais peut-être un éditeur, je veux dire un *vrai* éditeur. Dès la première ligne [. . .] la beauté écrasante de ce texte m'assaillit. Je lus *Molloy* en quelques heures, comme je n'avais jamais lu un livre. Or ce n'était pas un roman paru chez un de mes confrères, un de ces chefs-d'œuvre consacrés auquel moi, éditeur, je n'aurais jamais de part: c'était un manuscrit inédit, et non seulement inédit: refusé par plusieurs éditeurs. Je n'arrivais pas à y croire.
>
> That was the day I knew I would perhaps be a publisher, I mean a *real* publisher. From the very first line [. . .] the overwhelming beauty of that text waylaid me. I read *Molloy* in a matter of hours, like I'd never done before. Yet this was no novel published by one of my peers, one of those hallowed masterpieces that I, though an editor myself, would never have a hand in: it was an unpublished manuscript, but not just unpublished, rejected by several publishers. I couldn't believe it.[19]

Without putting in question the truthfulness of Lindon's anecdote, it is important to recall that Lindon's recollections have the advantage of issuing from a time when Beckett's symbolic value was widely recognized and had already long served as an anchoring point for the New Novel. What stands out is how this anecdote serves a certain purpose with respect to guaranteeing an image of Lindon himself and the Minuit stamp. The key underpinning of Lindon's account is his identification as a reader apt to recognize immediately and with conviction the value of texts missed or passed over by the rest of the field: as Lindon is mindful to reiterate, Beckett's manuscript had been rejected on numerous occasions. Lindon arrogates to himself ownership of the vision behind the various discourses of rupture and renewal identified in Beckett's work by critics. Indeed, rupture and renewal would become associated with Minuit generally from the late 50s on. The part of the citation that helps answer the question of what Beckett meant to Lindon in the early 50s comes in the last sentence, where Lindon connects the unpublished manuscript with Minuit's position in the field, or in his words, its position vis-à-vis his peers, confreres, competitors [indeed, the French term "confrères" suggests a brotherhood, a special relation among an intimate group]. "[T]his was no novel published by one of my peers," [. . .] "it was an unpublished manuscript." Lindon's nostalgia for this defining moment has to do with the opportunity to circumvent the conventional ways in which authors were coming to Minuit and bring in an outsider. In this, Lindon had found an appealing *modus operandi*: with relatively few exceptions, Lindon's choices would henceforth consist of gambles on unknown authors and outsiders to the field, and their "newness" would be the defining sign of their presentation.[20]

Lindon's account notwithstanding, it made sense to publish Beckett in 1951, though not on the grounds the New Novelists would later give in recuperating his work for their purposes. By virtue of his close association with the Minuit brand-name—skillfully orchestrated by Lindon and the New Novelists—Beckett would become always and *a priori* "the precursor," as one critic put it.[21] First, the value of publishing Beckett must be seen in relation to the problem of Minuit's indifferentiation within the field. Until 1950, Les Editions de Minuit—whether under Vercors or Lindon—did not publish a second novel by any one of its authors, and consequently, none—whether a financial success or not—could be held up as the sign of Minuit. Instead, Vercors was that sign: with his departure went Minuit's right to publish his work, as well. As I indicated at the end of the last chapter, one of Lindon's first tasks in taking over Minuit was to try to recast Minuit as *more* than the publishing house of the literary Resistance: this had proven to be a base of capital inadequate to ensuring Minuit's survival. Beckett turned up with a major set of completed and nearly completed texts: *Molloy*, *Malone Meurt*, and *L'Innommable* to start, with *En Attendant Godot* and the texts that would make up *Nouvelles et textes pour rien* on hand in the coming year.[22] Both demonstrably prolific and virtually unknown, Beckett was an entire literary project that Lindon could opt to invest in. At the same time, however, Lindon could not simply cease publishing Resistance texts and authors. Beckett's record of active participation in the Paris Resistance put him above reproach in a culture in which Resistance credentials were important capital. This element of Beckett's biography was helpful in lessening the impact of Lindon's steady move away from Minuit's identification with the French resistance—the trajectory I read in his reorganization of the Minuit catalog.

As one of Lindon's first additions to the catalog, Beckett was eminently defensible because he could be viewed as satisfying the exigencies of an intellectual culture imbued with Sartre's ideas. Yet Beckett's Resistance service was not the only way in which he had some degree of currency in the Sartrean realm: his first successful postwar publication in France was the prose piece appearing in *Les Temps modernes*. Much of the initial reception of Beckett's publications in the early 50s, up to and including the response to *Godot* in 1954, emphasized existentialist themes. It was possible to articulate Beckett's newness or difference from within a Sartrean frame of reference without expressing Lindon's "shock." Reviews of Beckett's writings published in *Les Temps modernes* in 1952 and 1953 are perhaps the most pertinent examples of this, if by no means the sole ones.[23] The Beckett of Lindon's shock, the figure of a certain kind of literary break, can only begin to be found in the play among literary journals in alliance with or against one another, as each makes interpretive claims on Beckett's œuvre: Maurice Nadeau and Bernard Dort in *Les Temps modernes*, Georges Bataille in *Critique*, Nadeau again in his own *Les Lettres Nouvelles*, and Maurice Blanchot writing for *La Nouvelle NRF*.

Nadeau's 1952 article on Beckett in *Les Temps Modernes* is a poignant illustration of the positionality's role in the development of different interpretations of Beckett's œuvre. The journal's predispositions or expectations can be read in the article's emphasis on Beckett's recuperability within an existentialist vision of humanity and of the role of the writer to expose the human condition. Focused on the trilogy, Nadeau's "Samuel Beckett, or The Right to Silence" ["Samuel Beckett ou le droit au silence"] traces the progressive disintegration of the narrators, identifying their trajectory toward "the opaque," "the undifferentiated," and "the unutterable," all recurrent themes of the various strands of Beckett criticism that would follow. What stands out in the article are the statements framing those themes as the components of an existentialist argument or assertion. There are several such statements throughout the text, reminding the reader what is to be made of Beckett's strange characters: "[a]n impressive and tragic spectacle [. . .], the most complete and ringing indictment of our condition ever formulated"[24]; "[h]is characters offer the spectacle of a humanity brought close to its animal condition by its sole quest for a miserable satisfaction of its needs."[25] In developing his conclusion, Nadeau goes the furthest in situating Beckett's difference within terms recognizable to *Les Temps modernes* readers. "Contestation of the world of man?" he asks. "We no longer have any doubt."[26] But, he goes on, Beckett's "protest" is an original one, because for as much as it expresses a "universal contestation" it also "contests itself." The texts' self-referentiality nonetheless does not diminish their share of intellectual engagement, culminating as they do in a "denunciation" of the "language 'of others,' powerless to express the reality of the unique."[27] The suggestion may seem too close to cliché, but one cannot help but associate these "others" to those inhabiting Sartre's hell; regardless, to situate Beckett as a critic of language—and especially literary language—is to argue that he belongs among the ranks of the Moderns familiar to readers of *Les Temps modernes*.

Within a year after the publication of that article, Nadeau revisits its themes in a text that appeared in *Les Lettres nouvelles* and reads like a rewrite of its predecessor. Like the earlier article, "Beckett's Last Attempt" ["La Dernière tentative de Beckett"] presents a reading of *L'Innommable* in relation to Beckett's previous novels, and identifies the same negative progression toward silence and paralysis. Yet in this version, Nadeau has eliminated all the vocabulary and assertions that gave his previous review its philosophical dimension: the discussions of "indictment," "protestation" or "contestation" are gone, and all references to "humanity" or "our condition" have been suppressed or, as in this example, paraphrased: "[d]oes one still recognize him too much as a representative of our species? So the author transforms him into Worm [. . .]."[28] Beckett intervenes in the reader's understanding of the narrator in order to prevent him or her from reading the narrator as a human figure: hence Nadeau suppresses his own urge and distances himself from his previous reading. He opts instead to all but retreat from interpretation and let the texts speak for and of themselves by adding many more textual citations to those kept over from the *Temps modernes* piece.

The critical emphasis has shifted from interpreting Beckett to characterizing his novels as an internally coherent system, the rules or stakes of which have less to do with the human condition than with their distance from such interpretation. As a consequence of this change, Nadeau is now unsure of what to conclude from Beckett's system, or rather, he is certain of only two possible outcomes:

> If literature is once again condemned, so too is the ambition to establish an identity between it and reality and literature must definitively go without a beyond. Or, on the other hand, if that ambition—mistaken once again—remains licit, its failure can very well also be called a success, given the result it lets us glimpse. In Beckett's case, it's surely an extraordinary success.[29]

This passage—and the trajectory of interpretation behind it—sheds light on how Beckett became a major reference for a number of the influential literary figures associated with Editions de Minuit in the early 1950s, from Bataille and Blanchot to Nadeau and—as I discuss later—Barthes. They each saw enormous potential in what Nadeau calls Beckett's "failure," a breakdown in traditional mimesis that may finally sweep away all the "amateurs of tired truths or vampires."[30]

The interpretive shifts in Nadeau's writings on Beckett are framed by his moves in the literary field, moves which provided the young editor at Editions de Minuit with new room in which to maneuver. *Les Lettres nouvelles* supplied Lindon with critical encouragement and support, almost immediately rewarding him for his investment in Beckett. At the same time, however, Lindon already had at his disposal authors and critics who could—and did—review Beckett in their journals: Blanchot in *La Nouvelle NRF* and Bataille in *Critique*. Both of these men were published Minuit authors prior to the discovery of Beckett, and both were also part of Jean Paulhan's author list at Gallimard. Before turning to *Critique* and its contribution to Lindon's revamped Minuit, first it is important to describe the challenge Gallimard posed to Lindon's editorship in these early years.

Beckett was an important "first" discovery for Lindon, because he was not a member of the stable of authors brought to Minuit because their manuscripts were rejected by Gallimard. George Lambrichs, a friend of Jean Paulhan, had worked at Gallimard before joining Vercors at Minuit after the war; his relationship with authors and personalities linked to the Gallimard network was central to the circulation of manuscripts from established literary sources at Minuit during Vercors's tenure and into that of Lindon. Unlike Lindon, Lambrichs was a well-connected insider; for instance, his involvement with projects like *Troisième Convoi*, a literary review that published five issues between 1945 and 1951, put him in contact with an entire cluster of the literary field, including its editor, Michel Fardoulis-Lagrange, as well as René de Solier, Arthur Adamov, Georges Bataille, René Char, Charles Duits, and Georges Henein, all authors published by Minuit during the same period of time.[31]

Anne Simonin's account of the contentious relationship between Minuit and Gallimard reminds us of what was at stake for Lindon in finding the kind of identification he describes when he read Beckett for the first time.[32] Her analysis elucidates a series of moves made by Lindon and Gaston Gallimard in the first years of the 50s to outmaneuver one another in battles over authors; they culminated in legal proceedings that ultimately ensured Minuit's contractual rights over its authors against the pressures applied by Gallimard. One quote shows us Gallimard plotting with his agents—in the fashion of something like a mogul of literature—to steal cultural capital from other publishers. He addresses Paulhan:

> If you were to have some free time, you could play the following game with Marcel Arland: draw up a list of all the writers published elsewhere and that it would be desirable for us to have. I will make my own list as well. Then we will put our two lists together. . .[33]

Gallimard's ruthless "game" makes new, smaller publishers like Minuit potential instruments of concentration of literary capital at Gallimard. Recently tried and censured by the Comité d'épuration—the quote dates from 1947—he was orchestrating his return or recovery from that censure. As regards Les Editions de Minuit, this equated to luring back to Gallimard authors who had been published at Minuit at the behest of Vercors, Paulhan, or Lambrichs. Without intending to make too much of this letter, I believe it indicates two important points: first, Gallimard's focus on acquiring positions of value already in place in the field is a strategy that leaves the challenge of recruiting and developing new value to others, and from positions, if Minuit's is any indication, of extreme financial instability. Bourdieu would much later categorize Minuit as a producer of long-term values: ones not immediately recognizable due to an initial gap in cultural capital, but that "paid off" in the long-term.[34] He was describing a significant aspect of the Minuit experience in the 50s, only in categorical terms that do not refer the reader to how that position was in fact an imposition thrust upon Minuit in specific circumstances. Hence Anne Simonin's analysis, which—as her subtitle "the duty of insubordination" indicates—first traces the story of Minuit's unyielding wartime sense of duty, and then posits a parallel sense of mission on the part of Lindon to not yield to Gallimard.[35] In this context, Lindon's "discovery" of Beckett has an additional valence. The experience of shock he describes can be understood variously as the shock of the new, the shock of encountering brilliance—presumably both meanings Lindon intended—or, as I have attempted to suggest, as the shock of discovering the "moi, éditeur."

3. Publisher of *Critique*

This section focuses on the significance of Lindon's decision to bring Bataille's fledgling journal into the Minuit catalog. I discuss the addition to Minuit's capital that *Critique* represents—and how it began to pay off directly for Lindon's editorial strategy—and the symbolic place of *Critique* within a strategy of generic organization made manifest in the design of the Minuit catalog. Like the adoption of Beckett, the publication of *Critique* merits reflection in terms of its meaning with respect to the literary field; despite the claims concerning the history of *Critique* by one specialist, who argues that *Critique* was not "a publisher's journal," the gamble on *Critique* and its difference with respect to other journals is what makes it very much a Minuit project.[36]

Before examining *Critique*'s place within Lindon's reorganization of Minuit, it is important to evaluate the capital represented by the incorporation of the figure of Georges Bataille. Bataille's incorporation is joined, from the very first, by the additional association with Blanchot, as well. Bataille's initial involvement with Minuit precedes the publication of *Critique* and was meant to result in a collection called "L'usage des richesses" ["The Use of Riches"].[37] Begun in 1949, Bataille's collaboration resulted only in the publication of his own two-volume *La Part maudite*, a text by Kojève on Hegel, and Jean Piel's essay in economics entitled *La Fortune américaine et son destin*. Blanchot's book on *Lautréamont et Sade* was published in the same year as the Bataille collection was introduced, but, interestingly, is listed under a separate rubric, vaguely titled "Essays."As I will show, as Lindon rewrote the Minuit catalog, these groupings would be subjected to several revisions.

Within a two-year period, Bataille became a substantial presence in the direction of Lindon's publishing. A novel (*L'Abbé C*), a three-part piece of literary criticism (*La Haine de la poésie*), the "*L'usage*" collection; additionally, his *Histoire de Rats* (part of *La Haine de la poésie*) was issued as a "Deluxe Work," with illustrations by Giacometti. Bataille represents Lindon's first major authorial investment prior to Beckett. After 1951, however, Bataille's association with Minuit was limited to his involvement with *Critique*. Still, the array of types of writing Bataille contributed during this period mirrors Bataille's ambitions for *Critique*, and had, I suggest, an enormous influence on Lindon's conception of Minuit, as well as his organization of its publications. Bataille's specific vision for *Critique* greatly inflected Lindon's efforts to develop the Minuit label in this first phase.

Bataille spent much of *Critique*'s first years—it was begun in 1946—looking for a publisher and trying to secure the journal's finances. The historian of *Critique*, Sylvie Patron, cites a circulation of under three thousand copies in the immediate postwar years—with a mere five hundred subscribers in 1949—as contrasted with *Les Temps Modernes*, which varied from twelve to eighteen thousand copies per issue, depending on whether or not a text by Sartre was in the contents.[38] Unlike the journals Bataille had participated in previously—such as the radical *La Critique sociale* or the surrealist *Documents*—*Critique* had more erudite pretensions. These can be perceived both in how Bataille pitched his own writings in the journal as well as in the style, range, and depth of the editorial choices made in its first half-dozen years at Minuit. In his very brief "introduction" to *La Littérature et le mal*, a collection of essays for the most part published in *Critique*, Bataille evokes the "serious character" of the journal. The determining context for understanding Bataille's emphasis on seriousness is the dominance of Sartre's *Les Temps Modernes*. This seriousness is illustrated by the journal's complete dedication to the critical essay and the absence of original literary works: this format distanced *Critique* from the doctrinaire character of *Les Temps Modernes*.[39] The astonishing variety in subject matter accomplished the same task, putting polemical, anti-Sartrean pot-boilers by Bataille side-by-side with more sober economic discussions by Jean Piel. Here I have in mind Bataille's "Jean-Paul Sartre and Jean Genet's Impossible Revolt" (from October and November 1952) and Piel's "Towards a World Economy Founded on the Gift" (from the first Minuit issue of *Critique*, 1947).

At work in Bataille's *Critique* is the expansion of critical discourse to include more than literary concerns. No immediately recognizable philosophical stance—aside, perhaps, from Bataille's own confusing anti-existentialism—could define the journal. Nor could the identification of a neatly circumscribed group of collaborators do so, with the possible exception of

Blanchot: Sylvie Patron makes an argument for identifying "the Bataille/Blanchot years," although it is difficult to detect a Blanchot imprint in texts from this period other than in his own. In addition, the emphasis given to opening to international input, whether in the form of contributions by foreign scholars or in articles on texts only available in foreign languages, is an editorial strategy bent on rivaling Sartre's international capital. In the era of the rapidly developing Cold War, *Critique*'s efforts to lay claim to a unique brand of intellectual internationalism were another way of avoiding identification with any single political program and of constructing the journal as an alternative to Sartre's group. In other words, *Critique*'s particular form of difference from *Les Temps Modernes* strives for a generic break with the format that *Les Temps Modernes* exemplifies. This can be read in Bataille's presentation of *Critique*, which in this case is not a manifesto along the lines of Sartre's "Introducing *Les Temps modernes*," but a two-page masthead that appears in every issue as well as every Minuit catalog.

The masthead as it appears in the catalog is a telling index of the various strategies I have pointed out: the allure of high-powered, intellectual seriousness; the extremely broad range of subject matter; the claim of greater import and depth to each individual article; and the international scope. At stake in this outmaneuvering of *Les Temps Modernes* is the claim of a more serious, intellectual habitus. Bataille's presentation is as follows:

> Since 1946, *Critique* offers to its readership through its studies devoted to works published the world over the most broad and precise information one can expect from a journal.
>
> From the importance of the subjects tackled and

> the works analyzed, from the scale of its studies, that go well beyond the context of simple reports, reaching at times twenty-five pages in length, and finally, from its international character, *Critique* has no peer in any other publication.
>
> Its French and foreign collaborators alike are highly qualified, each one in his or her own field. Taken together, their work delivers to every cultivated man the essential part of what he needs to know: the most recently acquired results in every activity of the mind, whether it involves literary or artistic creation, philosophical research, or historical, scientific, political or economic knowledge.
>
> It is possible to serve general knowledge without emptying its content: this is what *Critique* proves by publishing articles worthy of nourishing scientific debate without ceasing to be accessible to an enlightened public and to awaken its interest.
>
> *Critique* follows a formula that makes it an outstanding link:
>
> – between the literary and scientific worlds;
>
> – among experts in a variety of fields;
>
> – between men of science and the cultivated public;
>
> – among different countries.[40]

Critique's difference could not be more heavily emphasized: no other review matches *Critique* as the authoritative forum for the cultivation of the contemporary reader, offering the work of "highly qualified" "experts" covering *the* gamut of intellectual "fields." No realm of intellectual activity, in the presentation's claims, is left out, although Sylvie Patron has suggested that, in practice, the journal's subject matter followed very specific patterns.[41] The generic names given for these "fields" signal that other journals occupy outdated positions, and fail to change with the currents of intellectual progress: at stake is "literary creation" and "philosophical research," not literature and philosophy, offered in superficial doses that empty ("vider" in the original) the essential ingredients of any modern and intelligent reader's edification. The readership is likewise endowed with the *Critique* difference: "enlightened," "cultivated," and given to recognize the value of the journal's purview.

Critique's claim on capital is expressed in terms of a unique and rigorous scientificity, the success of which hinged on its appeal among readers; however, some evidence suggests that in the early 1950s such appeal was still yet to develop. In part, Critique's poor circulation numbers may be attributed to the continued predominance of other journals, such as *Les Temps Modernes* and *Esprit*. Their strength, along with the immediate and immense success met by *L'Express* when it was launched in 1954, indicates that *Critique*'s innovation in genre would have to wait for other changes to take place—changes in readers' loyalties and habits—for its claims to be successful.

Two more elements of the presentation of *Critique* need mentioning, as they are typical features, as we will see, of the Lindon catalog: one is the substantial list of excerpts of critical praise provided just beneath the text cited above; the other is a paragraph consisting of forty-one names of "Principal Collaborators." As is customary, both have been edited with an eye toward marketing considerations. The sources of acclaim are an intriguing glimpse at the kind of readership *Critique* could lay claim to in the early years of the decade. Five of the seven blurbs are from prestigious international literary and scientific sources, named with their cities of origin: "*The Times Literary Supplement*, Londres,"

"*Scrutiny*, Cambridge," "*Journal de Genève*," "*Flandre Libérale*, Gand," and "*Il Politechnico* (sic), Milan." Of the two French quotes, which appear first, one is from François Mauriac writing in *Le Figaro* and the other from *Esprit*: Mauriac's is one of just two in which the author is named (the other is the Italian Carlo Bô). Mauriac's praise from *Le Figaro* is the shortest of all of the excerpts, but the significance of a resounding endorsement from Mauriac—he calls it "the best made journal in print today"—with the cultural capital his position represents would not be lost on contemporary readers and clearly justified its inclusion. *Esprit* also calls it the best journal of the day, and underscores its seriousness and academic scope: "all of France's universities should subscribe their students to this journal." This quote has the brilliant touch of demarcating *Critique* in its difference from *Esprit* itself, indicating at once that, while it is the "best journal of the moment," its readership is actually more circumscribed than that of *Esprit*. Including the *Esprit* quote is an effort at turning that expression of their difference to *Critique*'s advantage, especially in light of the description of *Critique*'s readership.

The international praise for the journal is an important element of the case for the journal's "critical" difference. Evidence that the journal was read, appreciated, and recommended abroad lent it valuable cachet, helping its argument as an alternative to the major journals of its day. The blurbs from abroad are much longer than the two French excerpts, with the longest taken from *The Times Literary Supplement*, whose quote is especially emphatic about the dominant position of *Critique* with respect to the "intellectual vitality of Paris." The *Times* quote also reiterates the generic distinction of the journal: "[i]t is devoted entirely to criticism, that most fecund kind of criticism that finds its substance in contemporary French and foreign production. That substance can be found across the journal's range of rubrics and each of its authoritative essays." The quote goes on to underscore both the intellectual freedom of each writer and the editorial consistency represented by their "solid arguments." The intellectual charge behind much of the praise quoted is anti-Sartrean: if Mauriac puts *Critique* above *la Table ronde*, it is in recognition of *Critique*'s greater potential to dethrone Sartre's *Temps modernes*. In this respect, other of the excerpts are much more blatant, such as that of Carlo Bô: "[t]his journal is perhaps the most interesting thing to emerge from France since the war." While it is impossible to determine who edited the presentation—presumably either Bataille or Lindon, who had taken charge of promoting the journal—the use of these blurbs recalls Lindon's use of them in other Minuit publications. Lindon often employs the willingness of critics to be "brutally honest," their crass simplicity buttressing the sophistication of the presentation while simultaneously expressing what that presentation cannot be permitted to.

The last component of the presentation, the list of primary collaborators, is at once the most superficially opaque and the most editorially constructed of all. The majority of the individuals named had published only one, perhaps two, articles in *Critique*; still, they are listed as "principal collaborators." What justifies the choice? Again, it is a matter of reinforcing the image of variety, professionalism, and internationalism promoted in the presentation and echoed in the critical praise. It is just as important that the list be long as it is that there be figures likely to be recognized by potential readers—although non-recognition, in the context of *Critique*'s claims to authoritative specialization and international reach, also has a role in casting *Critique*'s new and particular form of value.

I will return to the usefulness of *Critique* in the first phase of Minuit's history in the section below on the critical reception of Lindon's new Minuit. In the further assessment of Lindon's role in shaping the Minuit label, I first turn from the characterization of *Critique* as a model for the re-conception of the intellectual journal—opened to a broad range of intellectual disciplines and apparently untainted, so it is claimed, by editorial subjectivity—to looking at ways in which the Minuit catalog comes to embody Lindon's careful deliberation about similar questions of intellectual literary activity. Between the promotional material from 1951 and the 1956 catalog, Lindon professionalized the Minuit catalog along lines similar to the logics of *Critique*'s presentation, and developed techniques for establishing Minuit's distinction that engage with the demands of the French literary field of the 50s in very savvy ways. His techniques and strategies re-draw the picture of French intellectual culture so as to privilege the topos of renewal and innovation that he cultivates for his stable of writers.

4. Minuit's Difference

By 1956, five years after first publishing Beckett, six years after bringing in Bataille and *Critique*, and—as I shall discuss in detail further on—three years past Robbe-Grillet's entrance, Lindon's editorial position had begun to take shape and accumulate cultural capital. Still, the coherence of a program had not yet appeared, as evidenced by the page-two text of the 1956 Minuit catalog. In later years, the page-two piece served as one of Lindon's most impressive tools for constructing the unity of his editorial position and for asserting his claims on cultural capital. Published eight years into Lindon's tenure, the 1956 catalog presents the image of a publisher and a house that have not yet made their mark. Its presentation on page two is a subtle narrativization of Lindon himself as literary novice or outsider making a go at the professional habitus of publisher. The logic of Minuit's difference is placed in the figure of the publisher and in his "adventure."

The presentation text on page two of the 1956 catalog establishes the connection between Minuit and the person of Jerôme Lindon I have thus far attempted to underscore in this chapter. Some of the traits I have described come through, including the modest image of the humble servant of literature:

> La publication d'un livre requiert la mise en œuvre des principales activités humaines: intellectuelles, et c'est l'auteur; techniques, et c'est l'imprimeur; commerciales, et c'est la librairie. L'éditeur, dans cette harmonie, on dirait qu'il ne sert à rien. Lui, pourtant, aurait tendance à croire qu'il participe à l'essentiel: artiste ou savant, il juge le manuscrit, l'accepte, le refuse, quelquefois suggère une correction; technicien, il conçoit la Présentation, choisit le papier, le format, le caractère, l'illustration; commerçant, il assume tous les risques, assure la publicité et la diffusion, entretient de bons rapports avec les journalistes et publie des catalogues.
>
> D'avoir tant de têtes gêne quelque peu l'éditeur, et souvent il ne sait guère où il va. Tel essai critique qu'il destine aux esthéticiens fait l'objet d'une adaptation à Hollywood, tel roman d'amour proposé aux foules essuie un échec commercial mais suscite une thèse sociologique en Sorbonne. C'est le domaine de l'imprévisible, ainsi que son nom l'indique, "librairie" étant, comme on sait, un peu de la famille de "liberté."

Aussi l'éditeur se résoud-t-il (sic) tout bonnement à éditer ce qu'il aime lire, et son programme s'exprime, comme celui du "nègre" de l'histoire, par cette formule dont il ne faudrait pas sous-estimer l'importance: "continuer."

~

Publishing a book requires the implementation of the primary human activities: the intellectual ones are the work of the author; technical ones, the printer; commercial, the bookstore. To this harmony, one might think the publisher adds nothing. The publisher, on the other hand, tends to think their role is essential: artist or *savant*, he judges the manuscript, accepts or refuses it, sometimes suggesting a correction. As a technician he conceives the presentation, chooses paper, format, characters, illustrations; as a businessman he takes on all the risk, ensures advertising and distribution, maintains good relationships with journalists and publishes catalogs.

Wearing so many hats can be challenging to editors, and they often do not know which way to turn. A critical essay meant for aesthetically inclined readers gets adapted into a Hollywood film, a love story meant for a mass audience is a commercial failure but becomes the subject of a dissertation in Sociology at the Sorbonne. It is the realm of the unforeseeable, just like the name *librairie* [bookstore] suggests, since—as it is well-known—the term comes from the family of words of "freedom" [*liberté*].

And so the editor resolves simply to publish what he likes to read, and his enterprise is summed

> up—much like that of the "negro" in that old story—by a term whose importance cannot be underestimated: "to carry on."

To continue publishing, that is the aim: a humble program for a publisher of books targeting the intellectual elite. Lindon is playing at a kind of arch modesty that stands in striking contrast to the multiple efforts at persuasion in the catalog contents that follow. Just as persuasive as the array of blurbs and excerpts—and perhaps in some ways even more so—Lindon's modesty conveys grace and elegance, and forms a skillfully understated address of the reader. His purpose seems to be to set the reader in a position to "judge" the results of Lindon's efforts, even while so much of the catalog furnishes the reader with selected, edited judgments. Still, Lindon's message provides some glimpse into how he perceived his position and the variables weighing on his chances of success in 1956. The importance given to journalists, with whom he must maintain "good relationships," is very significant among these variables, as demonstrated by the reproduction of critical praise from a great variety of presses throughout the catalog. Lindon makes tremendous effort to put external sources of authority and legitimation to work.

A second element of the slightly disingenuous image-making at play comes in the evocation of the spontaneity and improvisation (jokingly evoking a pseudo-etymological link between the French terms for "liberty" and "bookstore"—a witty wink at the educated reader, who of course knows that there is no link between the words) built into the business of making and selling books. The spontaneity in reception evoked by Lindon masks the one circumstance that goes unmentioned, but which is clearly subtextual—the case of non-reception, where, rather than unintended audiences receiving a text, there is none at all. Underlying the mention of two humorously unlikely cases of reception—a critical essay made into a Hollywood film, a romance novel inspiring a thesis in sociology—is the offer of complicity between reader and publisher. We are invited as intimates.

Hardly knowing "which way to turn," the publisher as described in this piece resolves to keep up the work of publishing, powerless as he is before the unpredictable nature of the trade. All bets being off, the publisher contents himself with simply publishing what he likes. If we grant this small text the status of "confession," it serves to position a human interlocutor across from the reader: the "I" of the text is submitted for the judgment of the reader, who is called upon precisely to evaluate the work of the publisher, himself present in, or made present by, each of his books. Lindon concludes with a joke that brilliantly encapsulates the kind of readerly address I've identified throughout in the piece. With urbane charm, Lindon's text names its writing subject as "the negro in that old story," a winking reference to an anecdote about an African soldier serving in the French army who is told by one of the presidents of the Third Republic to "Continuez" or "carry on." Readers who understand the joke enjoy a kind of insider collusion with Lindon.

Lindon's blend of humor and charm extends an invitation to the reader to become a sympathetic judge of Minuit's publisher, depicted as a cordial fellow member of the literati making a go at the "bewildering" world of book publishing. His comical performance of modesty functions as a *captatio benevolentiae*, a friendly capture of the reader's attentions and sympathies. This function is of a piece with the slightly different tone of the rest of the catalog, which is overloaded with information about the authors and their books: there are biographical notes on each author, some of which are extensive, and each novel title is closely followed by at least three (most have five or more) commentaries by reviewers, all journalists. The exaggerated quality of the catalog complements Lindon's staging of himself as publisher in that it underscores the efforts of the "negro" to provide his readers with all possible professional courtesies. We saw how the presentation emphasizes the complexity of the role of publisher—unable to adequately guarantee the conditions of reception for his books—and the public's lack of appreciation for that role. The catalog as a whole seeks to capture readers into the publishing adventure of Jérôme Lindon, the figure of wit mediating readers' encounters with the Minuit catalog. In successive catalogs, the figure of Lindon withdraws somewhat, as the *need* for such "personalized" strategies of persuasion diminishes. Nonetheless, that figure remains a presence on page two of the Minuit catalog. The strategies employed in this pre-New Novel catalog seem awkwardly personalized in comparison to the later catalogs. The changes to the catalog that were to accompany the New Novel phenomenon—examined in the next chapter—reflect the importance of the New Novel as the sign of Minuit's difference, displacing his narrative of a novice publisher's bafflement before the spontaneity of readership.

5. Critics: Robbe-Grillet and Barthes

We have seen several examples of Lindon's use of favorable criticism garnered in newspapers, journals, and magazines in the catalogs from the 1950s. Blurbs from reviews were meant as arguments for the value of the publications as well as demonstrations of the publisher's impact. For the most part, however, such criticism tends to have only a limited, short-term effect; moreover, in looking at the early 1950s, the profusion of blurbs stands out in contrast to Minuit's financial woes. The positive criticism did not sell many titles. In assessing the role of criticism in Minuit's position in the early 50s, it is important to pause over the emergence of certain crucial relationships that were to have an impact on Editions de Minuit in the long-term. Discussion of Alain Robbe-Grillet and Roland Barthes is a fitting conclusion to this chapter because the connections between these two figures and Editions de Minuit are illustrative of how a number of the initiatives I have presented thus far eventually worked to the benefit of Lindon and Minuit.

Alain Robbe-Grillet became part of Minuit's pool of writers a few years before he and Lindon developed their decisive collaborative relationship. Robbe-Grillet's earliest published writing appeared in *Critique* in 1951. Over the following three years he wrote a series of short book reviews under Bataille's editorship, the majority of which were reviews of Minuit titles or titles by Minuit authors published elsewhere. Although Robbe-Grillet has written little about his writings for *Critique*, in *Les Derniers jours de Corinthe* he explains his incremental entry into Editions de Minuit and leaves certain parts of the story untold. In 1950 he met Georges Lambrichs to discuss the manuscript of *Une Régicide*, which had been passed on to Lambrichs by Dominique Aury, friend of Jean Paulhan.[42] The novel would not be published until many years later, but their meeting encouraged Robbe-Grillet to return when the novel he was working on at the time, *Les Gommes*, was completed.[43] His contact with Lambrichs also led to him submitting reviews to *Critique* the following year. Although his account of the period is vague, Robbe-Grillet describes days spent in Lambrich's office with a group of young authors inventing literary journals that were never published; days punctuated by the brief appearance of Lindon, a "spectre véloce [swift-moving specter]" who inspired a "hostile chill" in the room.[44] Lindon published the "periodic reviews" of the writers gathered around Lambrichs—including, as we know, Robbe-Grillet himself—but maintained a distance from them; they, in turn, viewed him as "a money man who, by definition, understood nothing of the literature."[45] Robbe-Grillet's characterization of Lindon in 1950-1951 is very evocative, and suggests perhaps that Lindon was wary or skeptical of writers that he himself had not brought in—the authors left over from Vercors's era, or those Lambrichs supported:

> Jérôme, de son côté, ne tentait rien pour se faire aimer dans ce petit monde; sans doute aurait-il même allègrement supporté d'y être haï. Esprit aigu à l'image de ses traits physiques, rigoureux, dominateur, volontiers solitaire, méfiant à l'extrême, n'aimant à partager avec autrui ni ses responsabilités ni son pouvoir, il ne lui déplaisait pas de faire régner autour de lui un climat de crainte diffuse [. . .]."[46]
>
> ~
>
> As for Jérôme, he did nothing to ingratiate himself to the small group; no doubt he would have been delighted if they hated him. A mind sharp like his physical features, rigorous, dominating, gladly solitary, extremely distrustful, opposed to sharing either his responsibilities or his power with others, he was happy to let reign around him a climate of diffuse fear [. . .]."

Lindon's remoteness may have corresponded to a distrust that extended to Lambrichs as well, since he was the sole competitor for power in the house and because he represented, by his proximity to Gallimard and Gallimard's authors, an outside influence or potential threat to the independence of Lindon's Minuit. Perhaps for these reasons Lindon grew dissatisfied with Lambrichs's editorial direction and role; Lambrichs seems to have lost ground as Lindon's friendship with Robbe-Grillet developed into an alliance. He was fired in 1954.

According to Robbe-Grillet's account, his friendship with Lindon dates from 1952, when they began to discuss the publication of *Les Gommes*. The Robbe-Grillet Lindon encountered that year was more than just an unpublished novelist with a manuscript: his short reviews in *Critique* reveal a critic-in-training. As rudimentary as those early texts are, they served as stylistic exercises that prepared Robbe-Grillet to play a certain role, with Lindon as literary interlocutor; they also prepared the way for the clear change in critical stance that occurred in Robbe-Grillet's writing in 1955. That year—the year his second novel, *Le Voyeur*, was published—marks his change from reviewer to polemicist and theorist and coincides, importantly, with his new service as "lecteur" ["reader"] at Editions de Minuit. These new roles—theorist, lecteur—are discussed in detail in the next chapter; in these preceding years, Robbe-Grillet managed to ally himself with his "distrustful" and "solitary" editor and lend his developing literary convictions to Lindon's project of re-orienting Minuit's editorial direction. Letting go of Georges Lambrichs indicates that Lindon no longer sensed a need for his editorial input or the capital he represented. In Robbe-Grillet's view, Lindon's choice as replacement for Lambrichs—Jacques Brenner, who was not to stay long—reflected how important his own influence had become: "I imagine our director was distrustful of the exclusive quality of my literary choices—even though he was broadly in agreement with them—and wanted to counterbalance them with the very different choices of calmer writers more respectful of tradition."[47]

Robbe-Grillet's reviews from the period 1951-1954 show a number of early traces of the novelist and theorist of modern literature, and point to the significance of his growing influence with Editions de Minuit. His review of a crime novel in 1951 displayed some of the interests that informed the contemporaneous writing of *Les Gommes*, and suggests that part of the appeal of the detective novel genre for him stemmed from its displacement of worn-out exercises in bourgeois morality, as well as its occasion for uncertainty, misdirection, and "truquages" [illusion]. He begins by proposing that the genre has new cultural significance: "The crime novel [. . .] now plays the role [. . .] once held by the love story" and as a consequence "bourgeois morality cedes its role to the penal code—more serious, perhaps—or less antiquated?"[48] The shift from the love novel to the crime novel has done nothing to change the dominance of the themes of truth and deceit: "Reality does not for all that take on the too reassuring quality of the police report and the questionable margins truth likes to surround itself with are preserved: they are no longer the lies of an unfaithful spouse or the accusations of the jealous lover but rather rigged stories, alibis, false testimonies . . ."[49] Expressions like "bourgeois morality" suggest that he is taking part in the idiom of the day in collegial fashion—unlike the aggressive strategies of his later theoretical writings—and making the case for the text's critical significance within that idiom. These articles read like fairly standard reviews, which is why they come across as "exercices de style;" note, for instance, the typical stylistic conceit in this line: "[this text] maintains a fairly constant jovial form of expression that reassures us as to its author's future [. . .]."[50] Still, Robbe-Grillet does occasionally try out expressions of literary dogma in which one recognizes the later theorist and editor. Describing Jean Cau's 1950 *Le Coup de la Barre* (Gallimard) he writes that "we find this essential observation: what matters to the writer is above all literature, and not morality, class struggle or theology."[51]

His anti-engagement principle explains his appeal for the editors of *Critique*, who were for many years the only ones to publish his articles.

Other traces of Robbe-Grillet's later thematic and critical leanings appear intermittently, in inchoate form: "As for time—the main character of any novel, it is said—it therefore acquires a singular acuity [. . .]."[52] In the absence of a recurring critical approach or vocabulary, what surfaces is a preference for novels that present some stylistic difference or innovation—or at least a preference for novels for which the case of stylistic innovation can be made. That predilection is essential for assessing the significance of his growing relationship with and influence on Lindon, and his developing sense of belonging to Editions de Minuit. Lindon's decision to replace Lambrichs with Brenner is an indication of how Robbe-Grillet's particular leanings transformed the editorial dynamic at Minuit, and suggests the extent to which his in-house capital stemmed increasingly from his modernist inclinations.

A title Robbe-Grillet reviewed in 1952, René de Solier's *La Meffraie*, appears to have caught his attention for reasons that point to his literary tastes as well as his loyalty to the publishing house. Solier's novel was published by Editions de Minuit—in his capacity as reviewer Robbe-Grillet was developing a sense of the kind of literature Minuit should publish, as well as how to present it to *Critique*'s audience. In addition, Solier's novel features an utterly antipathetic main character: "The character is odious, [. . .] M. de Solier has chosen to make the man perfectly insupportable to us, and the whole book truly distinctly irritating." This and the other formal traits to which Robbe-Grillet attaches importance—a style of description that proceeds "meticulously, scientifically, like under a microscope," narrative switches from third- to first-person "to garner more surely the hatred of the reader," and an explicit deliberation on language ("the use of a vocabulary 'invented' or simply 'diverted from its meaning'")—show the beginnings of the editorial sensibility gaining ground at Editions de Minuit in 1952 and 1953.

In those same years, Robbe-Grillet entered into a collaborative relationship with Lindon with the publication of *Les Gommes*. With that novel's preparation for publication and its critical reception, Robbe-Grillet became a Minuit novelist in a full sense; an episode recounted in Anne Simonin's history of the publishing house sheds important light on what that meant for Lindon's Minuit.[53] Taken from unpublished correspondence between Lindon and Robbe-Grillet, the exchanges Simonin cites provide unusual insight into how their collaboration would form Minuit's signature marketing strategy. At issue between them was the presentation of *Les Gommes*, which was not selling due to a lack of critical attention. Some months after the book's release, Lindon decided to write (with Robbe-Grillet) a five-page brochure explaining the work. This was the first time, Simonin argues, that such a "lecture mode d'emploi" [instructions for reading] ever appeared in French publishing. The brochure was very successful: Jean Paulhan wrote to Robbe-Grillet congratulating him: "[. . .] the highest quality of a text like this is not that it is reasonable, or ingenious, or witty, it is that it makes you want to talk about it. And see, we don't stop." Encouraged, Lindon proposed making a jacket cover for *Les Gommes* that would include a photo very much in the vein of detective novel covers and two different strips bearing explanations of the novel's themes of "Oedipus" and "Time." Lindon's justification to Robbe-Grillet reveals a deft publisher, with very specific ideas of what attracts readers: "[. . .] the photo and the tape could attract quite a large audience, especially among people who know the book is good but assume it is some obscure and pesky work, like Kafka, Joyce or Beckett." Lindon imagines the potential reader's assumption that this must be an "obscure" and "bothersome" work, another like Beckett—well-enough known in 1953 to have come to signify the Minuit label at this early stage. In retrospect, this was an astonishing proposal: from early on in the house's clandestine years its novels' jacket presentation had—and still has—only rarely varied from the basic white design. A photograph, evocative of the detective novel genre, to reach out to a more popular audience?

Had Robbe-Grillet not rejected Lindon's idea and developed the following counterproposal, Les Editions de Minuit could very well have followed a radically different path, and become a very different publishing house. Lindon wanted to distinguish *Les Gommes* from Beckett's publications, at least in their inability to appeal to a wider readership as of yet. Was *Les Gommes* to set the stage for an entirely different editorial line than that represented by Beckett's work? A dual editorial strategy, reserving the blank jackets for the difficult, serious literature and glossy covers for novels of broad appeal? Robbe-Grillet's response to Lindon's concept was firm, direct, even imperious at times:

> [. . .] il me semble que nous avons donné nous-mêmes assez d'explication comme ça; il ne faut pas continuer dans cette voie [. . .]. Je le répète, et je voudrais bien que tu sois d'accord, il est essentiel que *toutes les explications que tu donneras soient endossées par une autorité littéraire*, aussi vague soit-elle [. . .]. Maintenant le gros point: la photographie [. . .]. J'y ai bien réfléchi, ta proposition de sujet délibérément policier présente trop de dangers. Tu sais que je n'ai pas hésité à donner dans ce genre-là à plusieurs reprises, et je ne le regrette pas malgré tout

ce qu'ont pu en penser Blanchot, Solier et les autres qui l'ont dit moins franchement. Mais là encore il ne faut pas charrier, [. . .] je ne crois absolument pas que l'on puisse compter sur des effets de ce genre-là pour autre chose que faire ricaner les petits copains et "ridiculiser les Editions de Minuit" comme ils disent! Il est évident que le public, même cultivé, n'est pas encore assez évolué pour pressentir que le genre "policier" est un des plus sérieux qui soit. Essayons de faire admettre la chose en douceur; au début il fallait bien choquer un peu, maintenant il s'agit de dorer la pilule.[55]

~

[. . .] it seems to me that we ourselves have given enough explanation like this; we must not continue on this path [. . .]. I repeat, and I would like you to agree, it is essential that any explanations you give be endorsed by a literary authority, however vague [. . .]. Now the big point: photography [. . .]. I have thought about it carefully, your proposal for a deliberately detective subject presents too many dangers. You know that I have not hesitated to do this on several occasions, and I do not regret it despite everything that Blanchot, Solier and the others thought of it and were less than frank. But here again, we must not kid ourselves, [. . .] I absolutely do not believe that we can count on effects of this kind for anything other than making our friends laugh and "making Editions de Minuit ridiculous" as they say. It is obvious that the public, even cultivated, is not yet evolved enough to sense that the "detective" genre is one of the most serious there is. Let's try to get this across with more finesse; at the beginning it

> was necessary to shock a little, now it is a question of gilding the pill.

In this conversation, the roles of author Robbe-Grillet and publisher Lindon seem reversed: the latter seems eager to popularize, whereas the former gives priority to how these moves could impact the symbolic capital of the publishing house. Robbe-Grillet restrains Lindon out of fear for what a cover photograph could do to the Minuit image, owing to a lack of sophistication on the part of the "cultivated public." Better to speak through a third-party, "a literary authority, as vague as that may be" to disseminate information about *Les Gommes*, and by extension, about Les Editions de Minuit. Robbe-Grillet stresses the importance of critical endorsement, which appears here as truly vital to maintaining control over the image of Minuit, over its prestige and class status. While his insistence anticipates the vital role critics would play on several occasions in Minuit's history, Lindon had already applied the principle by the printing of the 1954 catalog.

More significant, however, are Robbe-Grillet's remarks in favor of maintaining a single, consistent editorial line for the sake of satisfying certain preconceptions about seriousness and value. His rationale that they must win critics over to the *roman policier* by presenting *Les Gommes* as serious literature is tremendously revealing: it is a first demonstration of the kind of appeal to high literature—and claim on symbolic capital—that would become characteristic of Minuit's marketing strategy. Robbe-Grillet did not want to risk ridicule from some quarters of either his book or the imprint for the sake of greater sales. Despite the interest of some critics in the roman policier (he mentions *Critique* and *NNRF* critic Blanchot and Minuit author René de Solier) there are other critics ("our friends") who still need to be won over. He wished to shield his novel from a too-overt identification with a specific literary sub-genre, and in so doing effectively vetoed Lindon's initiative to diversify the editorial line. Minuit strategy would henceforth be directed at trying to "gild the pill": the gilt of seriousness enveloping the pill of the unexpected.

In his discussion with Lindon about the cover art and promotional texts for *Les Gommes*, Robbe-Grillet comes across as more than just a member of Lindon's stable of authors. He has gone from being an occasional book reviewer for *Critique* to serving as an interlocutor for Lindon, in a privileged relationship within the bounds of which he is able to offer his advice on Lindon's steerage of the publishing house. In the next chapter, I discuss Robbe-Grillet's role in the latter half of the 1950s as a reader and editor at Minuit. Before we can set aside the early 50s, however, it is important to address the impact of Robbe-Grillet's first two novels, *Les Gommes* and *Le Voyeur*, on Editions de Minuit, by pointing out the limited but vital critical response these novels generated.

In terms of their critical success, these novels had little in common: *Les Gommes* created relatively little interest, while *Le Voyeur* spawned a number of reviews and won the *Prix des Critiques*. The literary prize brought *Le Voyeur* further attention and it became a subject of controversy because of the violence hinted at throughout.[56] What the two novels did share, however, were a pair of vital critical links that secured influential support and encouragement for Robbe-Grillet, which in turn gave momentum to his rising stature and sway within Editions de Minuit. Each pair involves a small network of literary figures whose alliances created significant critical audiences for Robbe-Grillet: *Les Gommes* garnered the attention of Jean Cayrol, who in turn led Roland Barthes to read the novel, and, through his relationship with Maurice Nadeau at *Lettres Nouvelles*, Barthes helped bring Robbe-Grillet to the attention of an even wider audience. Barthes's articles in *Lettres Nouvelles* were likely part of what prompted Jean Paulhan to congratulate Robbe-Grillet for managing to get people to talk about his work. Shortly after Barthes's first article on Robbe-Grillet appeared, Nadeau invited Robbe-Grillet to print a prose piece in his journal. In addition, essays by Barthes on Beckett and Robbe-Grillet appeared in that journal in quick succession, anticipating the kinds of associations that would be common in later years. *Les Gommes* also caught the attention of Bernard Dort, whose article in *Cahiers du Sud* in 1954 would be the first of many on Robbe-Grillet's novels.

The publication of *Le Voyeur* activated a second crucial network, and for the first time brought to bear on a Minuit author a number of the important connections developed in the early 50s. With his ongoing interest in Minuit's fortunes, Jean Paulhan was predisposed to following Robbe-Grillet's career. He did not necessarily have Minuit's future foremost on his mind: Robbe-Grillet tells of Paulhan's attempts to lure him to Gallimard.[57] Those attempts coincided with Paulhan's solicitations for texts to publish in the *NNRF*. Paulhan's support added not only to Robbe-Grillet's exposure to readers of literary journals—by 1955 he had appeared in the pages of *Critique*, *Lettres Nouvelles*, and the *NNRF*—but helped create the "buzz" that the attribution of the Prix des Critiques lent to *Le Voyeur*. Winning that prize was a strong vindication of Robbe-Grillet's tactics, even if it did not result in the wide-appeal sales Lindon had sought for *Les Gommes*. *Le Voyeur* nonetheless sold well, very likely a first indication to Lindon that his strategies could pay off.[58] The support of other members of the Prix des Critiques jury made similar sense: as we have seen, by 1955 Georges Bataille and Maurice Blanchot had long been part of the Minuit "constellation." Bataille, editor of *Critique*, and his contributor—as well as published Minuit author—Blanchot were both invested in Minuit's bid for capital; their ability to exert symbolic capital outside of Minuit—as Gallimard authors and contributors to the *NNRF*, prize jury members—made them well-suited to serving as echoes of Robbe-Grillet's project to "gild the pill."

Roland Barthes wrote articles on Robbe-Grillet that were important for affirming the importance and seriousness of his writing. His essays in literary criticism in the early 50s are of much significance because they offer insight into how Robbe-Grillet's novels would later be characterized as major new additions to literary culture. Their particular assertions of value seemed to inform Robbe-Grillet's conception of his own writing and gave further definition to his nascent editorial project as he took on an editorial role at Minuit (see Chapter III).

Barthes owes his earliest opportunities to publish his literary criticism to Maurice Nadeau, whose changes in position among newspapers and journals in the early 50s (*Combat, Esprit, L'Observateur, Lettres Nouvelles*) determined where Barthes's writing appeared. By the time Barthes's first book, *Le Degré zéro de l'écriture*, was published in 1953, Barthes had earned notoriety for his series of "small mythologies" in *Les Lettres nouvelles.* As I discussed above, Nadeau's *Lettres nouvelles* presented itself as an attempt to depoliticize literature and criticism; while still imbued in these early years with Marxist critique, Barthes's work moved away from such emphasis fairly quickly, in part due to the forum Nadeau's publication provided. Despite the recognition that came from Barthes's articles, *Le Degré zéro de l'écriture* was vital in establishing his reputation among critics; reviews of the book were overwhelmingly favorable, and its publication marked Barthes's passage, according to one biographer, "from a limited, private audience to a public one."[59] Barthes's friendship with Jean Cayrol was therefore equally important at this early stage. A contributor at

Editions du Seuil, Cayrol was responsible for bringing Barthes's *Le Degré zéro* to publication, thus introducing Barthes to the publishing house he would stay with throughout his career.[60] Barthes's manuscript had been rejected by Gallimard, and Seuil's acceptance of it thrust Barthes into the same competition for capital as the contest that characterized Gallimard's relation with Editions de Minuit. Like Minuit, Seuil began during the war as a resistance publishing house, and Jean Cayrol, a concentration-camp survivor, was both a Seuil author and a member of the editorial committee. Nadeau's and Cayrol's backing was crucial to the success of Barthes's emergence as a respected critic; furthermore, they each supplied him with inspiration: Nadeau, through the space in his journal, and Cayrol through his own writings.

Barthes's interest in Cayrol's writing mirrors and illuminates his interest in Robbe-Grillet, and the ways in which he described the work of each reveal much about his own vision of literary value. While Cayrol's novels are referred to a handful of times in *Le Degré zéro de l'écriture*, Barthes devotes more detailed and specific attention to them in journal articles written before and after the book was compiled.[61] Published in *Esprit* in 1952 at Nadeau's behest, "Jean Cayrol et ses romans" puts key Barthesian terms and concepts on display for the first time. Barthes's article focuses on a trilogy Cayrol wrote and published between 1947 and 1950 with the title *Je vivrai l'amour des autres*.[62] Cayrol's writing exemplifies the kind of undoing of conventional novel-writing that Barthes will continue to argue for in his critical essays and praise certain authors for achieving:

> [L]e continu cayrolien n'est pas fait d'une intrigue, au sens habituel du mot; c'est un continu d'épisodes, de rencontres, de descriptions, dans lequel

> l'événement est ramené à une sorte d'état zéro, dont la minceur déconcerte [. . .] [C]e mouvement est sans triomphe, il ne s'agit pas d'un roman de l'optimisme, il ne s'agit pas d'une exaltation. Simplement, dans un temps intérieur infiniment reculé, repoussé par quelque cataclysme innommé—comme peut-être les camps—en deçà de l'humain, il y a une institution progressive de l'homme dans un monde déjà institué dans ses assises inhumaines (les objets).[63]

~

> [The] Cayrolian continuum is not made of a plot, in the usual sense of the word; it is a continuous series of episodes, encounters, descriptions, in which the event is brought back to a sort of zero state, the thinness of which disconcerts [. . .] [T]he movement is without triumph, it is not a novel of optimism, it is not about elation. Simply, in an infinitely remote interior time, pushed back by some unnamed cataclysm—like perhaps the camps—below the human, there is a progressive institution of man in a world already established in its inhuman foundations (the objects).

The "zero state" of Cayrol's texts reflects the stripping away of traditional plot, and with it psychology, sentimentality, and conventional modes of literary meaning (Barthes's term is *profondeur*, depth). References to the camps—the Nazi concentration camps like Mauthausen, from which Cayrol was liberated in 1945—punctuate the essay, and suggest an inchoate theory of Cayrol's writing as testimonial.[64] In Barthes's view, the experience of the camps, as an "unnamed cataclysm," seems to motivate Cayrol's reduction of textual representation to the "zero state." That reduction was of important philosophical consequence, particularly for an era—and a field—marked by existentialism:

> L'homme cayrolien, pour essentiel, pour éternel qu'il soit, n'est pas l'objet d'un humanisme. Le roman, c'est-à-dire l'acte littéraire, le saisit dans un état terrestre bien antérieur à celui où le prend en général la littérature classique; celle-ci s'intéresse à un homme socialisé par son passé et qu'elle regarde fonctionner dans le conflit de ses passions.[65]
>
> ~
>
> As essential, as eternal as the Cayrolian man is, he is not the object of humanism. The novel, that is to say the literary act, grasps it in an earthly state well anterior to that in which classical literature generally takes it; this one is interested in a man socialized by his past and whom it watches function in the conflict of his passions.

Barthes is forcefully asserting Cayrol's unique place in the contemporary literary landscape, out of reach of the realms of psychological or sociological interpretation (further on he writes that "the Cayrolian man is antecedent to all psychology and all sociology"[66]). Cayrol's characters inhabit a pre-novel, pre-socialized state, a zone in which Sartrean notions of committed literature also have no relevance or power.

Cayrol's texts, in sum, form the basis a whole set of textual concerns, strategies, and characteristics that become Barthes's mode of reading and literary interpretation in the latter years of the 50s. The principal categories of Barthes's reading are already in place here: he describes "Cayrol's objects," "duration," and "Cayrolian description." Like the plot, the objects in Cayrol's novels have been stripped down to their pure status as objects: "they have no secrets; they are flat, their essence is in their surface; the gaze follows them, but does not pierce them."[67] Hence, the description consists of a systematically external or objective gaze: "the Cayrolian description circumvents the object, exhausts all its images, all its surfaces, and only goes beyond them once it has been completely saturated by the gaze."[68] One of the crucial effects of these characteristics is to displace meaning with the narrativization of pure duration: "the Cayrolian novel [is] made up of the experience of a duration, not a message."[69]

By the time Barthes read Robbe-Grillet—first *Les Gommes*, in late 1953 or early 1954 and at Jean Cayrol's insistence, and *Le Voyeur* in 1955—his reading of Cayrol had become systematized and projected into a theory of writing. In his 1953 *Le Degré zéro de l'écriture*, he defines zero degree writing as "an indicative writing, or perhaps "amodal," "neutral," or "blank," that he posits as in opposition to "bourgeois writing."[70] Soon after reading *Les Gommes*, Barthes incorporated Robbe-Grillet into his shortlist of novels that exemplified zero-degree writing as he conceived of it. In the next chapter, I closely examine Barthes's reading of *Le Voyeur* in the essay "Littérature littérale," in which he identifies many of the same textual characteristics as those discussed above. In many ways, Barthes's reading of Cayrol anticipates his reading of *Le Voyeur*, but *Le Voyeur* reveals a more programmatic Barthes eager to cast the new literature as revolutionary. First, however, *Les Gommes* provided an opportunity for Barthes to expand the scope of zero degree writing by showing how Robbe-Grillet's novel was complementary to the innovative project heralded in Cayrol's writing.

In June of 1954, a short essay entitled "Pré-romans" in which Barthes compares Robbe-Grillet's *Les Gommes* with Cayrol's œuvre appeared in *France-Observateur*. In it, Barthes paints the broad strokes of a new literary movement and its authors. His essay is a valorization of both Cayrol and Robbe-Grillet for their problematization of literature, a problematization that is necessary:

> [L]a plupart des œuvres fortes, des œuvres neuves qui paraissent actuellement sont des romans problématiques, où la fiction se double d'une mise en question des catégories fondamentales de la création romanesque, comme si le roman idéal, le roman innocent étant impossible, la Littérature devait avant tout dire comment elle se fuit et comment elle se tue, bref comment elle se refuse.[71]
>
> ~
>
> Most strong works or truly new works currently appearing are problematic novels, where fiction is coupled with a questioning of the fundamental categories of fictional creation, such that with the ideal novel or the innocent novel being impossible Literature had above all to say how it flees and how it kills itself—in short, how it refuses itself.

There is an implicit historical notion of literature at work here, according to which unproblematized fiction is no longer possible; something like Cayrol's "cataclysm"—and just as "unnamed"—motivates Barthes's convictions about contemporary literature. The particular characteristics of Cayrol's fiction have become the basis for a prescriptive view of literature. In a slight shift of emphasis from his previous reading, Barthes describes Cayrol's contribution as that of a newly circumscribed novelist: "The function of the novelist is no longer endoscopic here, it is the very extension of a familiar but unusual world, one that it is yet to be born, and to which consequently the classic novel, the fully equipped novel would be an intolerable word and murderous."[72] The move in emphasis from description and duration to the relationship between the novelist and his world leaves those categories for Robbe-Grillet, whose contribution to the "explosion of the novel" Barthes terms as a new treatment of space and time, the first new treatment in over one hundred years of literature. His denunciation of major contemporary authors for their outmoded style is fierce:

> Robbe-Grillet travaille à introduire dans le récit un mixte nouveau d'espace et de temps, ce que l'on pourrait appeler une dimension ensteinienne de l'objet. Ceci est d'autant plus important, que littérairement nous vivons encore dans une vision purement newtonienne de l'univers: Camus ou Breton décrivent un paysage comme Chateaubriand ou Lamartine. Il y a longtemps que la peinture a résolu ce problème de la figuration simultanée des plans en mouvement. La Littérature pas encore.[74]
>
> ~
>
> Robbe-Grillet works to introduce into the narrative a new mixture of space and time, what one might call an Einsteinian dimension of the object. This is all the more important since in literature we still live in a purely Newtonian vision of the universe: Camus or Breton describe a landscape like Chateaubriand or Lamartine. Painting has long since solved this problem of the simultaneous representation of moving planes. Literature not yet.

To describe the alchemy of space and time in *Les Gommes* as a breakthrough in literary technique on a par with Einstein's revision of Newtonian physics is a very drastic means of asserting Robbe-Grillet's modernity over established figures in the literary field. Barthes is still some years away from identifying Robbe-Grillet variously as the proponent of "the school of the gaze [*regard*]," of "thingism [*chosisme*]," or of "literal literature." Beginning with his earliest occasions to read Robbe-Grillet, however, he clearly chose to assimilate Robbe-Grillet's writing into the conception of a new modern literature that had begun to take shape in his readings of Jean Cayrol and whose contours would continue to be defined through the novels of Robbe-Grillet.

Much later Robbe-Grillet would remark that Barthes's writings about his novels were more about Barthes than about the novels themselves.[75] While my discussion of Barthes's criticism in the early part of the 50s may to some extent support that claim, I think it important to conclude that discussion by asserting that in large part it hardly matters: Barthes's critical interest in Robbe-Grillet's writing was crucial to generating further interest in his work and to developing his credentials in the literary field. Barthes's ability to do so, in turn, hinged on the creation of new positions in the field prepared to endorse his pursuit of a new literature. In the next chapter, I examine how Editions de Minuit made the production of just such a new literature the linchpin of its entire publishing line.

CHAPTER III

Publishers of the New Novel, 1955 1960

> Certes, les auteurs font le renom de la maison qui les publie. Pourquoi ne pas voir que la réciproque est vraie tout autant?
>
> Of course, the authors make the reputation of the house that publishes them. Why not see that the converse is just as true?
>
> Alain Robbe-Grillet, *Les derniers jours de Corinthe*

In looking at the publishing activities of Jérôme Lindon and Alain Robbe-Grillet in the years 1957 to 1960, I broach a subject and a debate that have become major reference points of twentieth-century literary history and criticism. In 1957, the history of Editions de Minuit became in large part the history of the New Novel; as a result, Minuit began to acquire a pivotal role in literary publishing that would extend through the next decade and beyond. In 1957, Emile Henriot used the expression "New Novel" for the first time in an article attacking the ideas of Robbe-Grillet and Nathalie Sarraute, putting a name at last to the enigmatic creature that, as I showed in the previous chapter, had been in circulation among literary critics for a number of years. Editions de Minuit became identified with the New Novel, and in those years, the heyday of the New Novel's publication, Minuit rose in stature and cultural capital. It also inaugurated a lexicon of literary value by which the publications of the day would come to be critically measured—a lexicon that later merged smoothly, as I discuss in Chapter IV, with French structuralism. The ubiquitous nature of the New Novel as one of the foremost signs of France's cultural modernity, attested to today by its place in educational textbooks and by the sustained output of criticism on its authors, is evidence of Minuit's achievement. My aim in this chapter is to offer a contextualization of the New Novel that enriches our understanding of Minuit's role in its creation, as well as its place in Minuit's publishing. Namely, I suggest that Minuit established the New Novel as a new paradigm of literary value by using marketing techniques that were already recognizable as similar to those used in mass culture today. Doing so meant merging culture with commerce: a conjunction of editorial and promotional strategies, the New Novel was both a publishing product and a discourse intended to legitimize that product.

It is important to recall the weakness of Minuit's financial and cultural capital in a system whose rules heavily favor producers who are strong in both. Publishers who can afford a more polyvalent editorial strategy—and therefore a more varied booklist—are, in theory, more apt to capitalize on cultural change, or at the very least, hedge against unfavorable trends. Minuit's success with the New Novel hinged enormously on the readiness of literary culture to accept it, whether favorably or disapprovingly, as an icon of its modernity. While not immediate, and never true for all of its factions, that readiness reflected the field's approval of the posture of revolution and renewal asserted by the New Novel.

The subject of lively debate since its inception, to this day the New Novel continues to draw attention both in mainstream media and in critical circles. Several important critical studies underscore just how much is at stake in how we interpret the New Novel's success. These studies raise important questions about the contexts in which literary texts have traditionally been understood. They take the New Novel as something other than a result of textual strategies, and hence mark a departure from much New Novel criticism, which has tended to emphasize the formal traits that define the particular rigor and originality of the New Novel authors. I briefly mention two examples, Kristin Ross's *Fast Cars, Clean Bodies* and Nelly Wolf's *Une littérature sans histoire*, because—in addition to introducing various important variables at play in how the New Novel may be appraised—they illustrate some of the methodological issues that can arise when crossing literary criticism with historical or sociological inquiry.[1] Ross's and Wolf's work is also noteworthy because both appraise the New Novel negatively, and therefore represent another break with critical tradition: as I shall discuss in the next chapter, by and large most American critics of French literature have tended to support the New Novel—indeed, I show how espousal by American critics played an essential part in the New Novel's rise.

Both Wolf and Ross set the New Novel against the backdrop of a strongly determinant historical context: for Kristin Ross, it is the Algerian War (1954-1962). Ross characterizes the New Novel as a reflection of a culture strongly in denial of the horrors perpetuated in its name in Algeria. For her, the textual strategies of the New Novel mirror the will of the French to void the historical realities of the Algerian War and the culpability bound up with it. That voidance occurred via the dominant cultural theme of cleansing. Her argument about "Clean Bodies" identifies a discourse of hygiene that she uses to associate Roland Barthes's structuralist "New

Man" and the New Novel (via Robbe-Grillet's *La Jalousie*) with an assortment of examples drawn from across mass culture of France's "urge to cleanse."[2] For Nelly Wolf, the historical context for understanding the New Novel is the memory of Vichy and France's persecution of the Jews. Unlike *Fast Cars, Clean Bodies*, the focus of which is much more diffuse, Nelly Wolf's text is devoted entirely to re assessing the New Novel. Her argument is less nuanced and more polemical and indicts France as a whole in the late 40s and 50s for its "law of silence" with regard to its Fascist history and the deportation of the Jews. The New Novel is one manifestation of the law of silence, complicit with both the right wing Hussards and the left wing engaged intellectuals in building a wall of defense around "the unsayable."[3] There has been a deliberate "mystifying covering over of history," successful because of France's "collective aspiration to oblivion."[4] Though vaguely redolent of Rousso's analysis of the Vichy Syndrome, Wolf's thesis is a blanket condemnation.

Great caution is required when making claims about the connections between literature and cultural history. While their notions of historical analysis are very different, Ross and Wolf both neglect important factors that complicate the relationship between the New Novel and the production of cultural memory. Ross and Wolf are right to proceed from an implied relationship between literary production on the one hand and the shaping of cultural memory on the other. As we saw in Chapter I, the case of Sartre in the immediate postwar illustrated how a particular discourse of literary value can become dominant—for a time—in the service of a culture's demands. However, there is the risk of both exaggerating the symbolic importance of one single figure, as well as reducing positions to essential oppositions. Again, Bourdieu's theories are useful recourse.

The model of the literary field, with its defining principle of differentiation or positionality, is an important way of recalling that, at any given time, competing discourses vie for dominance. By taking the New Novel as symbolic of French literary culture as a whole, critics like Ross and Wolf overlook the conditions of its emergence and the ways in which its cultural significance changed with time. The meaning of the New Novel shifted enormously in French culture between its first mention in 1957 and 1958, and the early 60s. In framing the New Novel within the trajectory of Editions de Minuit, I seek to restore it to its humble beginnings and underscore its unique means of earning cultural capital. Additionally, as the product of one specific publisher, it is a vital component in a broader strategy of redeploying the literary genres that touches directly on the relationships Wolf and Ross sought to establish. The editorial strategies of Minuit, as I discuss later in this chapter, make the Algerian issue something of a moot point, marrying as they do the New Novel with a widely publicized position against the colonial war in Algeria. Kristin Ross discussed Barthes's and Robbe-Grillet's writings on the New Novel, rather than draw her conclusions from readings of novels that were promoted as exemplars of the New Novel, or compare those works to other Minuit publications that were garnering a great deal of attention in the late 1950s and early 1960s. Had she looked more closely, Ross may have been led to consider the differences between the critical discourse on the New Novel and the strategies for positioning that discourse on the one hand, and the issues of readability presented by the various works assembled under the heading of the New Novel on the other. She grants total confidence and representational authority to articles on the New Novel that hardly represent a uniform notion of writing, and even less a convincing expression of the New Novel. Taken as having always occupied centerstage of literary culture, Barthes, Robbe-Grillet, and the New Novel are presented as static symbols of an homogeneous structuralism. Nelly Wolf's identification of the New Novel with structuralism similarly reduces each to a static or synchronic event, and therefore critically enacts the very deed for which the New Novel is charged: evacuating history. The French structuralist "moment" comes several years after the New Novel; by the time the New Novel intersected with structuralism, it was already in its second generation and changing shape significantly (I trace out this relationship in Chapter IV).

Ultimately, their condemnation of the New Novel seems based in its refusal to satisfy implicit political or aesthetic convictions of a kind that it manifestly sought to put aside—views about literary commitment that recall Sartre's *littérature engagée*. Clearly, the New Novel should not be exempt from cultural critique, especially one that ponders its concurrence with the Algerian War and—perhaps equally importantly—De Gaulle's return to power. Nonetheless, such a critique need not smooth the rough edges of an ever divided literary field, nor base itself on an inflexible notion of the New Novel.

The New Novel marked the gradual move of its publisher and a number of its authors from the margins to the center, from capitally weak to culturally dominant. Minuit became the major publisher of elite intellectual culture by capitalizing on the increasing readiness of literary culture to accept the New Novel. Taking their cue from the history of literary movements, the Minuit authors deployed a discourse of cultural renewal to lay claim to capital. At stake was the promise of a newly realist mode of writing that would strip literature of old fashioned philosophical, political, and ideological constraints. The public roles of theorist and architect of Minuit's New Novel were both played primarily by Alain Robbe-Grillet.

1. Robbe-Grillet, Editor and Publicist

As the considerations that went into the marketing of *Les Gommes* in 1953 demonstrate (see Chapter II), Jérôme Lindon and Alain Robbe-Grillet had only begun to form some specific ideas about editorial strategy in the first half of the 1950s. It was only after the publication of *Les Gommes*, and in the vein of criticism that the book inspired, that Robbe-Grillet started to develop and publicize his own literary criticism. Still, his early articles—some of which were published with later ones in 1963, under the title *Pour un Nouveau Roman*—appeared only in the relatively small circulation journals *Les Lettres Nouvelles* and *Critique*. As I pointed out above, the critical success and controversy that met *Le Voyeur* in 1955 was a first demonstration of Robbe-Grillet's appeal among a growing number of critics; equally important, it increased his authorial stature enough for his next articles to reach larger readerships. A quick succession of articles followed the publication of *Le Voyeur*: in *L'Express* in December 1955, January and February 1956, as well as *La Nouvelle NRF* in July 1956. These articles are important expressions of an editorial strategy in formation, and document the initial discursive context in which Minuit's developing field position was being and would be promoted. For in early 1955, Lindon made Robbe-Grillet a co-editor of Minuit's literary publishing, and the two men's stature and symbolic capital were henceforth profoundly interconnected. His role as Lindon's primary collaborator—sustained to varying degrees over the subsequent thirty years—was widely unknown, due in part to Robbe-Grillet's own coy persistence, even into the late 1980s, in referring to Editions de Minuit as if it were merely his publisher, rather than a house he had helped to run.[5] It is as if the fact of his work as editor would have undermined his image as writer and head of a literary movement, and the authenticity of his claims made more questionable. Seeing Robbe-Grillet as a partner to Lindon casts his developing public image in a new light, as the parts of author and theorist overlap with those of editor and publicist.

From 1955 to 1959, Robbe-Grillet read many of the manuscripts submitted to Editions de Minuit and, unlike Jérôme Lindon, left record of many of those readings—Anne Simonin has counted six hundred fifty reader reports [*fiches de lecture*]—on file in the Minuit archives.[6] These reports are a very peculiar kind of reader report. In the two years preceding the christening of the New Novel, Robbe-Grillet's work as a reader went hand in hand with his evolving dialogue with critics over what the terms of literary value ought to be. In their overwhelming rejection of the submissions, Robbe-Grillet's reports shed some light on the practical application of his developing concept of the New Novel, the Minuit brand, and of a revised system of literary genres.

Simonin cites three categories Robbe-Grillet used to organize the over four hundred fiches covering novel manuscripts: "novels in the purest psychological style for the sentimental press [*presse de coeur*]," "novelesque novels [*romans romanesques*]," and "naturalistic novels."[7] Despite the appearance of a system, the categories of the fiches are fuzzy and seem to overlap; they show the extent to which the New Novel at Minuit remained somewhat ill-defined both before and after getting its name in 1957, and how vague Minuit's posture of renewal was until its christening by critics. From reading examples of his comments from each set, it becomes clear that Robbe-Grillet's categorization is hierarchical, going from bad to worse: the sole good category, "the future novel," appears only negatively in the reports.[8] The first category of novels was the easiest for Robbe-Grillet to dispense with; one example illustrates his intolerance of intellectual lightness that struck such works from his consideration. Clearly, certain novel genres would never appeal:

> Roman d'amour sans grand intérêt (pour personne, j'espère). Le narrateur (à la première personne) rencontre une jeune fille, l'épouse. Mais elle meurt bientôt, ce qui met fin, enfin, au livre. Insipide, mal écrit, plein de bons sentiments. Ça commence en Suisse, ça se poursuit dans une bonne vieille province française . . . Ça finit au panier.[9]
>
> ~
>
> A love story of no great interest (to anyone, I hope). The narrator (in the first person) meets a young girl, marries her. But she soon dies, which finally ends the book. Tasteless, badly written, full of sentimentality. It starts in Switzerland, it continues in a good old French province . . . It ends in the basket.

His summary suggests that the expression "psychological style for the sentimental press" refers to writing that is the furthest removed from the mode of literary renewal he seeks. While difficult to evaluate without access to the manuscript he was describing, Robbe-Grillet's remarks depict a very conventional work, with stable first-person narration, generic plot development—bordering on the romance novel—and stereotyped settings ("good old province"). That such traits of genre seem to have been anathema to Robbe-Grillet indicates the degree to which his input would invest Editions de Minuit in a single line of literary publishing. The question of whether or not Minuit could have sold a mass readership title appears to have never been raised—the example of *Bonjour Tristesse*, published by the comparably sized Julliard, comes to mind.[10] The attempt alone would have compromised the operative distinctions of value—and therefore class and taste—asserted in the development of the New Novel. Working as a Minuit editor in this way, Robbe-Grillet was a guardian of the Minuit brand before becoming the public champion of its New Novel.

At first glance, it is hard to tell what sets works designated in the second category ("novelesque novels") apart from those in the first. These examples are of manuscripts that do not come across as having been drastically different from the one referred to above, yet Robbe-Grillet's reactions to each make an interesting contrast:

> Roman psychologique type dans un décor de haute montagne. Pureté des cimes et ambiguïté des sentiments. Joie des ascensions difficiles. Accidents de cordée et aléas des histoires d'amour. Pas mal si on veut. A renvoyer sans commentaires.
>
> ~
>
> Typical psychological novel in a high mountain setting. Purity of summits and ambiguity of feelings. Joy of difficult climbs. Rope accidents and the vagaries of love stories. Not bad if you want. To be returned without comments.
>
> ~
>
> Roman romanesque à la première personne. L'amour, les problèmes . . . merde!! Mais quand même: un homme qui essaie d'y voir clair dans la vie. Ça et là des passages intéressants. Ça ne suffit pas. Le narrateur écrit une pièce où, sous une autre forme . . . , etc. Mais ça ne suffit pas.[11]
>
> ~
>
> Fictional novel in the first person. Love, problems . . . shit!! But still: a man who tries to see things clearly in life. Here and there interesting passages.

> This is not enough. The narrator writes a play where, in another form . . . , etc. But it's not enough.

The first evaluation, dated six months prior to the second, shows tired indifference in the presence of yet another stylistic exercise; by the time he read the later manuscript, the signs of the "novelesque" genre were a cause of frustration. The valuable portions of the text are unable to overcome the handicaps of genre: "This is not enough[. . .] it's not enough." Less immediately reviled on Robbe-Grillet's scale of value than the novels of "the purest psychological style," the "novelesque novels" are in fact ultimately worse, because their "novelesque"—read romantic, feminized, "sentimental press"—aspects stifle potential authors. Robbe-Grillet writes of another novel in this category: "[. . .] containing perhaps some interesting things. For later? No, the guy probably writes whatever and will evolve into the mundane."[12] Robbe-Grillet's use of the expression "novelesque novel" is telling. Shorthand for a number of genres of novels—if not, indeed, a fairly nondescript catchword applicable to nearly all—including sentimental novels, adventure novels, and even psychological novels, it anticipates the way in which his use of "new novel [nouveau roman]" later encapsulated a disparate set of novels. The tautology of "novelesque novel" is resolved by the implicit splitting up of the terms it consists of: Robbe-Grillet was in search of the "novel" that banishes the "novelesque." He was also in search of authors: with each manuscript he was evaluating its author for potential. Can this author be made to fit?

The third category of novels in Robbe-Grillet's system consists of "naturalistic novels." "Naturalism," like "psychology" and "novelesque novel," is another Robbe-Grillet catchword for a broad swath of literary ills. Nonetheless, the reference to Zola is not fortuitous: he dismisses naturalistic novels primarily for their claim of realism, but their political commitment has no place in the determination of value either. His particular conception of naturalism—as well as his rejection of it—is made more explicit in his articles than in the reports, since his dismissal of politically motivated fictions is very curt—at least in the examples available. Of one text he wrote:

> Roman romanesque naturaliste. De nos jours, en Russie soviétique, dans une ferme collective; en Espagne . . . ; et ailleurs. Mais du point de vue littéraire, ça change peu malheureusement.[13]
>
> ~
>
> Naturalistic novelesque novel. Nowadays, in Soviet Russia, on a collective farm; in Spain . . . ; and elsewhere. But from a literary point of view, it changes little unfortunately.

This unusually short evaluation does not even go as far as to indicate any main characters; instead, the description is limited to listing some of the spaces in the narrative, suggesting a vehicle for social realist themes. The "literary point of view" he cites is one which, in requiring a minimum of innovation, ignores considerations of content.

Anne Simonin claims that Robbe-Grillet saw more potential for steering naturalistic novels toward "the future novel" than in "novelesque" novels, since the former already bore "the mark of an interest in contemporary literature."[14] None of the novels published by Editions de Minuit appear to have such origins—only one of the authors whose works were reviewed by Robbe-Grillet in this fashion was ever published (Jean Thibaudeau). Still, Robbe-Grillet's aversion to naturalistic novels may have stemmed from their having been contemporary, in the sense of having an affinity with Sartrean engagement, without being (sufficiently) modernist—hence their potential to be drawn away from a retrograde literary style.

> Roman naturaliste moderne: un journaliste, un commissaire de police, un militant communiste, sont mêlés à une explosion rue de la Huchette . . . Un nord africain, le Parti, la femme du policier, les autres journalistes . . . , etc. Analyse vaguement existentielle, cafés et déambulations. Ecriture marquant quelques soucis de modernisme: ruptures, audaces diverses, cinéma. Des choses intéressantes. A inscrire en classe élémentaire![15]
>
> Modern naturalist novel: a journalist, a police commissioner, and a communist militant are involved in an explosion in rue de la Huchette . . . A North African, the Party, the policeman's wife, the other journalists . . . , etc. A vaguely existential analysis, cafes and strolls. Writing showing some concerns of modernism: ruptures, various signs of daring, cinema. Interesting things. To register in elementary class!

The manuscript in question, a strange hybrid of modernist "ruptures" and "existential analysis" shows promise, pending a veritable enrollment in training at the Minuit School. The association of terms here is telling: in the opposition Robbe-Grillet set up between "naturalistic novel" and "modern novel" or "modernist novel," the existentialist trait is of a piece with the text's naturalism, and needs to be unlearned.

The *fiches de lecture* are small snapshots where we see Robbe-Grillet implementing a system of critical reading in which the New Novel had a primordial—if always virtual—role.

Although it remained a rough shorthand for Robbe-Grillet's preferences, his system of categories was a means of staging the New Novel's difference from contemporary literary production. The critical lexicon of the reports reappears in Robbe-Grillet's articles dating from the period of his editorship, with more elaborate rhetoric. In turning my attention toward those essays, I show how Robbe-Grillet's contentiousness prepared the way for Minuit's literary publishing to become the focus of critical attention. Once that occurred and the New Novel started to gain in prestige, Robbe-Grillet and Lindon redoubled their activities aimed at consolidating the identification between Editions de Minuit and the New Novel.

The year 1955 marked the beginning of Robbe-Grillet's long career as an editor at Minuit and, with a long list of articles appearing in a broad range of publications, as an infrequent literary theorist. So infrequent were his theoretical articles, however, that he is better described as a polemicist, or, in the context of his editorship, a publicist: the bulk of his critical and theoretical writing dates from and relates to the development and consecration of the New Novel (1956–1963). As I discussed in Chapter II, Robbe-Grillet had gotten started by writing a considerable number of book reviews for *Critique* in the first part of the decade. In 1955, he ceased to publish reviews in preference for critical essay-writing that was, in some respects, imitative of Blanchot's *Chroniques* in *La Nouvelle NRF* and Barthes's regular contributions to *Les Lettres nouvelles*. I argued in Chapter II that the articles by Blanchot and Barthes on *Les Gommes* and *Le Voyeur*—in addition to other points of reference—were important support for and encouragement of Robbe-Grillet's development of an aesthetic. Their columns may have served as inspiration of another sort: that of using the forum of the literary journal to work out ideas on literature, art, and philosophy. Robbe-Grillet's articles from the period reflect the traditional logic of the journal article, but for very different purposes. The parcellary structure of Blanchot's *L'Espace littéraire*, composed entirely of *Chroniques* spanning a decade, nevertheless reflects an elaborate and developed critical investigation. The same can be said for Barthes's *Mythologies*. The comparable volume of Robbe-Grillet's is his *Pour un nouveau roman*, a very selective collection of his articles from the 1950s; these articles, as well as the texts that were not included, depict a wholly different set of rhetorical strategies and aims. From 1955 on, Robbe-Grillet made use of virtually every opportunity to promote a singular view of contemporary literature that advanced himself and his publisher as the future of French literary culture. Aimed at capturing the attention of the greatest number of critics and littérateurs, Robbe-Grillet's pieces were more polemical than critical; by carefully borrowing the signs and conventions of literary criticism, Robbe-Grillet worked on setting himself up as an authority on literary matters. The move from book reviews to polemical essays is one from description to prescription: in the expression "New Novel"—and its numerous predecessors, such as "the future novel"—Robbe-Grillet had a tool with which to condemn the literature of the present in the name of the literature of the future.

Robbe-Grillet's articles from 1955 and 1956 create the image of a veritable pamphleteer. Their belligerent tone and sweeping assertions had the doubly beneficial effect of dividing critics into two camps: supporters and opponents; in short, creating a recognizable—and recognized—field position, as nebulous or virtual as it was. Nebulous because, as evocative as they are, the pieces turn on fundamentally tautological argumentation. Robbe-Grillet's rhetoric cycles through a small set of theoretical terminology, terms he divides into opposed categories; because of the slipperiness of those terms, the reader is forced to adjust to personal definitions that reiterate Robbe-Grillet's claim on authority. Across the divide between "a new literature" and "the literary tradition," what ultimately stands out most is the image, posture, and performance of Alain Robbe-Grillet.

Robbe-Grillet's first article in *L'Express* is an good illustratration of his brand of pamphleteerism. "Littérature engagée, littérature réactionnaire"[16] exposes quite simply and directly the fundamental dichotomy that he would continue to manipulate in positioning Minuit and the New Novel. That dichotomy is set out in the title: Robbe-Grillet's task was to articulate a third, middle route between two extremes, those being Sartre's engagement and "pure entertainment," or "art for art's sake" ["l'art pour l'art"]. Robbe-Grillet dismisses Sartrean engagement first: "In other words, the social revolution should not be the only goal of the writer, it should not even be his first goal at all . . ." The reactionary right is then given even shorter shrift. With no figurehead cited, reactionary literature comes across as nothing more than a literature of entertainment: Robbe-Grillet wants to propose something different, something "which despite everything would not be a game."[17] Serious and important though not political—the alternative is a another kind of writerly engagement, whose contours are not well defined. Nonetheless, the desire to appropriate Sartrean vocabulary is clear: "Commitment, from this new perspective, regains its full value. Instead of being political in nature, engagement means a writer's full awareness of current issues in his own language, a conviction of their extreme importance, a willingness to resolve them from within."[18] He gives no indication of what such problems of language would be; instead he insists that literature should be the most important thing in the world to the writer—"even the only important thing."[19]

We have seen this strategy in Paulhan's anti-Sartrean discourse (examined in Chapter I), where redefining literature and the role of the writer was a way to discredit his political opponents; Robbe-Grillet lent a voice to that opposition without occupying a directly political position himself. It is not surprising that this anti-ideological concept of the writer had some appeal to both the moderate left and right—both interested in defining themselves against putatively more radical figures. *L'Express* was an appropriate and supportive forum for his claims, with its clear anti-Communist stance and broad centrist appeal—its most prominent contributors at the time were Merleau Ponty, François Mauriac, and Albert Camus, each of which had done intellectual battle with Sartre. As if acting on his own words, after his articles in *L'Express* Robbe-Grillet ceased to address his political critique so explicitly. While he continued to focus on attacking the left—citing Sartre and Camus almost exclusively—he moved the battlefield to primarily literary grounds.

"Une voie pour le roman futur" appeared in *La Nouvelle NRF* in July 1956, and was Robbe-Grillet's first article for the distinguished review; its sanction of Robbe-Grillet is not surprising, given the approval Blanchot and Paulhan had already expressed in arguing to award Le Prix des Critiques to *Le Voyeur* the year before. Robbe-Grillet's articles in *L'Express* that appeared earlier that year had contributed to his legitimization, and his winning the Prix de la Fondation del Duca (1956)—a large cash prize awarded in recognition of his (two) novels—saw his value among many journal editors rise. The title of this exemplary piece sets the stage for how he will develop his position throughout: the entire matter of finding "a path for the future novel" poses that the craft of writing novels is so fraught with problems that a way must be cleared for "the new." The same broad category—here called "the future novel"—is signified variously throughout the articles, and that variation was one of Robbe-Grillet's main rhetorical strategies of the pre-Nouveau Roman years. He constructs the need for—and value of—this abstract category by applying a list of negatives to the whole of contemporary literature. And because "the future novel" remains abstract, the reader is prompted to evaluate Robbe-Grillet's theoretical authority against his authority as a writer. Recognized as standard means by which writers develop their cultural capital—and sell their books—the journal article, in Robbe-Grillet's hands, became a way to stage Minuit's entrance into the literary realm.

The first paragraphs of "Une voie [. . .]" begin to describe the problem evoked in the title, proposing that "an entirely *new* literature" may not yet be possible, and indeed has not yet been possible, despite many attempts. The repeated efforts of the previous thirty years failed because they did not get the support of a readership "comparable to that of the bourgeois novel"—as a result, "the only conception of the novel that has currency today is in fact that of Balzac."[20] The previous intellectual masters and innovators had failed: in one fell swoop, the contemporary novel is portrayed as old, outdated, and—via the suggestion of Marxist critique in the phrase "bourgeois novel"—ideologically suspect. In the same breath, Robbe-Grillet divides the literary culture of the previous three decades between the pandering traditionalists and the fringe of unsuccessful experimenters: the entire edifice of literary value is obsolete and stifling. The concept of the "'good' novel" has not continued to evolve, but instead has held onto "sacrosanct psychological analysis" that dates back centuries.[20] The best selling authors of the day might just as well plagiarize *La Princesse de Clèves*. Nonetheless, there is hope for "new literature": Robbe-Grillet claims, cryptically, that "[it] is already seeing the light of day, and that it will represent—by completing itself—a more total revolution than those from which romanticism or naturalism were born."[22] The oppositional myth is in full display, with the figure of *chef d'école* not far behind.

By not citing instances of the new literature or engaging in readings of examples, Robbe-Grillet ended up promoting a concept that, for its very indistinctness, engaged the interests of critics keen on having their say in the dissemination of the new. Part of Robbe-Grillet's success came from the value—inherent to the market of ideas—of claims about literary history. The literary equivalent of "the next big thing," "new literature" activated evaluative judgments of the past and normative judgments of the present that were critics' means of exerting their capital and shaping the reproduction of the literary field. The radical vision Robbe-Grillet promoted was a challenge to literature, literary history, and critical authority.

Among his targets—which included virtually all of contemporary literary production (minus presumably his own)—are Sartre and Camus, the moderns of the previous decade. They were the only contemporary non-Minuit writers that Robbe-Grillet discussed in any detail, and he did so regularly. In focusing on *La Nausée* and *L'Etranger*, Robbe-Grillet took aim at two of the of the period's most famous and widely read works written by prominent author intellectuals of the left. At once an acknowledgment of their significance—Robbe-Grillet operated under the principle of attacking only those whom it would be the most useful for him to attack—his criticisms of them were an attempt at appropriating their prestige. In this light, the title of Robbe-Grillet's first (and at the time unpublished) novel seems highly suggestive—*Le Régicide*. Robbe-Grillet's drama of ascension painted him as the marginal herald and hero of a literature to come, one that could only exist by usurping the power of the discredited signal bearers of a compromised literature.

The image of Robbe-Grillet as marginal hero is inscribed

in his sweeping portrayal of literary culture as fundamentally inert and blind to inspiration. The entire edifice of literary production is to blame for the stagnation of literature—"from the publisher to the most modest reader, including the bookseller and the critic."[23] The literary field is inherently closed upon itself, unable to recognize or understand the new: "the entire literary organization in place [. . .] can only fight against the unknown form trying to impose itself [. . .] a new form will always appear more or less an absence of form."[24] The tyranny of the old is that those with the power to crown the new are the least interested in doing so: "hence the specialists of the novel (novelists, critics, or too frequent readers) will undoubtedly be those who will experience the greatest difficulty in breaking out of the rut."[25] The "specialists"—including readers who are too well read!—are caught in a tainted system that will always reject the revolutionary. Authority in questions of literary value, in their hands, is poorly placed.

Like a true insurgent, Robbe-Grillet puts some of the clichéd vocabulary of revolution to work against the backdrop of the permanent crisis of literature. It is hard to imagine how "without some radical change"—without a "more total revolution" than those of the past—the art of the novel can avoid demise. Never mind the incompatibilities between that notion and the apparent self-sufficient inertia of "the literary organization," and the stately march of ongoing literary history, in which a place for "the future novel" is already foreseen. At stake is nothing less than the very possibility of "freedom": "it is *freedom* [*liberté*] that should at least be possible, and that is not."[26] So much of Robbe-Grillet's position rests on that highly charged word. Forty years later, in his reminiscences of the period (in *Les Derniers jours de Corinthe*) he makes a subtle double judgment of these articles, at once downplaying them as "my little theoretical articles" and assigning them an important role in making a new "wind of freedom"[27] perceptible. In one respect, his 1994 assessment is in harmony with mine: the effect of the articles on the literary field was important. The details of his arguments—namely, the discourse of positionality, their theoretical volatility, and evocative lexicon of literary criticism—are to him unimportant, yet, in my view, they are what explain his success in precipitating the next reconfiguration of the literary field and taking center stage in it.

Robbe-Grillet's belief in his fundamental claim that he was liberating literature is one element of the New Novel myth that he refused, even in the "temps révolu" of the autobiographical novels, to revise. In 1954, Robbe-Grillet equated literary freedom with the freedom of the reader to see "the world around him with free eyes."[28] "Thingism," "Objectivity," "School of the Gaze": these are some of the names given by critics in the late 50s to Robbe-Grillet's emphasis—visible for the first time in "Une voie pour le roman futur"—on detaching description from interpretation. His argument conceives itself as an attack on "literary" types of meaning: the reader's freedom can only be actualized by stripping away narrative's traditional habit of instrumentalizing the world for false purposes. Committed literature is just one more manifestation of the artificial interpositions and interferences inherited from "the psychological and naturalist tradition."[29] The "literary phenomenon" is being displaced by the "optical adjective," thus signaling an end to the interpretive systems that literature presses upon the reader and delivering her back into direct contact with the being-there ['*être là*'] of the world.[30] While the distant reference for Robbe-Grillet's theory is ultimately Heidegger, the close reference is Roland Barthes, whose essay on *Le Voyeur* published a year before "Une Voie [. . .]" had christened Robbe-Grillet's novels as a "literal literature."[31]

In the vein of his earlier articles, Barthes's latest piece provided a store of concepts from which Robbe-Grillet drew much inspiration. Indeed, Barthes's text—published, importantly, in Minuit's house journal, *Critique*—put forth the basic vision of literary culture that we read in Robbe-Grillet, and, to a striking extent, prefigured—or perhaps directly "inspired"—Robbe-Grillet's theoretical stances in the articles. "Literal literature" presented *Les Gommes* and *Le Voyeur* as a singular "great novelistic exploration," and set those novels against the "traditional novel" in order to announce a new literature and a new experience of reading.[32] The set of negations Barthes read in the novels is substantial, and each of them is subsequently taken up by Robbe-Grillet. Anti-traditional, anti-bourgeois, anti-psychological: Barthes identifies and valorizes the signs of a marginal literature that he endows with the potential to redefine literature as a whole.

> Un roman de Robbe-Grillet ne se lit pas de la manière à la fois globale et discontinue dont on 'dévore' un roman traditionnel, où l'intellection saute de paragraphe en paragraphe, [. . .] comme si la lecture, dans son geste le plus matériel, devait reproduire la hiérarchie même de l'univers classique [. . .].[33]

~

> A Robbe-Grillet novel cannot be read in the way that is both global and discontinuous in which we "devour" a traditional novel, where the intellect jumps from paragraph to paragraph, [. . .] as if reading, in its most material, had to reproduce the very hierarchy of the classical universe [. . .].

Novels that invite their co-optation into "the classical universe," and therefore allow their unfettered consumption, participate in the bourgeois system of material—and cultural—reproduction. Robbe-Grillet's treatment of objects renews "the art of description" in disallowing such ideological complicity; material objects are no longer made mere expressions of human sentiment but instead occupy "an implacable space."[34] The basic component of the "literature of the finding" ["littérature du constat"] is "the properly optical nature of the fictional material"; later he terms it "Robbe-Grillet's optical system."[35] It is a system capable of exiling "the Civilization of the Soul" that constantly threatens to take over his novels and recuperate them via psychology: "an entire psychological order threatens to take over [investor] the novel" nonetheless, "Robbe-Grillet's novel therefore remains perfectly outside of a psychoanalytic order."[36] Barthes's interpretation of Robbe-Grillet fits his novels into the critical project of *Degré zéro de l'écriture*, as seen in Chapter II. Literary renewal is achieved through a "zeroing" out of the traditional elements of fiction. In the path from *Les Gommes* to *Le Voyeur*, Robbe-Grillet abandoned one such cumbersome fictional support: "in *Les Gommes*, the objective world was supported by an enigma involving a criminal inquiry [. . .] in *Le Voyeur*, there is no longer any qualification of the story; it tends toward zero, to the point that we can hardly name it."[37] Description wins out over plot, suspending the determinacy of meaning, allowing objects to manifest pure exteriority: "objects appear as a sort of zero theme of the argument. The novel takes place in this narrow and difficult area, where the anecdote (the crime) begins to rot, to 'intentionalize' the superb stubbornness of the objects to be merely there."[38]

In the autobiographical fictions Robbe-Grillet published in the 1980s, he repeatedly sought to distance himself from Barthes's writings about him. The circumstances and strategies of those efforts notwithstanding, the texts from 1955 and 1956, in addition to the reader reports, show how close they were. Indeed, Barthes served as a *maître à penser* for Robbe-Grillet, furnishing him with a vision of literature that he in turn applied as a co-editor at Minuit and in his "little theoretical articles." In Barthes's critical and theoretical valorization of his works Robbe-Grillet found a logic for Minuit's publishing that he utilized in his fiches de lecture, as well as a theoretical narrative for Minuit's position in the field that he reiterated in his articles. His adoption and polemical adaptation of Barthes's ideas were brilliant marketing moves: in their simultaneous proclamation of and call for a new literature, the articles reinforced Barthes's signs of literary modernity as grounds of judgment and value. All that was missing was a slogan that would effectively activate the associations Robbe-Grillet was putting into place. This missing slogan was provided by Emile Henriot, member of the Académie Française, in *Le Monde* in 1957, when he dubbed Robbe-Grillet's *La Jalousie* and Nathalie Sarraute's *Tropismes* exemplars of "the new novel."

Robbe-Grillet's campaign was undeniably successful, as evidenced in several ways: first, the increase in frequency and length of his theoretical articles, as well as the importance of the journals in which they appeared. Second, a dramatic rise in the number of articles treating the subject of a new literary movement, and its increasing association with Robbe-Grillet. By May 1957, the order of associations had sufficiently solidified for it to be reflected back on Robbe-Grillet in Emile Henriot's landmark *Le Monde* essay.[39] This first major echo provided a national forum for Robbe-Grillet's positioning to be played out, and made a valuable contribution to his pursuit of cultural capital. In addition, after the essay "Nature, humanisme, tragédie"—his longest—appeared in the *NNRF* in 1958, Robbe-Grillet greatly reduced the frequency of his journal articles, contenting himself more and more with other means of self- and brand-promotion.

By Henriot's lights, his article on "the new novel" should have damaged Robbe-Grillet's nascent prestige and discouraged Minuit's editorial line. Concluding that "it is without any profit for the reader," the article is explicit in rejecting Robbe-Grillet and defending the very notions of literary value Robbe-Grillet sought to overturn. Instead, following in the tradition of *succès de scandale*, Henriot's attack confirmed Robbe-Grillet's oppositional image: the elder, conservative statesman of literature—the Academician was 68 in 1957—might have done more harm by espousing Robbe-Grillet and Sarraute. Their theses were not destined to appeal to many established field positions, center, left or right, but represented an ostensibly de politicized alternative. Contrary to his best intentions, Henriot ended up publicizing Robbe-Grillet's and Sarraute's theories, further doing Editions de Minuit a tremendous service by *connecting* the two authors' works, despite the eighteen years separating them—Minuit's 1957 re-edition of *Tropismes* combined two new prose pieces with those published in 1939.[40] Even more generously, Henriot gave an accurate review of Robbe-Grillet's arguments as well as a summary of Robbe-Grillet's recent rise in capital, contributing to the development of his public image. As would become a pattern in much of the criticism on the New Novel, Henriot subordinated Sarraute's work to that of Robbe-Grillet, offering just one paragraph of commentary at the end of the piece and hardly distinguishing her ideas from Robbe-Grillet's. The advantages of the initial, auxiliary connection from Robbe-Grillet to the other Minuit authors—as I discuss in Chapter IV—would far outweigh this and other disadvantages.

As a member of several juries and selection committees, Henriot had had the opportunity to follow Robbe-Grillet's career, and had apparently attempted to block his progress in a number of instances—both for the Prix des Critiques and the del Duca prize. Writing on the occasion of the publication of *La Jalousie*, Henriot tells the story to show how rapid the rise of Robbe-Grillet's success was:

> On a fait la part belle à Alain Robbe-Grillet. On lui a donné il y a deux ans le Prix des Critiques pour son roman *Le Voyeur*. Il a obtenu l'an dernier la bourse de la fondation Del Duca (sic). Une interview dans l'Express et une étude sur le roman dans la Nouvelle Nouvelle Revue française lui ont fait faire depuis quelques mois figure de chef d'école, et il a sinon encore des disciples, des admirateurs qui le suivent et qui croient en lui.[41]
>
> ~
>
> We gave pride of place to Alain Robbe-Grillet. He was given the Prix des Critiques two years ago for his novel *Le Voyeur*. He was awarded the Del Duca Foundation (sic) scholarship last year. An interview in *l'Express* and a study on the novel in the *Nouvelle Nouvelle Revue française* have made him look like a head of school for several months, and while he does not yet have any disciples, he has admirers who follow him and believe in him.

He then criticizes these awards and honors, arguing that "the Prix des Critiques was wrongly awarded" and lamenting the "highlighting of a work in itself questionable"; as for the essays, they do help in reading *La Jalousie* ("its reading [. . .] is clarified") but "its doctrine" is unconvincing and "the novel, in itself, is not good." After summarizing the major points of Robbe-Grillet's articles, Henriot sets out to show how unsatisfying those points—and their execution in the novel *La Jalousie*—are for readers. The final verdict on quality comes from Henriot's concept of what readers want: books like *La Jalousie* threaten to kill the novel "by putting the reader off it."[43] In rallying to the cause of a certain kind of reader, however, Henriot unwittingly confirms the merits of Robbe-Grillet's argument, since Henriot's reader comes across sounding very much like the reader targeted in Robbe-Grillet's attacks.

It is not that Henriot has misunderstood Robbe-Grillet's polemic: "Robbe-Grillet believes that the time is over for the old-fashioned novel, the novel based on psychology [. . .] because psychology is artificial and subjective to the psychologist."[44] Rather, Henriot stands by the value of all the traditions Robbe-Grillet termed as "outdated notions": good literature "fires the imagination" and "moves the senses or the heart, or entertains the mind."[45] Robbe-Grillet teaches nothing about "man;" instead he uselessly complicates his novels: "his technique of a desired complication seemed to me of little interest, good only for confusing the reader."[46] He creates "so much trouble to understand and to annoy the reader that he is forced to contort the mind to find the key to [his] rebus."[47] As critical as Henriot's remarks are meant to be, they nonetheless echo Barthes's and Robbe-Grillet's distinction between literature that is "devoured" and the difficult experience of reading the "future novel." Ultimately, Henriot played right into Robbe-Grillet's hand; in the same breath he used to assert that there was nothing well-founded in Robbe-Grillet's theories, he confirmed that there in fact was.

In discussing *La Jalousie*, Henriot explains that there is a missing character, a presence never described or otherwise indicated, the husband who has been cheated on; however, in accordance with Robbe-Grillet's system, the author "does not have to state the feelings of his characters."[48] Approval or rejection of "the new novel" comes across as a choice for or against the conventions of psychological narrative. Gambling that, like him, the average reader would not see "what there is worth retaining from these abstractions and this systemic literature," Henriot casts his lot with what Barthes's termed bourgeois readerly expectations.[49] His mistake was to misjudge the broad cultural appeal of the oppositional posture his article reinforces.[50] Indeed, the last line of his piece captures his inflexible vision of taste in literary culture: the project of these new novels "is of no benefit [profit] to the reader, it only interests writers."[51]

Another of the benefits of Henriot's article for Robbe-Grillet and Editions de Minuit, it should be remembered, was the name "new novel" itself. Along with the name, Henriot inaugurated what would become a time honored practice of New Novel criticism: the weighing of readings of specific works against a set of theoretical notions that putatively define the New Novel. Henriot's article predicts how the "figure of the *chef d'école*" would soon come to rest on Robbe-Grillet's shoulders in the final years of the 50s. Through his theoretical writings—accompanied by Sarraute's *Tropismes* in 1957—Robbe-Grillet generated publicity for a product that—theoretically—did not yet exist; they amounted to claims of authority over what would qualify as "the future novel." His claims were unique in that in 1957 and 1958, Robbe-Grillet—as an editor at Minuit—and Lindon would begin to orient production to match his demands, as I discuss in detail below. In most other respects, his claims were not unique in literary criticism between early 1955—when *Le Voyeur* was published—and mid-1957, when Henriot's article appeared. Most literary chroniclers take it as part of their role to comment on the contemporary literary period, or at least on a figure taken as emblematic of it—doing so is at once an assertion of their acumen and a reinforcement of the collective sense of legitimate culture. A series of articles by Claude Mauriac in *Le Figaro* and *Preuves* beginning in late 1956 developed readings of "the new school" of "Aliterature";[52] similarly, Bernard Dort wrote about the new literature frequently in 1956 and 1957, alternatively calling it the "novel of the tabula rasa," "novel of a new genesis," or naming "blank novels [*blancs*]."[53] Nonetheless, like Henriot, these critics lent credibility and significance—in other words, cultural capital—to Robbe-Grillet still virtual project, regardless of whether their judgments were flattering or critical.

While critics continued to propose different names for the "new school," Henriot's label endured, sustained in part by the July 1958 *Esprit* devoted entirely to "the New Novel." By 1961 the term "New Novel" was common currency, appearing in the titles of articles from *Preuves*, *Arts*, *France Observateur*, *Critique*, and *La nouvelle critique.* Before publishing collection of texts under the title *Pour un nouveau roman* in 1963, Robbe-Grillet had already publicly adopted the expression in 1960: in two articles, "Le nouveau cinéma et le nouveau roman" and "Nouveau Roman, homme nouveau."[54] Jérôme Lindon, meanwhile, began to include the expression in the Editions de Minuit catalogs beginning in 1959. Most importantly, as I discuss in Chapter IV, the label had begun to appear in criticism abroad, in the United States (*Yale French Studies* 24, 1959), Germany (*Deutsche Rundschau* 10, Oct. 1960), Belgium (*Le Soir*, Brussels, 21 Dec. 1960), and Canada (*Revue de l'université de Laval* 16, 1961). Before examining the international character of the New Novel phenomenon, however, I first turn to the workings of publishing the New Novel at Editions de Minuit in the period 1957–1960.

2. Publishing the New Novel

In Chapter II, I discussed how Jérôme Lindon began to revamp Editions de Minuit into a more versatile publishing enterprise in the early part of the 50s. His strategies to reposition Minuit anticipated what the New Novel phenomenon would accomplish over the course of the late 50s and early 60s. Lindon's handling of the booklist left by Vercors and Lescure, his sponsorship of Bataille and *Critique*, and his publishing Samuel Beckett and Alain Robbe-Grillet were the first steps in remaking the Minuit label. In his editorial work and his efforts at capturing critics' attention, Robbe-Grillet brought important focus to Minuit's publications. Still, it was Jérôme Lindon who, in a near reversal of the roles played in the preparation of *Les Gommes*, decided in 1957 to limit Minuit's literary production to the New Novel—or to what would be presented under the sign of the New Novel. In 1958, Alain Robbe-Grillet proposed creating a series of "action novels" at Minuit; in his letter rejecting the idea, Lindon explains that: "Les Editions de Minuit is beginning—despite my best efforts—to become a real publishing house, producing a lot of books, some of which even sell."[55] Although Minuit's financial situation continued to be weak, Lindon's earlier initiatives had put into place a system of literary production that was profitable enough to allow him to continue searching for ways of creating capital. In the final years of the 1950s, the New Novel developed into a literary event on an international scale. Turning first to the New Novel as it appeared in Lindon's presentation of the 1960 Editions de Minuit catalog, I show what the group consisted of, and how it fit the image of intellectual culture promoted by Minuit. I then describe the steps—where there were any, other than merely moving authors to a new part of the catalog—taken to create the New Novel group. At its most concrete stage in the 1960 catalog, the impression of a coherent group became more understated by the 1962 edition, ironically at the same time that the New Novel dominated French literary culture and Editions de Minuit recorded its first profits.

Pierre Bourdieu would categorize Minuit publishing as composed of "risky long-term investments," and while I examine his relationship to Minuit in more detail in the next chapter, I draw on this piece of descriptive terminology in order to begin to assess Minuit's literary publishing during the period in question. In his chapter on "The Market of Symbolic Goods" in *The Rules of Art*, Pierre Bourdieu proposes describing literary production according to long-term and short-term cycles.[56] In his view, these two production strategies sufficiently differentiate publishers so as to envision them on a spectrum: on one end, the houses like Minuit, who publish titles that initially sell few copies, but in the long-term see significant increases. On the other end are publishers who produce quick earning titles whose returns drop off in the long-term. Long-term titles are those that have gained intellectual capital—which guarantees their long-term durability as symbolic goods—whereas short-term titles, or in Bourdieu's words, "safe short-term investments" are commercial successes that do not garner lasting value.[57] Bourdieu's terms are charged with an implicit value hierarchy that at once simplifies Minuit's catalog and glorifies its intellectual credentials. It is as if he wants to keep safe commercial publishing and risky intellectual literature as far apart as possible. What complicates matters is that, to some extent, most publishers display a combination of these strategies without always being able to accurately anticipate the cycle titles will have. It seems misdirected for Bourdieu to make Minuit the archetype of long-term intellectual publishing strategy, since it is difficult to conceive of any point in its history when that description would accurately apply, particularly in the 1957-62 period that Bourdieu draws his examples from.[58] Lindon's additions to the Minuit brand in the early 50s—as in the latter half of that decade—included both titles that achieved long-term value and some that were safe and short-term; still others were safe *and* long-term. More generally, like for any publisher, it was in Lindon's interest to work for the development of both short- and long-term capital from every part of his booklist.

Rather, the truly distinguishing feature of Minuit publishing was its use of the New Novel to "package" its literature. Its theoretical cultural "rupture" distributed innovatory appeal to each of the Minuit authors, and the capital garnered by some would benefit all. The quote from Robbe-Grillet opening this chapter reveals the relationship between authors and their publisher embodied in the New Novel: "Of course, the authors make the reputation of the house that publishes them. Why not see that the converse is just as true?"[59] The only caveat to add is that before the New Novel, Editions de Minuit did not yet have the capital to "make the reputation" of its authors. Part product line and part theoretical statement, the New Novel was a mode of capital relay among authors and between authors and publisher.

The 1960 Editions de Minuit catalog, published in December 1959, is an impressive snapshot of the production of the New Novel. As the catalog's keystone, the New Novel lends an overarching coherence to the entire catalog and publishing imprint. The generic difference of the New Novel becomes Minuit's difference, giving a new cast to each of Minuit's publications—including the many publications that pre-dated the New Novel. We find Lindon's Minuit finally realized in the 1960 catalog; it is now a "real publishing house," each of its rubrics an expression of the house's distinctiveness. The catalog's most valuable commodity is on prominent display: with the market for novels being much larger than that for poetry, theater, or the humanities and social sciences, the New Novel receives first priority and occupies the first dozen pages. The New Novels are listed under the rubric "French Novels" ["Romans Français"]—in the absence of the logic of a New Novel group, the inclusion of Samuel Beckett's translated prose there would be somewhat baffling. As in every Minuit catalog, the selection of author photographs in the margins seeks to create or reinforce certain associations, and thus lays bare editorial and promotional strategy. In this instance, the photographs are clearly meant to foreground the New Novel group and signal its breadth, with photos of Robbe-Grillet, Claude Simon, Michel Butor, and—most interestingly—the two Gallimard authors Nathalie Sarraute and Marguerite Duras. Even though they had published just one title each at Minuit by that time, Sarraute and Duras have photographs in the catalog, while authors published in the same period or who had more titles (like the older author François Boyer) do not. The emphasis given to Duras is a particularly striking instance of Minuit strategy, since her connection to the New Novel became a matter of considerable controversy between herself and Robbe-Grillet, with her rejecting any involvement with the New Novel. (I return to the case of Duras presently.)

The introduction to the catalog, written by Jérôme Lindon, is an effective promotion of the image of French intellectual culture Minuit has to offer: one characterized by a combination of literary innovation and political engagement. The core of that image lies in its articulation of intellectual liberty—the New Novel—and its defense—the collections "Under Oppression" ["Sous l'oppression"] and the new, extensive set of "Documents." Recounting Minuit's clandestine beginnings, Lindon equates that heroism with his current publication of accounts of the Algerian War, citing the French government's seizure of two titles:

> Les Editions de Minuit ont été fondées à Paris, en 1942, par Pierre de Lescure et Vercors. Assurer la publication clandestine d'œuvres littéraires qu'auraient interdites la censure nazie, tel était l'objet que se fixait la nouvelle maison d'édition. Depuis *Le silence de la mer* jusqu'à *Nuits noires* de Steinbeck, en passant par des œuvres de Jean Paulhan, Eluard, Aragon, F. Mauriac, Jean Cassou, André Gide, etc. . . . , les Editions de Minuit s'efforcèrent de témoigner que l'occupation n'avait pas éteint toute liberté dans les lettres françaises. Vercors continuera d'animer la maison jusqu'en 1948. Elle est dirigée depuis cette date par Jérôme Lindon.
>
> La libération de 1944 n'a certes pas supprimé tous les périls que risque de courir en France la défense des libertés. La publication et la saisie, en 1958 et en 1959, de *La Question* d'Henri Alleg et de *La gangrène* en sont une preuve.[60]
>
> Les Editions de Minuit was founded in Paris in 1942 by Pierre de Lescure and Vercors. Ensuring the clandestine publication of literary works that would have been prohibited by Nazi censorship was the object of the new publishing house. From *Le silence de la mer* to *Black Nights* by Steinbeck, including works by Jean Paulhan, Eluard, Aragon, F. Mauriac, Jean Cassou, André Gide, etc . . . , the Editions de Minuit endeavored to bear witness that the occupation

> had not extinguished all freedom in French letters. Vercors continued to run the house until 1948. It has been managed since then by Jérôme Lindon.
>
> The liberation in 1944 did not, of course, remove all the dangers that the defense of freedoms risks running in France. The publication and seizure, in 1958 and 1959, of *La Question* by Henri Alleg and *La gangrène* are proof of this.

In 1962, Lindon published the minutes from his trial for publishing Alleg in a slim volume called *Provocation à la désobéissance* as a means to further document Minuit's audacious engagement. Until then, that purpose was served by the Minuit catalog, along with the free publicity created by the seizures themselves and the famous "Manifesto of the 121" originated by Minuit authors.[61] The seizures were of "Documents": Editions de Minuit was subject to a total of eleven between 1958 and 1962, when the Algerian conflict was finally ended. Creating the "Documents" was a way to construct continuity with Minuit's clandestine history, and bring the symbolic capital to be gained from being a target of State censorship to bear on its entire imprint.[62] In 1960, the "Documents" collection was mostly comprised of titles dealing in some respect with the Algerian War, eight of eleven with titles like *La question algérienne* and *Pour Djamila Bouhired: Plaidoyer pour une jeune Algérienne comdamnée à mort.*[63] They were accompanied by three Holocaust and deportation testimonials, Rousset's *L'Univers concentrationnaire*, Micheline Maurel's *Un camp très ordinaire*, and the French edition of Elie Wiesel's *La Nuit.*[64] Maurel's book won the Prix des Critiques in 1957, Minuit's second in a row; Wiesel's became an international bestseller and probably the mostly widely known of the Nobel laureate's writings. Publishing books on Algeria and the Holocaust simultaneously was highly provocative, pairing the unpopular genre of Holocaust narratives with texts criticizing France's presence in Algeria. The addition of several older titles to this newly formed collection illustrates how Lindon mixed strategies of short- and long-term production. Paulhan's *Lettre aux directeurs de la résistance* (1951) is poignantly recontextualized through its appearance next to Jean Cassou's *La mémoire courte*, winner of the 1953 Prix de la Résistance. In adding these to the list of more recent texts, Lindon made use of the Algerian context to create a pedigree of ideological resistance that was Minuit's—split off and listed in a rubric called "Under Occupation"—but until then not his own.

Published in 1957 and 1958, the "Documents" coincided with the recruitment of the New Novel authors. The catalog presentation turns next to naming that group, and just as in the case of the "Documents" series Lindon cites a lineage to suggest a firm personal editorial vision:

> Mais dès 1948, la direction des Editions de Minuit s'est efforcée de constituer les éléments d'un fonds d'édition qui ne reposât pas seulement sur des positions idéologiques ou des combats historiques. Ce fut en 1951, la publication de Molloy, par Samuel Beckett, celle des Gommes, par Alain Robbe-Grillet en 1953. Plus tard, Butor, Robert Pinget, Nathalie Sarraute, Claude Simon, Claude Ollier, entre autres, contribuèrent à leur tour à la formation d'un groupe littéraire nouveau, que faute de mieux on appelait "le nouveau roman" et dont la réputation dépassa vite nos frontières.[65]

> But as early as 1948, the management of Editions de Minuit endeavored to constitute the elements of a booklist which was not based only on ideological positions or historical struggles. It was in 1951, the publication of *Molloy*, by Samuel Beckett, and that of *Les Gommes*, by Alain Robbe-Grillet in 1953. Later, Butor, Robert Pinget, Nathalie Sarraute, Claude Simon, Claude Ollier, among others, contributed in their turn to the formation of a new literary group, which for lack of a better term was called "the new novel" and whose reputation quickly spread beyond our borders.

Echoing Robbe-Grillet's writings and statements about "the future novel," Lindon's lead in brings to mind the criticisms leveled at the New Novel by Nelly Wolf and Kristin Ross that I cited at the beginning of this chapter. But here the New Novel comes after the description of Minuit's history of "ideological positions" and "historical battles," and is implicitly presented as a counterpart to them. This is where the case for literary autonomy—and for the Minuit stamp to stand for that autonomy—found its most compelling argument. Critics of the New Novel have failed to take this specific productive context into account—a context of marketing and promotion to be sure, but also and most importantly a context of consumption. For consumers of the New Novel in the late 50s and early 60s, buying and reading a New Novel meant endorsing a small publisher doing battle with the government. By staging the New Novel as a kind of resistance to ideological pressure, Lindon cast its consumption as support for intellectual freedom in the literary field. Through the commitments of his "Documents," Lindon supplied the means and justification to situate his literary group beyond those concerns.

The selection of authors Lindon highlights is very specific, covering all of the authors who appeared with him in what has become known as the "family photo" taken in 1959. These same authors were continually listed on the flap copy of Minuit publications to reinforce their connection—a connection that bound the authors and their works to the "reputation of the house" and to the effectiveness of the New Novel as a brand. The allusion to the New Novel's success abroad ("whose reputation quickly spread beyond our borders"), which I discuss in the next chapter—evokes the unusual role foreign instances of recognition and capital building played in making the New Novel's success in France.

The titles that were promoted as part of the New Novel group represented nearly all of Minuit's literary publishing in the several years prior to the 1960 catalog. That there were publications and authors left out indicates the desire to continue publishing some authors of general appeal in addition to the New Novel. Few of them would continue to appear in the catalog, with one notable exception: Boris Vian's 1956 *L'Automne à Pékin*.[66] The identification of Minuit and its authors with the controversial new trend is in this sense the short-term strategy alongside the longer-term aim of developing Minuit's capital as a broad spectrum publisher. Hence, in the paragraph following the list of the New Novelists, we find a partial inventory of the minutely chiseled set of rubrics dividing the remaining categories of Minuit's publishing:

> Outre une première liste consacrée à ces romans, le présent catalogue contient 24 rubriques diverses, correspondant généralement chacune à une collection: Théâtre (avec *En Attendant Godot*), Romans étrangers (Faulkner, Melville, Arthur Miller), Poésie (Eluard, Jouve, Ungaretti), Critique (Jaspers, Jean

> Paulhan), Philosophie (Bataille, Clausewitz), collections "Documents," "L'homme et la machine", "Forces vives" (avec les ouvrages de Le Corbusier), "Vieux Paris" (avec ceux de J. Hillairet), "Vieilles Villes", "Aleph", consacrée au judaïsme, et enfin la collection "Sous l'oppression", reproduction fac similée des volumes parus pendant la guerre.[67]
>
> In addition to a first list devoted to these novels, this catalog contains 24 various rubrics, each corresponding to a collection: Theater (with *En Attendant Godot*), Foreign Novels (Faulkner, Melville, Arthur Miller), Poetry (Eluard, Jouve, Ungaretti), Criticism (Jaspers, Jean Paulhan), Philosophy (Bataille, Clausewitz), the collections "Documents," "Man and Machine," "Living Forces" (with the works of Le Corbusier), "Old Paris" (with those of J. Hillairet), "Old Cities," "Aleph," devoted to Judaism, and finally la collection "Under Oppression," facsimile reproductions of the volumes published during the war.

This division of the catalog into rubrics was an important element of Minuit's marketing strategy. From rubric number two, "Limited Editions for 'Discerning' Readers"—costlier vellum editions of selected literary titles—to number seventeen, "International Library of Sociology of Cooperation"—comprised of eleven titles on economics—the appeal is to a varied, educated elite readership, even one highly specialized. The chief exception is the continued presence of Hillairet's nine volume history of Paris, despite the fact that it was undoubtedly not a best-selling series. Lindon's conclusion reinforces the point, once again marrying erudite publishing to intellectual engagement:

> Riche de 300 titres disponibles, ce catalogue un peu éclectique est celui d'une maison d'édition indépendante qui reste modeste dans son économie comme dans son organisation. Puisse t il exprimer le souci principal de ceux qui en assument la responsabilité: dégager, à l'écart des conformismes et des pressions de toute nature, les voies des recherches fécondes et des luttes indispensables. Ce n'est probablement pas tout à fait par hasard si l'on trouve associés ici les noms et les œuvres d'hommes aussi fondamentalement différents que Samuel Beckett et Henri Alleg, les prêtres ouvriers et Ben Gourion, Alain Robbe-Grillet et Le Corbusier.[68]
>
> With 300 titles available, this somewhat eclectic catalog is that of an independent publishing house that remains modest in its economy and organization. May it express the main concern of those who take responsibility for it: to open up—away from conformisms and pressures of any kind—the paths of fruitful research and indispensable struggles. It is probably not entirely by chance that we find associated here the names and works of men as fundamentally different as Samuel Beckett and Henri Alleg, the worker priests and Ben Gurion, Alain Robbe-Grillet and Le Corbusier.

"[F]ruitful research" and "indispensable struggles," Beckett and Alleg—Minuit is the articulation of intellectual research and responsible political engagement. "It is probably not entirely by chance" that Minuit's casting of literature as research—against "conformisms and pressures of any kind"—appealed to many. Here was David against Goliath, "modest" and "independent," battling for independent literature.

With this description in mind, it seems pertinent to ask: how independent, autonomous, or free of pressures *were* the Minuit authors as they became New Novelists? In the paragraph describing the New Novel group, Lindon asserts that the later authors—Butor, Pinget, Simon, Sarraute, Ollier—"contributed in turn" to Minuit's editorial line. Naturally, the story is more complicated; what Robbe-Grillet and Lindon both termed "freedom" was, for some of the authors at least, a new kind of constraint.

For example, there are plenty of reasons to suspect that Robbe-Grillet's editorial involvement with the editing and publication of Claude Simon's *Le Vent* (1957) was decisive in making Simon's work fit the editorial mold of the New Novel. That suspicion—given Simon's enormous productivity and worldwide success—raises broad questions about the effect of their passage through Minuit and the New Novel on Simon and the other authors. In Simon's case, Robbe-Grillet himself would later drop hints regarding that effect in a devilishly timed piece that appeared in *Paris-Match*. Titled "The Timid Dragoon" and published shortly after Simon's receipt of the Nobel Prize for Literature in 1985, the article jabs at Simon's stalwart literary persona, suggesting Robbe-Grillet's own share of responsibility for Simon's career, one Simon was too timid to make on his own.[69] Appropriately enough the article caused a stir, the best indication—in the absence of access to original manuscripts—of there being truth in Robbe-Grillet's claims. In any case, his comments at least acknowledge that the New Novel was in part the result of recruitment:

> J'ai connu Simon en 1956, c'est-à-dire à l'époque où Jérôme Lindon et moi-même recherchions des

romanciers novateurs à forte personnalité pour les regrouper aux Editions de Minuit, afin d'engager un combat commun au profit de talents très divers [. . .]. J'ai alors eu entre les mains, par hasard, le manuscrit d'un roman qui m'a tout de suite transporté d'enthousiasme. C'était *Le Vent* de Claude Simon [. . .]. J'ai aussitôt voulu rencontrer cet auteur, qui me semblait promis au plus grand avenir. Et je lui ai demandé pourquoi son roman, emporté du début jusqu'à la fin par une violence narrative comparable à celle de l'ouragan, se trouvait coupé ça et là (et à mon sens affaibli) par d'étranges ruptures de ton, accompagnées de soudaines baisses d'intensité: des chapitres intercalés dans le cours du récit et rédigés d'une écriture beaucoup plus sage, plus traditionnelle, dont le but visible était d'expliquer à la critique sous-développée des choses qui, cependant, passaient avec plus de vigueur et de persuasion dans les rafales de la tempête.[70]

~

I got to know Simon in 1956, that is to say at the time when Jérôme Lindon and I were looking for innovative novelists with a strong personality to bring them together at Editions de Minuit, in order to engage in a common fight for the profit of very diverse talents [. . .]. By chance, I had in my hands the manuscript of a novel which immediately filled me with enthusiasm. It was *Le Vent* by Claude Simon [. . .]. I immediately wanted to meet this author, who seemed to me to have the greatest future. And I asked him why his novel, carried from beginning to end by a narrative violence comparable to that of a hurricane, was interspersed here and there (and in

> my opinion weakened) by strange breaks in tone, accompanied by sudden drops in intensity: chapters interspersed in the course of the narrative and written in much wiser, more traditional writing, the visible purpose of which was to explain to the underdeveloped critics things which were passing with more vigor and persuasion in the gusts of the storm.

"The Timid Dragoon" is an allusion to Simon's service as a cavalryman in World War II; associating that experience with other aspects of Simon's life—like his hobbies as winegrower, downhill skier, and other physical pursuits—Robbe-Grillet is out to deflate Simon's heady avant-gardist reputation. His gently teasing play on Simon's title—vent, ouragan, rafales—puts across an image of a hesitant innovator: someone who, like some of the authors Robbe-Grillet described in his reader reports, just needed a little training and encouragement.

Simon was material to work with; unlike Sarraute, Pinget, and Butor, he experienced an initiation or an apprenticeship in order to become a suitable Minuit author. Sarraute's sole publication with Minuit was her 1957 *Tropismes*, so she was never subject to editing by Lindon and Robbe-Grillet; also, as Robbe-Grillet's "co-conspirator" she was on more equal footing than the others. Robbe-Grillet recounts in *Les Derniers jours de Corinthe* how, in the summer of 1957, he met Sarraute at a colloquium and together they decided they should "make an alliance." Butor, who expressed substantial hostility against Robbe-Grillet's theoretical declarations, never published another novel at Minuit after *La Modification* (1957). He moved to Gallimard, presumably to distance himself from Robbe-Grillet, which meant he could continue—like Sarraute and Duras—to belong to the group and gain from the association while exercizing his own authorial freedom.

His series of critical essays, *Répertoire I, II,* and *III* were published by Minuit, and helped sustain his link to the New Novel throughout the 60s. Pinget, whose manuscripts came to Robbe-Grillet and Lindon by way of Samuel Beckett, predated the New Novel, since he came to Minuit in 1956 with a substantial set of manuscripts and books previously published by Laffont, which were subsequently published as New Novels; they included *Graal Flibuste* (Minuit 1956), *Mahu ou le matériau* (Laffont 1952, Minuit 1957), *Entre Fantoine et Agapa* (Laffont 1950, Minuit 1958), *Baga* (Minuit 1958). One of the most prolific of the Minuit authors, Pinget was ironically the least well-known New Novelist, despite having been the easiest fit with the editorial line. The last member of the older generation who should be mentioned, Marguerite Duras, had a fitful relationship with Editions de Minuit and the New Novel, although her reticence did not diminish their effect on her writing.

Both Claude Simon and Duras were experienced writers by 1957. Duras had five novels at Gallimard, and was well-liked by many critics; favorable reviews appeared in various journals, including *Critique* (by Jean Piel), *Les Temps Modernes,* and *Lettres Nouvelles.* She was a regular point of reference for Françoise Giroud in *L'Express* as an example of an important woman writer of whom the reading public was wrongly ignorant.[71] Simon, similarly, had four titles in print—*Le Tricheur* (1946), *La corde raide* (1948), published by Editions Le Sagittaire; *Gulliver* (1952) and *Le Sacre du Printemps* (1954), published by Calmann-Lévy—but had enjoyed no critical acknowledgement prior to the publication of *Le Vent* in 1957. As in Pinget's case, everything Simon published from *Le Vent* forward came out with Minuit, and he embraced the New Novel label—an embrace that meant forsaking the direction of his early career in favor of the changes wrought by the New Novel. Would Simon have won the Nobel Prize for Literature in 1985 had he not undergone capital reconversion by Editions de Minuit? There is no question that his incorporation was fruitful for him and his publisher, as witnessed by his extraordinary long-term productivity and success. It was announced in May 2002 that a selection of his best novels—chosen by Simon himself—would be published in La Pléïade. Publication in the prestigious Bibliothèque de la Pléïade is one of the highest honors a writer can receive, and signifies their entrance into an important "pantheon" of French literature.

How Simon's pre-Minuit publications were handled in the catalog and in flap advertising is unusual, and heightens one's sense of his having undergone a conversion to the New Novel. In the 1960 catalog and in lists printed in novels in the early 60s, mention is made of just the earlier two of the four novels. *La corde raide* and *Le Tricheur* were purchased by Minuit, and implied to be available, when in fact they were not reprinted for many years. *Gulliver* and *Le Sacre du Printemps* were not acquired, are never cited, and by Claude Simon's vehement request will never be re-published.[72] The references to earlier novels lent him credibility as a writer and lent Minuit credibility as a publisher of quality—nevermind that the list of his works left out parts of his corpus, apparently deemed incompatible with his refashioning as a New Novelist.

It made sense for Minuit to bring Duras into the fold of the New Novel. She stood out as a good prospect since she was an author who had already earned some recognition as a literary innovator: Colette Audry, writing in *Les Temps Modernes* in 1953, identified *Les Petits Chevaux de Tarquinia* as "a challenge to psychological literature," whose subtle handling of silence, uncertainty, and deception describes a "painful collective experience, experience where almost nothing happens but where nobody knows exactly where they wound up."[73] Bernard

Dort—a frequent critic of Robbe-Grillet—very likely contributed to her recruitment when he wrote about her work in 1955:

> Les héros de Marguerite Duras sont posés devant nous sans être qualifiés. Ils *sont là*. Ils parlent, ils agissent (peu), ils commentent leurs actions. Le cours du récit est lent, coupé de tâtonnements. L'auteur n'explique rien.[74]
>
> ~
>
> The heroes of Marguerite Duras are placed before us without being qualified. They are there. They speak, they act (little), they comment on their actions. The course of the story is slow, cut off by trial and error. The author does not explain anything.

These aspects of her work explain why to Robbe-Grillet the editor saw her writing as rich in potential; still, she needed to be made into a Minuit New Novelist. This was a brief but equally decisive move in her writing career. It was decisive on two vital—and now familiar—fronts: first, her putative membership in the New Novel movement added enormously to her intellectual prestige, as in Simon's case. Winning the Prix de Mai for *Moderato Cantabile* in 1958 boosted her reputation as a writer and advanced her considerably toward a career as an avant-garde film-maker. Like Robbe-Grillet, Duras began expanding into film in 1958, and the success of their endeavors—he won the Prix de Venise in 1961, the product of her collaboration with Alain Resnais, *Hiroshima mon amour*, became an art-house classic—secured them increased national and international renown, as well as linked the New Novel to the New Wave. Her ability to produce what would be a prolific—and often difficult—body of literature and film was indubitably a result of her association with the New Novel, the site of which was the publication of *Moderato Cantabile*; ten years would pass before she published at Minuit again.

The second decisive aspect of that association was literary: it is commonplace among critics of Duras's œuvre to discern a turning point in her work between *Le Square* in 1955 and *Moderato* in 1958.[75] Taking my cue from Robbe-Grillet's comments about Simon, however, I offer the speculation that such a formal and stylistic transition may well have been influenced by her new association with Robbe-Grillet and Lindon. Unfortunately, if manuscripts of *Moderato* pre-dating publication are still in existence, they have thus far been out of my reach. My hypothesis draws some support from the fact that no such manuscripts can be found in her personal archives, now deposited at the Institut de la Mémoire Contemporaine (IMEC), although there may be something in the Minuit archives. My speculations are further fed by the discovery that Marguerite Duras kept nothing in her files from any of the work predating the spring of 1958. Is there an implicit statement about her previous and later work inscribed in this? Did she perceive a clear career-related and/or artistic caesura between them?

A look at the manuscripts that are publicly available, however, turns up an interesting set of relations between the version of *Moderato Cantabile* published by Minuit and Duras's subsequent film-adaptation of it. Over the course of ten manuscripts dating from 1958 and 1959, Duras revised *Moderato Cantabile* for the screen, and in the process re-conventionalized the book's narrative, as if the foreignness of the new medium had prompted her to restore what may have been removed during the original book's editing.

The film version of *Moderato Cantabile* reads as if Duras was grappling with the editorial lessons that made *Moderato Cantabile* a New Novel. The more convincing point of transition in her work comes immediately after the screenplay of *Moderato Cantabile*, in the development of *Hiroshima mon amour*: in *Hiroshima*, a broad rewriting of *Moderato Cantabile*, she applies the New Novel techniques she struggled with in the screen drafts of *Moderato Cantabile* to a virtually identical plot structure. Consequently, by examining the changes and notes in the development of *Moderato Cantabile* from novel to screenplay we have an exceptional window onto how the New Novel functioned as an editorial strategy at the most important stage in the life of the Minuit imprint—and of the group—as of 1958.

That the markers of a text's belonging to the category of the New Novel are in one sense fairly trivial (amounting to the suppression of information normally supplied) but, in another sense, have significant consequences, becomes clear when one looks at the material Duras restored in revising her novel as a film. Elements of characterization resurface in the screenplay whose erasure from the novel helped it signify the New-Novelesque abstraction of character—what one critic perceived as signs of "social alienation" and the description of mankind at its "zero degree of existence." Anne Desbaresdes accompanies her child to and from his piano lessons; during one lesson there is a murder in the street below. Intrigued, Desbaresdes begins to frequent the bar where the incident happened; she makes her inquiries of another visitor there, a man named Chauvin, and an unusual, unspoken passion develops between them. Desire hovers over their series of encounters at the bar, until it vanishes as enigmatically as it came. Composed primarily of dialogue between the couple, the novel is as oblique in its characterization and description as the two characters are in voicing their situation. Pared down to a murmur, the narrative proceeds through the minute events of everyday activities, suspending supposedly bourgeois expectations regarding setting—where and when does this take place?—character—who are these people, what do they look like?—and, most interestingly, motivation—why do these things happen? The last question reconnects *Moderato Cantabile* to Robbe-Grillet's cause célèbre that time and again we encounter illustrated in this first phase of the New Novel, and mentioned in critical accounts from Robbe-Grillet to Henriot and critics supportive of the Minuit school. The virtue of the campaign against "sacrosanct psychological analysis" is in attaining realism by removing layers of psychological pre-determinations from narrative discourse. In a similar way to Robbe-Grillet's *La Jalousie*, the Minuit edition of *Moderato Cantabile* stages that refusal of explanation within the context of a narrative that has no other subject-matter than the psychological weight of the relationship between its two main characters.

Duras's drafts reveal conflicting inclinations: on the one hand, to restore features that were dropped from the book, and on the other to reiterate New Novel theory to both her filmmaking collaborators and the viewer. She underscores that the focus is placed entirely on the actors' rendering of the novel's dialogue: "All the drama—I cannot see it any other way—will be in the conversation that goes on between Anne and Chauvin. It's all in the theatrical delivery of the last lines."[76] Elsewhere, she insists on the need for indeterminacy. Her rhetorical question, reminiscent of Robbe-Grillet, reveals how her own understanding of the text has been shaped by the New Novel: "[. . .] *why would we know more clearly than them what is going on in them*? As long as what is happening in them, from the beginning and which we have *exposed*, but never explained, does not come under psychological analysis?"[77] In another manuscript stage-direction, she repeats that: "We know nothing at all about the respective moods of Anne and Chauvin. We just know a denouement is approaching that we know nothing about."[78] But even as she seeks to emphasize the spectator's ignorance in this way, she adds a line to the end of the film that seems to want to have it both ways, explaining what the characters themselves cannot know: "This is how Anne Desbaresdes and Chauvin will separate forever, in the early morning, in complete ignorance of what happened between them, in the terror, shared by all those who have known their history, that it ends differently."[79] In light of her strict rejection of explanations such as this, this authorial intervention is surprisingly analytical and amounts to a lapse into interpretation; it is as if Duras permitted herself some psychological analysis by refusing others the right to analyze themselves. She names the atmosphere of "horror"—the condition that makes for the story's drama, and hangs over the characters throughout—that in the novel is never so explicitly tied either to the couple's parting or to the murder at the beginning.

Thusly, what we are allowed to know about the characters changes dramatically between the novel and the film. It includes the addition of details that do not appear in any way crucial to the screenplay—that is, details that seem to have always been present, despite their absence from the Minuit edition. In the novel, the characters' social status—indeed, their entire lives outside of their exchanges with each other—were undefined, remote, irrelevant, even non-existent. We do know that Desbaresdes is married, we do not know that she is married to an industrialist who is the wealthiest man in town—or even that the town is Blaye, on the edge of the Gironde in the Bordeaux region. Indeed, the husband acquires a speaking part in the film, in a scene of domestic discord over the piano lessons for their child—who, incidentally, is named Pierre. Rather than depict Anne and her son walking everywhere, the film shows their car and driver; additionally, we learn that Desbaresdes's clothing is "extremely elegant." The signs of class and wealth that appear in the film suddenly add a dimension of social taboo to her curiosity about the murder that has taken place and her visits to the working-class part of town. A whole psychological geography emerges, one shaded with a rather conventional romanticism: "This is the time when Anne D. leaves her villa on Bd de la Charente in luxury and order, rule and respectability."[80] Similarly, Chauvin's characterization is much more complete in the screenplay. We are shown his home, shown evidence that he is married, told that he works for Anne's husband—all details never given in the book, where Chauvin is shrouded in mystery, reduced to a name, a voice, and a set of interactions that "expose" more than "explain" the character. Interestingly, Duras loses track in the manuscripts of what we know about him, giving hints as to his social status in the description of his room, when we have already been told he is an engineer at the Fonderies de la Côte. His room is a "[c]omfortable and tidy room. The photo of his wife is on the nightstand. A suitcase is open on a table where he has started to throw away his laundry in bulk. The rest can be seen stacked in the half-open cabinet. Next to the suitcase, on the table there is an underwater rifle and a mask. And a briefcase (which serves to make it clear that Chauvin is not a worker)." As sparse and vague as the screenplay's descriptions are, all of these realia—and even its mere role in communicating aspects of the characters' social and psychological existence—are totally missing from the novel, presumably in conformity with the editorial line of the New Novel.

But the manuscripts present more than just the settings left out of the novel. The working-class world the main characters move through goes from being an indistinct background to becoming a virtual third character of the story. Duras envisions several scenes in which the couple is literally surrounded by workers returning home from their shifts at her husband's factory. The workers know her, since—as we learn—she is "the main event of the city," and their seeing her with Chauvin plays an important role in their relationship—indeed, being seen is an important thematic element of their story. In certain instances, the working-class characters provide us with views of Desbaresdes that suggest her glamour or even sexuality; primarily, however, they reflect her psychology. Duras describes a minor event in the bar during the couple's first meeting when a pool ball rolls over near Desbaresdes; a boy comes to collect it and notices her: "He looks at this extremely elegant woman with a sort of stupor, he looks above all at the contrast between the order and the regularity that this woman exudes and her outfit, between the order and the regularity of this woman and the expression which is now beginning to inhabit his face."[81] In other instances, the workers surrounding them seem like an urban crowd through which Desbaresdes and Chauvin recognize themselves and each other; the crowd is threatening, its arrival always signaled by the factory siren that punctuates Desbaresdes's days. The ends of the factory shifts are "gunshots" ["*coups de feu*"] that hold some fascination for her: "Anne Desbaresdes watches the workers heading to work under the black smokestacks of the foundries. This is how we know it is dawn. [. . .] She always has her forehead pressed against the glass while the tide of workers becomes intense, and at the end of this immense perspective of the corridor a door opens slowly."[82] The foil provided here by the anonymous social world might have done nothing to change one critic's praise of Duras's narrative of "social alienation"; but it does raise a new set of questions and interpretative possibilities that the Minuit edition of *Moderato Cantabile* did not. Whether or not critics would have made much of the story's strong notes of haut-bourgeois bad faith, it seems clear that the more conventionalized version envisaged in the screenplay would have had difficulty passing as a New Novel. Erasing the conventional signs of a story of cocuage re-centered the novel on Duras's talent for delicate and subtle dialogue. The traditional elements of description are gone: the couple moves in something of a vacuum, reduced to the quiet expression of their transitory desire. It was this spare, ethereal, indistinct aspect that captivated many of the critics in 1958, and it was used to explain Duras's relationship to the New Novel: "This explains the quality of the new novels which we struggle to identify; unless to say that they are cinema since they project the pure event, the encounter, the shock of faces and things in movement in a universe where everything is only a face, to the detriment of man."[83]

Minuit publishing *Moderato Cantabile* in 1958 sufficed for Duras to become associated with the New Novel; important figures—including Robbe-Grillet—helped reinforce that connection when they chose to reward the novel with the Prix de Mai. The jury comprised of Roland Barthes, Georges Bataille, Maurice Blanchot, Jean Cayrol, Bernard Dort, Louis-René des Forêts, Maurice Nadeau, Bernard Pingaud, Jean-Pierre Richard, Robbe-Grillet, and Nathalie Sarraute was almost entirely made up of faces familiar to anyone associated with Editions de Minuit, from authors published by Minuit to critics who had written about the New Novel (including Nadeau [*Lettres nouvelles*], Pingaud, Dort, and Richard). They exemplify what Bourdieu refers to as the "discoverers" when he characterizes the role of those agents in the literary field who contribute to producing belief in the artists they "discover."[84] Their choice represented a significant recognition of the edited form of *Moderato Cantabile*, and helped create Duras's place in the first group of New Novelists, as did her inclusion in articles on the New Novel in the 1958 issue of *Esprit*.

However, despite her recruitment and publication by Minuit in 1958 and her critical success notwithstanding, in the years that followed, Duras held herself aloof from the New Novel as a school, refusing the label of New Novelist and turning down invitations to appear alongside the New Novel authors at conferences. While this aloofness is unlikely to have cost her any symbolic capital, it may have cost something financially. In a telephone exchange with the literary scholar Marie-Claire Ropars, Duras divulged her great sense of frustration over the financial success that met the New Novel authors and of which she had been deprived.[85] Their books sold, while her belonging to a "community of shame" went inadequately rewarded, that is up until Minuit published her international bestseller *L'Amant* in 1984. Of course, she had nonetheless accumulated the critical attention to accede with the other New Novelists to a position of tremendous critical prestige and stature.

The 1958 issue of *Esprit* devoted to "Le Nouveau Roman" was an important moment for Minuit and the New Novelists, but not because it necessarily convinced its readers of the value of the authors associated with the new literary movement. *Esprit*'s confirmation of the movement's existence was enough for it to gain momentum. The issue's first article is Olivier de Magny's "Panorama d'une nouvelle littérature romanesque," a presentation that went further than Robbe-Grillet and Lindon could have even wished: all of the Minuit authors are mentioned, including Beckett and Duras (the subject of an article titled "Marguerite Duras et le 'roman abstrait','" focused entirely on *Moderato Cantabile*), with non-Minuit authors Jean Cayrol, Jean Lagrolet, and Kateb Yacine included as well. Magny was not naive about the role of Minuit in his "Panorama": "Let us note in passing the role played, if not claimed, by these editions in the birth of the myth of a new school of the novel." Nonetheless, he worked to identify the constituents of "a new literature of the novel."[86] Whether as *literature* or *school*, the myth had its first legs. By taking the New Novel beyond the Minuit group to include other authors, Magny also originated another traditional element of the New Novel phenomenon: the debate over who rightly belonged to the group and who did not.

Les Temps Modernes contributor Bernard Dort, writing in the same *Esprit*, reinforced a second important trait of the early years of the New Novel, one we saw in Henriot: the disproportionate attention given to Robbe-Grillet as "chef d'école." Ideas taken from his articles and his public appearances dominate the initial critical engagement with the New Novel authors. Dort's article "Des romans 'innocents'?" makes passing reference to Sarraute's arguments from *Tropismes*, but makes no reference to any of her novels, any of the other authors' works, or even Robbe-Grillet's. There is no need to do so, Robbe-Grillet having given him enough to determine that "For our novelists, it is therefore a question of making appear, or rather to make us recognize a new reality—a reality which was until then masked by what Robbe-Grillet calls the 'myths of depth' or by what Roland Barthes would call bourgeois mythologies."[87] Like Henriot, Dort sought to attack Robbe-Grillet; instead he extended the life of Robbe-Grillet's critical persona, granting him the status of "chef d'école" on the one hand, and making of his ideas a *way in* to understanding contemporary literary production on the other. In other words, Dort, Henriot, and other critics fed right into Robbe-Grillet's strategies as editor and publicist.

Robbe-Grillet, then, was able to shape the critical reception of the authors associated with the new literary movement, giving critics a means of talking about those authors that would constantly evoke the existence of non New Novelistic authors, whose works could be used alternatively for comparison or contrast—often enough a little of both. This is precisely the kind of work that came to characterize New Novel criticism, and again examples can be found in the 1958 *Esprit*. "The refusal," "taking distance from lived experience," "the ambiguity of 'I' and 'he,'" "the putting 'into parentheses' of psychological preoccupations": so many expressions to identify the novels and authors of a literary revolution heralded, edited, and then promoted by Jérôme Lindon and Alain Robbe-Grillet. In just a few years, the number of articles in the press and in critical journals dealing with Minuit authors exploded. Controversial, attacked by elements on the right and the left, winning literary prizes, selling titles at home and abroad, the New Novel helped Minuit become a "veritable publishing house." Starting out so well, the New Novel had been a risky short-term investment that paid off; in the next chapter, I examine how it navigated the cycles of cultural production in the 60s to enter a long-term production cycle of cultural capital.

CHAPTER IV

Minuit and the Institutionalization of the New Novel, 1962-1967

> Twenty-three years and two wars, for a publishing house, is no longer the prime of youth.
>
> Editions de Minuit Catalog, 1965

This chapter explores the ways in which the New Novel phenomenon sustained itself through the decade following its introduction in the late 1950s. The factors that contributed to the New Novel's success are illustrative of a remarkable conjunction of demand for what the New Novel was taken to represent. In examining those factors, I aim to uncover the unique set of circumstances that allowed Minuit and the New Novel to have such a profound impact on French and international cultures. In many respects, this success rewarded Lindon's efforts to define and assert Minuit's difference in the literary field beginning in the early 1950s, and culminated in firmly establishing the small publisher in the firmament of French publishing houses. In addition, in the 1960s the New Novel secured Minuit as a figure for the independence of French intellectual culture—a status that would be tested in subsequent decades, as I discuss in the next chapter.

The previous two chapters demonstrated how Robbe-Grillet's activities as editor, novelist, and editorialist in the mid- to late-1950s contributed to his value as a rising star and to spreading the "New Novel" name in literary culture. Throughout the 60s, Robbe-Grillet worked to keep the focus of attention on the New Novel and the New Novelists. As in previous chapters, these efforts must be viewed against the dual backdrop of Editions de Minuit's editorial strategies and broader changes in the literary field.

Certain of Minuit's publications proved to be very provocative. Before 1963, the New Novel had drawn the attention of critics and publishers from far afield[1]; when Robbe-Grillet published *Pour un nouveau roman* in that year, the New Novel acquired a manifesto. A number of critics were immediately preoccupied with either attacking his theses or defending them in readings of novels that appeared to support Robbe-Grillet's polemic. Also in 1963, Editions de Minuit published the first critical monograph on a New Novel author, and in so doing inaugurated a series of publications meant to help secure the importance and reputation of the New Novel and/or New Novelists, in all cases writers published by Minuit.[2] These publications were of a piece: the success of the New Novel and its writers was aided by texts that argued for their importance as indices of contemporary or "modern" French culture.

Pour un nouveau roman gathered a selection of Robbe-Grillet's essays from the 50s in one place, thereby historicizing Minuit's "cause." Despite its forward-looking title, *Pour un nouveau roman* signaled that the New Novel had already come into existence, and set the stage for critics to negotiate the matter of which authors, which books, and what literary signs constituted the New Novel. In the Minuit catalog, *Pour un nouveau roman* was described—for several years at least—as the "manifesto of the New Novel."[3] Our literature is a failure and so is our appreciation of it: for Robbe-Grillet's polemic to appear valid, critics needed to debate the questions of what had changed in literature and who reflected that change. As I will show, this was precisely what much criticism in the early to mid-60s sought to do, and, regardless of the variety of its analyses and conclusions, it eased the New Novel's path into the textbooks and school manuals, sites of official narratives of literary history that would teach the New Novel to subsequent generations of pupils and university students.

No less crucial to Minuit's success at home was the evidence the publisher could cite of its novels' success in translation around the world. Once again, the Minuit catalog was Lindon's platform for showcasing the scale of the New Novel's global reach. The editorial strategies behind the publication of Marguerite Duras's *Moderato Cantabile*—first in French and then in English translation—serve as a case in point. That novel was integral to creating visibility, momentum, and readability for the New Novel movement abroad. Analysis of stylistic choices made by the translator of *Moderato Cantabile* offers perspective on the novel's success in English. *Moderato Cantabile* underscores the role and importance of the New Novel's success in translation abroad in Minuit's publishing history and editorial strategy.

The New Novel could not have followed this particular path to canonization if it had not been seen as a part of broader changes in French culture. While the emphasis in textbooks is almost always on how the New Novel represented a change in literary technique, it is implied that such a change in turn represents, in metonymical fashion, something else: the modern French genius, its reaction to the problems or realities of contemporary French life, and so on. Weighing in on this was not just the rapidly-expanding critical discourse on the New Novel, but also the set of associations created for it by its publisher. Here once again the role of Minuit as publishing house was vital: the close identification of the New Novel with Minuit meant that the New Novel would be associated with Minuit's newest turn in editorial direction, its turn to the humanities and social sciences.

The period was marked by the rise of structuralism and of new major intellectual figures, and by a peak in interest in their intellectual culture on the part of many French. One of the key episodes of the history of French structuralism, broadly defined, was the feud [*querelle*] between Roland Barthes and Raymond Picard that was initially played out in the pages of *Le Monde*, illustrating the cultural prominence given to what—under different circumstances—might have seemed a somewhat parochial debate over critical methodology. Instead, their quarrel acquired great symbolic importance, betokening a divide between new, rigorous, and would-be scientific approaches to human knowledge and experience on the one hand and the staid, conservative, and traditionalist university-sanctioned school of thought. The structuralist *querelle* engendered a very revealing conflict between camps of Editions de Minuit editors and contributors that illustrates both the polarizing power of the structuralist moment and the means at Lindon's disposal to profit by it, while keeping Minuit at a distance.

1. The Rising Star of the New Novel

As Lindon wrote in the page-two text of that year's catalog, by 1965 Minuit was no longer in its youth. Nor was the New Novel. Indeed, as virtually the publisher's sole literary undertaking in the 1960s, the New Novel strongly marked Minuit's period of "maturity." As of the 1960 catalog, a large number of Minuit's earlier literary booklist items had been removed; the authors cut out included those with whom Lindon's contacts were described by Robbe-Grillet as distant, aloof, and impersonal, such as Alfred Kern, André Dhôtel, or Charles Duits.[4] The New Novel itself "matured" by becoming an increasingly recognizable set of literary practices; Minuit matured by paring down its literary offering to a more recognizable set of authors. This section traces and attempts to characterize the editorial strategy of the New Novel in this second phase.

The New Novel's momentum was not somehow "natural" or self-sustaining: it was created by the success of Lindon's and Robbe-Grillet's publishing initiatives within a given cultural environment. But before they could be promoted as New Novels, Minuit novels had to be written and published. The period of 1958-1967 was very prolific for Minuit's main authors: Robbe-Grillet published six titles, Claude Simon four, Robert Pinget seven, and Samuel Beckett five. Though he gave no more fiction to Minuit after *La Modification* in 1957, Butor published part of his series of criticism at Minuit, first in 1960 (*Répértoire I*) and then in 1964 (*Répértoire II*). This helped make sense of the inclusion of his Minuit œuvre on all of the various materials to promote the New Novel that Minuit published in this period, thus sustaining the notion of a New Novel group (I examine one such example below). The number of texts published is impressive on its own, but it is also of note that, in many cases, these are very long novels. Additionally, in Robbe-Grillet's case, he was editing for Minuit and publishing his own texts in between writing and directing films. The authors who—like Butor—stopped publishing at Minuit were no exceptions to the rule of general productivity.

Sarraute and Duras who, as we saw in Chapter III, were so instrumental in the formation and introduction of the New Novel, were prolifically writing for their publisher, Gallimard.

Lindon's ability to sustain this steady output of texts demonstrates that, at the very least, he was confident enough to make a continued, long-term investment in his authors. In the absence of statistics on sales of the publications from this period, other evidence suggests that Lindon was getting significant returns from his earlier investments; the same evidence suggests that he knew that the new titles could very well increase the sales of the older ones. Graphs published in the 1965 Editions de Minuit catalog trace the sales of three works published in the 50s, Beckett's *En Attendant Godot*, Butor's *L'Emploi du temps*, and Robbe-Grillet's *La Jalousie*. *Godot* and *La Jalousie* each show both a regular and substantial increase in copies sold annually from 1959 to 1964, with only a slight dip for each in the year 1962-63. Each book's sales in 1963-64 were well over triple their sales in 1958-59: from 1,200 to 4,600 units for *Godot*, and from 950 to 3,500 for *La Jalousie*. The graphs' author, Pierre Bourdieu—who will be the subject of later discussion—added the dates of certain events alongside each graph, inviting the reader to consider correspondences between increases or dips in sales and potentially relevant contributing factors. For instance, Butor's peak in copies sold coincides with his winning the Prix Renaudot for *La Modification* in 1957. *L'emploi du temps* then dropped steadily in sales from 2,100 copies in the first year to an average of 700 per year between 1960 and 1964. Despite the consistent appearance of Butor's name and works on Minuit's publications lists as part of the New Novel group, sales of *L'Emploi du temps* remained much lower than those of the other authors' works. The data point to no single explanation, but does the drop-off in copies sold relate to the lack of subsequent Butor novels at Minuit?

Had Butor's name not managed fully to emerge from Robbe-Grillet's growing shadow? Or was *La Modification* the only of his three Minuit publications to see the benefits of the group association? Whatever the combination of causes was, it is no contradiction of Minuit's group strategy for certain titles and certain authors to reap the rewards of association before others.

Equally notable is the juxtaposition of the sales of *La Jalousie* with the date of the release of *L'Année dernière à Marienbad*, suggesting that the film's success spurred demand for the novel. Further below, I will discuss the reproduction of the graphs in the catalog as a very particular kind of argument for Minuit's legitimacy; for now, the important lesson the sales graphs offer is the importance of momentum. By maintaining a regular publishing rhythm for his authors, Lindon could hope for increases in sales of their previous titles, as well as of titles of the other New Novelists. At the same time, Lindon could expect to see sales of the older titles foster sales of the new ones, especially as more and more critical attention was focused on New Novelists. The older and newer novels framed an evolution to the New Novel that needed interpretation: as I will show in section two of this chapter, Lindon grasped the importance of the criticism that sought to make the case for the New Novel œuvre. In commissioning Ludovic Janvier's study of the New Novel, *Une Parole exigeante: le Nouveau Roman* in 1963 (published in 1964), Lindon tried to distribute critical support from Robbe-Grillet—who was the subject of his own Minuit-published monograph, *Les Romans de Robbe-Grillet* the same year—to some of the other primary New Novel authors, including Simon and Butor.[5]

The catalog graphs also show, quite simply, that demand for certain Minuit publications grew increasingly in the first half of the 60s. *Godot* had passed its tenth anniversary and was selling more than ever; seven years on, *La Jalousie* continued to generate capital as a long-term investment. Minuit and the New Novel were selling well. Furthermore, as they sold, the older titles were providing capital to reinvest further in the New Novel venture. In the claims they make on the history and significance of that venture, the ancillary titles I have mentioned—Robbe-Grillet's *Pour un nouveau roman*, Morrissette's *Les Romans de Robbe-Grillet*, and Janvier's *Une Parole exigeante*—were an important component of that reinvestment. Along with Minuit's steady stream of new novels, they contributed to producing a sense of a New Novel phenomenon, vaguely initiated in the recent past, that was continuing in the present.

One of the curious aspects of Lindon's ongoing bet on his New Novel authors is that it was virtually his only literary gamble of the 1960s, a decade during which no new members were successfully admitted to the core group of authors associated with the New Novel in the late 50s, as the odd new author to appear in the catalogs of the period rapidly disappeared. No new author published more than two novels at Minuit between 1960 and 1970: the New Novel had become a permanent regulating function of Minuit's literary publishing. This may or may not have already chagrined Jérôme Lindon in 1965, when he was clearly conscious of needing a successor to the New Novel generation. In his introductory text to the 1965 catalog, Lindon describes the success of the New Novel phenomenon, and then suggests that a new turning point has been passed in Minuit's history. He puts a clever spin on Minuit's publishing situation, as if to give existence to a successor generation by sheer force of will:

> Vingt-trois ans, pour une maison d'édition, et deux guerres, ce n'est plus la prime jeunesse. La Résistance et le conflit d'Algérie appartiennent désormais à

l'Histoire de France et les petits livres qui les ont jalonnés demeurent surtout aujourd'hui à nos yeux comme des témoignages, directs ou transposés, sur ces époques: du *Silence de la mer* à *La Question*.

Le Nouveau Roman lui-même est entré, sinon dans l'Histoire, au moins dans beaucoup de bibliothèques. Il a envahi les collections de poche. Les étudiants américains apprennent le français dans une édition intégrale d'*En attendant Godot* ou de *La Jalousie* (avec notes en anglais). On peut lire *La Modification* en langue slovaque, *Moderato Cantabile* en langue boer, *Le Palace* en portugais, *Tropismes* en norvégien, *Comment C'est* en finnois, *Graal Flibuste* en serbo-croate et *La Jalousie* en coréen. Ça représente, pour cette petite vingtaine de romans et nouvelles, quelque deux cent cinquante éditions étrangères. Cessant d'être considéré comme une mystification, le Nouveau Roman ne risque-t-il pas d'être devenu une institution?

Heureusement, n'ayant jamais cessé d'être, aux yeux de tous ses contempteurs, “dans l'impasse”, il n'a jamais cessé non plus d'en sortir. D'ailleurs, à côté des grands écrivains des années 50 surgissent déjà ceux des années 60. Le succès de *L'Opoponax*, de Monique Wittig, qui a obtenu en 1964 le prix Médicis, est significatif à plus d'un titre.

A part ça, les Editions de Minuit ont fait paraître en 1963, et réédité en 1964, un monumental *Dictionnaire historique des rues de Paris* qui a quelque chance, comme le dit Le Monde, de marquer une date dans l'histoire de notre capitale.

~

Twenty-three years for a publishing house and two wars is no longer the prime of youth. The Resistance and the conflict in Algeria now belong to the history of France and the little books that have marked them remain today in our eyes as testimonies, direct or transposed, of these eras: from *Silence de la mer* to *La Question*.

The New Novel itself has entered, if not into history, at least into many libraries. It has invaded pocket collections. American students learn French in a full edition of *En attendant Godot* or *La Jalousie* (with notes in English). You can read *La Modification* in Slovak, *Moderato Cantabile* in Boer, *Le Palace* in Portuguese, *Tropismes* in Norwegian, *Comment C'est* in Finnish, *Graal Flibuste* in Serbo-Croatian and *La Jalousie* in Korean. It represents, for this small twenty novels and short stories, some two hundred and fifty foreign editions. Ceasing to be regarded as a hoax, does the New Novel not risk having become an institution?

Fortunately, having never ceased to be, in the eyes of all its scorners, "at an impasse," the New Novel also never ceased emerging from it. Besides, alongside the great writers of the 1950s, there are already those of the 1960s. The success of *L'Opoponax*, by Monique Wittig, which won the Medici Prize in 1964, is significant in more ways than one.

> Apart from that, the Editions de Minuit published in 1963, and reissued in 1964, a monumental *Dictionnaire historique des rues de Paris* which has some chance, as *Le Monde* says, of marking a date in the history of our capital.

Monique Wittig and Tony Duvert two years later were the only new entrants published in the 60s to continue to publish at Minuit in the 70s. Wittig, as Lindon later admitted, was a particular source of disappointment for him, as she did not fit herself into Lindon's demanding production cycle of a new title approximately every 2 years.[6] Daniel Boulanger, who wrote *Le Gouverneur polygame* in 1960, and Lucciola Koechlin, author of *L'Agenda* in 1962 are just two examples from a series of failed attempts in Lindon's search for the "great writers" "of the 60s." Claude Ollier, who would later be added to the ranks of the New Novel, published *L'Eté indien* in 1963 before moving on to different publishers.[7]

Lindon's text is a reminder to readers of Minuit's various contributions to French history: History with a capital "H" in the first case, literary history, and Parisian history. This concern for Minuit's place in history, as we have seen elsewhere, traverses the Lindon Minuit catalog. His text asserts the merit and the continuity of those contributions, while it thematizes Lindon's search for a new beginning. The wars are behind us, both Minuit and France; Minuit's anti-Algerian War strategy is henceforth a part of France's history books, which give witness (*témoigner*, *témoignages*) to the unbroken line from Vercors's *Silence* to Alleg's *Question*. In his signature modest wit, Lindon moves cleverly from mention of Minuit's record of resistance to an assessment of the success of the New Novel. His joke about the New Novel perhaps not having entered into history affirms that it is both contemporary and ongoing, while indeed having historical impact. Despite its detractors, the New Novel has sold and acquired its own force; so much so that it must continue to evolve in order to avoid falling into institutional impasse. Lindon's text nicely displays the full range of his ambitions for Minuit; alongside the great writers of the 50s and the ongoing tradition of *témoigne*, Lindon hopes to introduce the new generation. However, as I will show in the next section, Lindon's new generation would not be literary, but rather critical. Meanwhile, the need to escape identification with the New Novel seems to have already begun to make itself felt as early as 1965.

In citing the historical impact of the New Novel, Lindon emphasized its success at ending up on readers' bookshelves. Above, we saw particular titles selling healthy numbers of copies; one factor that contributed to this good commercial showing was also a major part of the New Novel's capital success in France: its international success.

Jérôme Lindon was scrupulous about documenting and citing the number of translations published for each title and the languages in which they were published. Asserting its international scope became a vital part of Minuit's promotion of the New Novel. By all means, Lindon did not create the circumstances in which success abroad translated into success at home. The New Novel's voyage to the US in particular engaged an entire set of favorable circumstances that no cultural producer could have anticipated, much less orchestrate. Still, Lindon's use of international success to strengthen the case for the New Novel in France is an index of how much could be made of that kind of boom. Implicit in the charts and tables used to track Minuit's international hits is the suggestion that, for the world outside of France, its New Novel was a leading sign of serious contemporary French culture. The authors' international reputations were a roundabout means of entry into France's elite for both them and their publisher; after that, debates over the value of their work might ebb and flow, but their centrality as subjects of debate would not. The New Novel's international success kept it largely in France's cultural spotlight, as a matter worthy of debate. Coupled with growing critical literature on the New Novel, translation was a crucial factor in the New Novel's passage into the canon of French literature and cultural history.

In the early 60s and into the 70s, the Editions de Minuit catalog was laden with evidence of the New Novel's international scope and reach. In the 1950s, Lindon had honed his technique by introducing photographs in both the catalog and the *extraits de catalogue* (smaller printed excerpts of specific parts of the catalog for distribution) showing Beckett's French *En Attendant Godot* beside five translated editions. In the 60s, the catalogs grew in size and number of photographs, and included other types of reproductions as well: a section of a Beckett manuscript on one page, Robbe-Grillet's drawing of the city in *Les Gommes* on another, etc. An exciting complement to the rather drab author photos, these enhancements draw readers' attentions to the creative processes at play in the books' conception and writing. The photographs of New Novels next to their foreign language editions signify their supposedly universal value.[8] To add further proof of that value, Lindon printed a photograph in 1962 showing a loose assortment of press clippings on the New Novel in English—the *Yale French Studies* issue on "Midnight Novelists and Others" appears there—Dutch, and French.

The most striking evidence appears in the 1965 catalog. In place of the photograph of the translation covers, in this catalog Lindon began to publish a chart of Minuit translations and new editions and their country of publication. Thirty-one countries are listed across the top of the chart, covering most of the Western world as well as Japan, South Korea, India, South Africa, Turkey, Brazil, and Argentina. In addition, at the right side of the chart Lindon added alternative French editions—"Scolaire," "Luxe," "Poche," and "Club"—to indicate when a title was republished for some special collection, such as *le Club du livre*, *Editions de Poche*, etc. In all, then, each of the Minuit publications could have potentially resulted in thirty-five new editions. Down the left side are listed Minuit's primary publications: Beckett's prose and his two most famous plays (*Godot* and *Fin de Partie*), Butor's three novels (*Passage de Milan*, *L'Emploi du temps*, and *La Modification*), Duras's *Moderato Cantabile*, five titles by Pinget, eight titles by Robbe-Grillet, Sarraute's *Tropismes*, and Simon's four novels (twenty-nine in all). Dots across the grid indicate which titles were translated and published in which countries. In all, the twenty-nine titles had generated almost three hundred foreign and alternative editions, averaging just under ten different editions per title.

The chart is an extraordinary glimpse into certain types of demand for Minuit and the New Novel. It also explains certain habits and strategies of presentation that heretofore might have been the cause of some puzzlement. Why did Lindon insist, throughout the 60s, on maintaining the same group presentation formed in 1958, with authors (Butor, Duras, and Sarraute) who had quickly stopped publishing at Minuit? Not every author and title was an international success. It turns out that Butor's *La Modification* and Duras's *Moderato* were Lindon's top two sellers abroad: as of 1965 *La Modification* had been translated in twenty-one countries and had two alternative French editions; Duras had sixteen translations and three new French editions. Both books had spawned more editions than either Beckett's *Godot* or any of Robbe-Grillet's titles, despite Robbe-Grillet having been the most active promoter of the New Novel as well as the figure most often associated with it. Why were Beckett's works always so prominently displayed along with the New Novels? Of the seven authors, Beckett was the most translated, with eighty-five foreign and alternative editions. After Beckett, Robbe-Grillet could also boast of a substantial overseas presence, with sixty-seven different editions of his writings in circulation. Robbe-Grillet also had the most books sold in "Scolaire" and "Poche" editions (four titles in six different collections). The numbers and pattern of translations help to explain the persistent appearance of these authors and their books together in Lindon's promotional material. As Lindon's best successes abroad, these titles had the greatest claim to make on cultural capital in France. This was one way in which international success shaped the New Novel, by confirming both a date of birth—1958, when Duras's, Sarraute's, and Butor's last publications were still recent—and a continuity, expressed in the subsequent writings of Robbe-Grillet, Pinget, and Simon.

The chart became a mainstay of Lindon's catalogs. In later versions, Lindon simply added the recent publications of the same group of authors. They show how responsive the international book market was to new New Novels, and how quickly after their initial French publication Robbe-Grillet's, Pinget's, and Simon's books would be published abroad. In the year and a half between the publication of *Pour un nouveau roman* (1963) and the preparation of the January 1965 catalog, the book of essays had generated eight translations and one "Edition de Poche" (a smaller, cheaper format pocket edition). Robbe-Grillet's 1965 *La Maison de rendez-vous*, his first novel in six years, went quickly into translation, with thirteen different editions by early 1967. Simon's *Histoire* had eight translations within a year of publication; similarly, Pinget's *Quelqu'un* reached seven foreign editions in a short period.

International success cannot be measured solely by the number of foreign editions garnered by the Minuit books. Rather, the impact of that success varies according to the size of the markets involved and the financial and symbolic capital created within them. Examining Lindon's chart by country reveals certain patterns in demand, as well as some striking variations. The most consistent pattern indicates that countries in which Beckett's novels had been translated also invested heavily in Robbe-Grillet's and Simon's works, leaving out Pinget altogether and Butor's first two novels. This strongly suggests the importance of Beckett's earlier reputation in bringing the New Novel overseas: the association of Beckett and the New Novel was ultimately mutually beneficial, but initially, perhaps, more helpful to the New Novel.[9] Many countries exemplify this pattern, including Italy, Sweden, Great Britain, Germany, and the United States. With the addition of the five novels by Butor, Duras and Sarraute, these countries were the most complete importers of the Minuit literary catalog. Many less consistent importers also followed the Beckett-Robbe-Grillet-Simon pattern, such as Denmark, Portugal, and Spain. Variants include Japan, where all of Robbe-Grillet's and all but one of Simon's titles went into translation, while none of Beckett's prose did. Poland, Switzerland (presumably Swiss German-language editions), and Romania follow Japan's pattern, only with fewer publications of each author's works.

Lindon's chart does not simply show the international reach of the New Novel. It also demonstrates Minuit's strategy of promoting the New Novel in France as an international phenomenon. We saw above how this is echoed in the catalog's page-two text; Lindon *translates* the corpus of foreign editions into the weight of an institution: "It represents, for this small twenty novels and short stories, some two hundred and fifty foreign editions. Ceasing to be regarded as a hoax, does the

New Novel not risk having become an institution?" While willfully exaggerative, Lindon's evocation of the New Novel as becoming something of an institution is not entirely false. As we have seen, by the mid-60s the New Novel had markedly increased its sales in France, had entered foreign literary markets, and had become Minuit's signature editorial line. The foreign dimension of the New Novel was an important feature of Editions de Minuit's own institutionalization—its passage out of "the prime of youth." In order to grasp some of the extent to which access to foreign markets could represent an institutionalization of the New Novel, I now briefly turn to the case of its success in literary culture in the United States at the end of the 1950s and early 1960s. A remarkably broad embrace of the French New Novel brought Minuit and its authors to the foreground of a then-fashionable American cultural francophilia. Combined with other factors, this led to a very clear institutionalization—within growing French departments at universities and colleges across the country—of Minuit's New Novel.

While a number of disparate factors fed into the American admiration for French culture in the 60s—from the demographics of the postwar Baby Boom and Cold War geopolitics to the popularity of French New Wave films—there may always remain something inexplicable about the trend. A very important piece of the puzzle, however, has to do with the dynamics of the American literary field, and the sharp rise in the late 50s of a small but very influential newcomer to the field, Barney Rosset and his Grove Press.

Accounts of the cultural and political upheaval of the American 1960s often refer to the landmark court cases of the 50s as events that anticipated that upheaval. One such case, *Brown v. Board of Education*, very clearly anticipated the Civil Rights Movement that would so dramatically alter the landscape of American race relations.[10] Another such case involved the prosecution of Allen Ginsberg's "Howl" by the City of San Francisco in 1957. Lawrence Ferlinghetti, now--famous owner and publisher of City Lights Books, was the Beats' publisher in the west, and introduced several important Beat writings.[11] After the successful defense of "Howl" and the Beats became national news, Rosset became the eastern pole of Beat publishing, editing titles by Kerouac, Burroughs, Terry Southern, and others.[12] The censorship trial of "Howl" provided the Beats with a broad notoriety and countercultural appeal; more importantly for our purposes, it galvanized Barney Rosset's sense of publishing direction. In championing the cause of anti-censorship, Rosset gave shape and purpose, as well as countercultural cachet, to an editorial line that had hitherto been, in the words of Grove Press historian S.E. Gontarski, "amorphous."[13] In publishing the Beats in the late 50s, Rosset created Grove's first major success,[14] which fueled his search for controversial, risqué, and provocative books. This was the editorial strategy and context within which the New Novel was introduced to American readers.

There are reasons to believe that Rosset's editorial direction was only amorphous in its public perception. A pair of clear lines appear in Grove's pre-Beat publishing: French literature and literary criticism on the one hand, and modern European theater. Prior to publishing the Beats and the New Novel, Rosset had established important contacts in Paris that clarify how he developed ties to Minuit and the New Novel. As a student at the New School for Social Research, Rosset worked with Wallace Fowlie, who pushed Rosset's interests both classic and contemporary French literature. At Grove in 1955, for instance, such disparate authors and titles as Zola's *Earth*, Larbaud's *Poems of a Multimillionaire*, *Germinie* by the de Goncourt brothers, and a study of Apollinaire were published.[15] Fowlie also appears twice in Rosset's booklist, as he published a study of Rimbaud at Grove in 1953 and an anthology of French poetry in 1956.[16]

Through one of his professors—perhaps Fowlie—Rosset came into contact with Sylvia Beach in the first years of his ownership of Grove Press.[17] Owner of Shakespeare and Co. on the Left Bank, Beach had been a well-known figure among anglophone expatriate writers in the 1920s and 30s. Her bookstore had become—and remains today—an institution unto itself, a pilgrimage site of sorts for expatriate writers on their quest for freedom of expression.[18] In addition, Shakespeare and Co. was the primary outlet for the publications of Paris-based Olympia Press, which published literature unavailable in Britain or America due to its scandalous content, from now-canonical titles and authors—such as Henry Miller, Anais Nin, and Vladimir Nabokov—to anonymous erotica. Olympia Press's publication of Nabokov's *Lolita* was an important precursor to the Beat episode in America, bringing the issues of censorship into focus on both sides of the Atlantic.[19]

Olympia Press's publisher, Maurice Girodias, greatly influenced Barney Rosset's initial publishing initiatives. One of the tastes they shared was for erotic literature, but Rosset only began publishing erotica after the Beats.[20] Still, Rosset's determination to bring a complete, unexpurgated *Lady Chatterly's Lover*—an Olympia publication—to the United States very likely originated from his contact with Girodias. His publication of *Lady Chatterly's Lover* in 1959 was followed by his winning a court decision against the US Postal Service granting his right to distribute the book by mail. The *Chatterly* case was a direct application of the "Howl" precedent; when the government appealed, a US Court of Appeals upheld the first decision in May 1960.[21] Girodias also brought Henry Miller to Grove, which ultimately published many of his novels in America for the first time.[22] Rosset brought out *Tropic of Cancer* in 1961, again prompting an attempted ban by the Postal Service; this time the attempt was dropped without a trial. State- and city-enforced statutes continued to suppress *Tropic of Cancer* and other Grove titles; with the books legally available through the mail, such statutes were destined only to add to the books'—and their publisher's—"underground" appeal.[23] These publications and the controversy that swirled around them sealed Grove's reputation at the forefront of an ever-broadening challenge to traditional notions of art and morality.

Girodias's other great legacy to Barney Rosset was Samuel Beckett. Girodias saw several of Beckett's English-language manuscripts in the early 50s. He, Sylvia Beach, and Wallace Fowlie observed the success of *Godot*'s staging in French, and—presumably on their advice—Barney Rosset published the first American edition of the play in 1954. Rosset continued to publish Beckett, one title per year, for the remainder of the decade. At the same time, Beckett's prose captured the attention of a young American student named Richard Seaver, who, in 1955, orchestrated the publication of *Molloy* in English with Rosset and Girodias.[24] In 1959, Rosset made Seaver editor of Grove's *Evergreen Review*, and in so doing further established French literature as a priority in Grove's publishing.[25]

In 1958, Grove published Beckett's trilogy in one volume; Beckett's prose publication coincided with Grove's first Robbe-Grillet novel, *The Voyeur*—the first New Novel to be translated for American readers. The timing may have been somewhat coincidental, but Beckett's large presence at Grove does point to the kind of relay-function that his work served in helping the New Novel cross the Atlantic.[26] The inclination on the part of Grove's publisher and editors to recognize value in Robbe-Grillet's novels stemmed from its recognition of the value of

Beckett's writings. Furthermore, the fact that Robbe-Grillet's novel landed at Grove Press is vitally important to understanding the New Novel's American introduction. With the publication of *The Voyeur*, Rosset began to systematically incorporate the New Novel into his ever-more distinctly countercultural editorial line. The New Novel joined ranks with the sexual rebellion of Lawrence and Miller (among others) and the social rebellion of the Beats.[27] In that company, the New Novel could be sold both to those in favor of the cultural changes heralded by Grove's publications and to those who were prepared to espouse only less-controversial forms of artistic innovation. The focus of the New Novels on formal and literary categories of innovation made them easier candidates for mainstream critical endorsement.

Along with the numbers of translations highlighted on Lindon's chart, there are two additional indices of that mainstream endorsement that appear in the record of New Novel publishing in the US They show that, while Grove did not make itself synonymous with the New Novel—its strategy, as we have seen, was polyvalent—it was instrumental in creating a market for the New Novel in translation. Owing to the particular set of associations developed by the Grove label—free speech battles, the Beats, Beckett—the New Novel made a quick and successful entrance into American literary culture. The first clue comes from a 1963 edition of Sarraute's *Tropisms*, published by George Braziller. Printed on the book's back cover are six blurbs about five different Sarraute texts in translation. Several details about this back cover are striking. First, the number of texts in translation as of 1963 is a startling illustration of the speed with which her novels were imported. Second, the sources of commentary make a bold, clear statement about the mainstream address of the translations in America. The New Novel was by no means a purely academic phenomenon in the United States. The sources are as follows (in the order in which they appear): *New York Herald Tribune*, *Saturday Review Syndicate*, *The Yale Review*, *The New Yorker*, *Life*, and *The Massachusetts Review*. The list does lean heavily on a certain cultural dimension of the United States, but it is more regional than academic, coming predominantly from New England (*The Massachusetts Review*, *The Yale Review*) and New York. This regional imbalance reflects the hierarchical structure of American literary culture as a whole at the time. It is instructive for readers familiar with its contemporary manifestation that the exception to the regional imbalance, *Life* magazine, also weighed in on Sarraute's writing, calling her *The Golden Fruits* a "small scintillating book."

Around the same time as the English publication of *Tropisms*, other New Novels were entering additional American editions, but in their original French. In his page-two text of the 1965 catalog, Lindon referred to the American students who were learning French from Robbe-Grillet's *La Jalousie* "(avec notes en anglais)." In the sections below I discuss the critical response to the New Novel and its entrance into French schools. The New Novel found its way into American schools and universities several years before doing so in France. I mention this fact here to distinguish between literature that only sustains itself as a subject of debate between academics and literature that not only captivates an academic readership but also becomes its pedagogical tool. In the transition from subject of academic debate to teaching device, these publications became institutionalized symbols of contemporary literature. The Macmillan Series of Contemporary French Literature, edited by Germaine Brée, illustrates my point well: its considerable emphasis on prose published by Minuit was an endorsement of the publisher's and the New Novel's capacity to represent modern French literature.

The circumstances favoring the importation of the New Novel into culture in the US at the end of the 50s and into the 60s were numerous, and I have only pointed to some here. My purpose in discussing the New Novel in the United States has been to highlight the value of its successful translation to the momentum and cohesion of the New Novel at home. The New Novel's relatively speedy transatlantic crossing brought important new capital to its authors and their publisher, both financial—through the multiplication of original and ancillary editions—and symbolic, inasmuch as its international scope gave it the appearance of becoming an institution. In this respect, the arguments Lindon made in his promotional material for the New Novel are not wish fulfillment but reasonable and substantive assessments.

Just as Minuit's success in the American literary field owed much to Grove Press capitalizing effectively on other literary cultural movements and trends, Minuit's long-term success in France must also be understood in relation to a set of favorable circumstances taking shape in French literary culture in the early 1960s. We saw Grove's unique editorial deployment of Minuit titles in translation; although Minuit's literary publishing became closely focused on the works of the New Novelists, their novels were part of Lindon's broad editorial strategy. In Chapter III, I examined the strongly implicit complementarity between Minuit's emerging New Novel strategy and its anti-Algerian War activism. Lindon's "Documents" series helped make the case for a broad new image of French intellectual culture. In the aftermath of the Algerian conflict in 1962, and Minuit's trial a matter of historical record, that image had to be updated. Lindon's publishing followed a particular progression from the New Novel in literature to scholarly publishing. The next sections follow Marguerite Duras's Minuit novel *Moderato Cantabile* from its publication in French into

English, and then examine the steps Minuit took to modernize its claim on French intellectual culture through its expansion into the humanities and social sciences.

2. Duras's *Moderato Cantabile* in Translation

My purpose in discussing the New Novel's claims to the world stage has been to highlight the value its success in translation brought to bear on the momentum and cohesion of the New Novel at home in France. Duras's name belongs on just one Minuit title in the 50s, and, as noted above, Duras had no particular interest in her work being considered part of the New Novel. Nonetheless, throughout the period *Moderato Cantabile* is featured prominently in the Minuit catalog, and the New Novel gained by its success. In the last chapter I discussed the editorial sense it made for Minuit to bring Duras into the New Novel's fold. We saw how the film version of *Moderato Cantabile* reads as if Duras was grappling with the editorial lessons that made *Moderato Cantabile* a New Novel. Consequently, in looking at the changes and notes from developing *Moderato Cantabile* from novel into a screenplay, we found an exceptional window onto how the New Novel functioned as an editorial strategy at the most important stage in the life of the Minuit imprint—and of the group—as of 1958. Elements of characterization resurface in the screenplay whose erasure from the novel helped it to signify the New-Novelesque abstraction of character—what one critic perceived as signs of "social alenation" and the description of mankind at its "zero degree of existence." Richard Seaver's translation of *Moderato Cantabile* was published in 1960 by Grove Press in New York. Many features of Seaver's translation confirm Laurence Venuti's charge that a logic of "fluency" and "transparency" dominates the translation of texts into English.[28] The dominance of an imperative for fluency has resulted in a culture that values translations that represent a form of "domestication," that eliminate foreignness and difference.[29] Going further, Venuti accuses the market for translation of a fundamental narcissism, of "producing cultures in the United Kingdom and the United States that are aggressively monolingual, unreceptive to the foreign, accustomed to fluent translations that invisibly inscribe foreign texts with English-language values and provide readers with the narcissistic experience of recognizing their own culture in a cultural other."[30] Venuti's aim is to call for a practice of translation that resists these dominant values, refuses to "domesticate" foreign texts, and challenges the target language culture (24 and infra). Seaver's translation dates from what Venuti identifies as the "apex" of translation in America, (250) when the market for literature in translation in the United States was at its most open. Reading Seaver's work in terms of adaptations, deletions, re-appropriations, and foreignness, there is evidence of both a logic of domestication and strategies of foreignness. The success of *Moderato Cantabile* as an introduction to the French New Novel should be understood as a result of the mixed translation practices evidenced in the English text; ultimately, Seaver's work shows a taste for both the fluency offered by Duras's text and for a measure of difference.

Given Richard Seaver's capacity as reader for Grove Press and editor of Grove's *Evergreen Review*, one can expect his translation to echo the literary qualities he identified in the source text, or even to amplify them. Indeed, Seaver's *Moderato* reflects a reading of the Duras text that privileges syntactical and semantic simplicity. This spirit seems to motivate the translation's numerous deletions (lines of both dialogue and description) and stylistic simplifications. The following is an example taken from the end of a paragraph near the end of the novel, and shows how the translator smoothed out a part of the text by deleting a short adjectival clause from the middle of a sentence. The French reads "Un choeur de conversations diverses, assourdies par la pudeur, emplit le café."[31] In English, "The café resounded with the chorus of various conversations."[32] There is no obvious syntactic motivation for this deletion; instead, it appears that the translator chose to delete the somewhat disjunctive portion of the sentence for the sake of streamlining the paragraph. The deleted clause introduces a striking contrast in the term "assourdies" which works in opposition to the sentence's main verbal group, "un choeur" . . . "emplit le café." The disjunct in English between "resounded," "chorus," and "muffled" must have been judged an unnecessarily complicated turn to the sentence. Though a minor deletion, it removes the link tying the chorus of conversations to the main characters, Anne and Chauvin, of whose presence in the café everyone is aware and made uncomfortable by. Furthermore, in harmony with the values of the New Novel and its reception cited above, Seaver's deletion removes an instance of psychological explanation, scaling back, even if slightly, the descriptive assertions of the narrative.

There are a number of similar deletions, seemingly motivated by a desire to simplify sentence structure, remove redundancies, and smooth out the text's style. Unlike the example above, however, some of Seaver's deletions and adaptations are rather problematic, and go too far in removing particularities of the source text. Above we saw just how critical to the shaping of *Moderato Cantabile* as a New Novel was the question of narrative authority: in her screenplay manuscripts, Duras is highly conscious of not narrating or describing events, feelings, attitude, etc., and merely showing them. The narrative voice of *Moderato Cantabile* is meant to be at once omniscient and not, thus the persistent and regular recourse in the French text to expressions of doubt that serve to undermine the notion of omniscient narrative authority and push the reader to interpret as much as possible from the dialogue. Deletion of many of the adverbial expressions like "apparamment," "peut-être," "sans doute" from the English may have seemed like minor losses for the sake of shortening sentences and sustaining a smooth, *fluent* text, but their loss diminishes the consistency of the narrative's use of them and the examples that remain risk becoming less readable in these terms.

An important question faced by Duras's translator is sentence length: namely, the French *Moderato Cantabile* consists primarily of very short, simple sentences. On the one hand, this fact makes translation easier, and mitigates Seaver's efforts at shortening and simplifying some of the rougher edges of the text: there is no question that *Moderato Cantabile* lent itself to a greater portability and readability than the syntactic challenges found in a Simon. On the other, it introduces the problem of when to combine sentences. Short sentences can mean choppiness, and in many cases this appears to have troubled Seaver enough to merit stitching clauses together with commas:

> La dame hocha la tête, la désapprouvant de tant de douceur. Le crépuscule commença à balayer la mer. Et le ciel, lentement, se décolora. L'ouest seul resta rouge encore. Il s'effaçait.[33]
>
> ~
>
> The lady shook her head, disapproving such tenderness. Dusk began to sweep over the sea. And the sky slowly darkened, except for the red in the west, till that faded as well.[34]

The adaptation here of three short descriptive sentences into one makes the temporality simpler by substituting a preterite ("faded") for the French imperfect tense ("s'effaçait") and considerably accelerates the description. In the source, the "lentement" motivates the periods separating each clause: the reader is forced to pause at the end of each sentence, reading slowly, and the marked time of reading relays the notion of time passing for the characters. By removing the second verb ("resta") and introducing "except" and "till" as armatures of the sentence, Seaver has avoided a certain choppiness, increased fluency and smoothness, but at a certain cost to the difference of the source text. The stakes of this practice are high: combining too many of Duras's sentences would have domesticated the text entirely, and broken it away from the New Novel values it is meant to clarion: silence, uncertainty, ambiguity, lack of explanation, etc. Similarly, in some of Seaver's dialogue deletions, flow is privileged over respect for the source's fragmentary nature.

Not all of the translator's decisions, however, tended toward fluency, flow, and smoothness. Indeed, in contradiction with the aforementioned measures, Seaver retained many aspects of the original text, from short choppy sentences to long, overloaded ones, including a French-style use of nominatives. These and other aspects—the use of the French term "patronne" to refer to the café owner, the retention of the few French place names—help to "foreignize" the translation, and conflict with the elements of domestication present in the text.

Duras's style in French makes ample use of commas to introduce information appositively into sentences without coordination. What results are sweeping sentences, with clauses set off in suspension by commas that overburden the sentence structure but create a poetic rhythm. French is far more tolerant of such style than English. For instance: "Il joua à faire tourner son verre dans sa main afin de lui faciliter les choses, de lui laisser l'aise, comme il crut comprendre qu'elle le désirait, de le regarder mieux"[35]; "He pretended to turn his glass in his hand to make things easier for her, put her at ease, as he suspected she wanted him to, so she could look at him more easily."[36] The translator has worked to retain the original comma structure and pattern of clauses, and "cheats" just a little to make his sentence work grammatically (with the use of "so"). Elsewhere, his efforts are less successful. In this example, Seaver resorts to dashes to retain Durassien syntax: "L'appartement de Mlle Giraud était suffisamment haut, au cinquième étage de l'immeuble, pour que le champ de ses fenêtres donnât de très loin sur la mer"[37]; "Mlle Giraud's apartment was high enough—it was on the sixth floor—so that its windows overlooked a wide expanse of ocean."[38] Unlike the comma structure in the original, the use of dashes is rare enough in Seaver for this occurrence to strike the reader as odd, and to make the apposition of information in his sentences stand out even further.

The French predilection for nominatives also creates problems for translators seeking to adhere closely to the style of source texts. Again, the result is the introduction of a degree of foreignness into the target-language. In this example, Seaver has eliminated the comma structure, but retained the abstraction present in the source: "En bas, quelques cris, des appels maintenant raisonnables, indiquèrent la consommation d'un événement inconnu"[39]; "Below, a welter of shouts and orders proved the consummation of an unknown incident."[40] The unusual use of "proved" and the nominative "consummation" jump out as awkward and unidiomatic. The addition of "welter," a term idiomatically linked with waves seems meant to help by connecting metaphorically with the narrative's obsessive description of the sea in the previous pages, but fails to aid the abstract construction.

The examples taken from the translation of *Moderato Cantabile* show how important the translator's role as cultural mediator is, and how seemingly minor decisions about sentence-length, punctuation, vocabulary, and deletions reflect a culture's threshold and taste for cultural difference. As we have seen, Seaver was not unwilling to make changes where he felt translation could effect improvements in line with his reading of the text's value: some increase the text's foreignness, some increase its fluency. In many other places, he kept very close to the original, and sought at times either to maintain the basic sentence structure of the source or respect its vocabulary. By avoiding the temptation to combine short sentences, delete seemingly redundant dialogue and roughnesses, and rewrite awkward constructions Seaver allowed elements of the text's foreignness to pass into English. Ultimately, by not disrupting *Moderato Cantabile*'s readability Seaver's mixed translation practice allowed Duras's text to transport a particular notion of the New Novel to American readers successfully.

Through the mixture of effects of domestication and of foreignness, one can observe a threshold of taste for cultural difference and the "exotic" in Seaver's translation of *Moderato Cantabile*. As one of the most successful New Novel titles in translation, the case of *Moderato Cantabile* shows how the priorities of Minuit coincided with those of the novel's English translator, resulting in the strange circumstance of a novel that publicized and popularized an avant-gardist literary movement in a very direct, highly readable literary style. In the next section, Minuit trades on the New Novel's success to expand its claims on intellectual capital by developing an extensive catalog of scholarship in the humanities and social sciences.

3. Minuit and the *Sciences Humaines*

The New Novel grew in stature and prestige throughout the early and mid-60s.[41] In so doing, it sustained Editions de Minuit, and provided the important financial and symbolic capital that fueled another significant change in editorial strategy: Lindon's turn to the *sciences humaines*, a term that encompasses the humanities and social sciences. While *Critique* had been an ongoing and thriving humanities and social sciences undertaking, only in this period did Lindon begin publishing the book series by the same name under the direction of Jean Piel, the journal's editor. Before examining the various external components of Minuit's and the New Novel's success in the 60s, I consider Minuit's initiatives to expand its scholarly publications in philosophy, sociology, economics, and history significantly. With Jean Piel, the other primary figure, responsible for this expansion was Pierre Bourdieu, who edited a collection at Editions de Minuit beginning in 1964 called "Le Sens commun" ["Common Sense"], which added a major new dimension to the Minuit catalog.[42]

In the initial phase of Bourdieu's long stint at Minuit—his collection spans the 70s and 80s, and ends in 1992—he added his own touch to the publisher's promotion of the New Novel. In previous chapters, we saw how changing marketing and promotion techniques in the Minuit catalog registered changes in editorial strategy. We saw the ways in which Lindon deployed Minuit history to identify his new publications with French history (the French Resistance during Nazi occupation, opposition to the Algerian War) and a tradition of Minuit quality. Already a showcase for the New Novel, in Bourdieu's hands the Minuit catalog became a heavily documented argument for the prestige and impact of the New Novel. But at the same time, Editions de Minuit became the context, and testing-ground, for

Bourdieu's thinking about intellectual autonomy, cultural production, and the culture of the intellectual elite. In the various kinds of documentation that appeared in the Minuit catalog from 1966 to at least 1971[43] one finds signs of these interests. His experience at Minuit was thus split between his agency in the historical processes of legitimization and institutionalization (of Minuit and the New Novel) and his observation of those processes.

No details have surfaced in the literature about Bourdieu's arrival at Editions de Minuit in 1963 or 1964, including how, exactly when, or why. Evidence strongly suggests that for Bourdieu, a large part of Minuit's appeal stemmed from its daring stance against the Algerian War. By 1963, Bourdieu had a long record of publications on Algeria.[44] In addition, Bourdieu respected Minuit for its journal *Critique*, where he could find research from further afield than the French university. In an interview from 1985, Bourdieu cited his admiration for the *Critique* of 1950s, "then in the middle of its best years, with Alexandre Koyré, Eric Weil and others writing for it; in it, you could come across both wide-ranging and precise information on work being done in France and abroad."[45] The combination of Minuit's anti-Algerian War credentials and its intellectual appeal captures why Bourdieu and Minuit were a logical fit: in joining Minuit as a publishing scholar and editor, Bourdieu brought an editorial project that was aggressive, bold and intellectually serious. In the first year of his contribution to Minuit, Bourdieu published both a new ethnographic title on Algeria—*Le Déracinement: la crise de l'agriculture traditionnelle en Algérie*—and his first of several major works on the French education system, *Les Héritiers: les étudiants et la culture*. These titles established Bourdieu's presence at Minuit, and a short time after their initial publication Lindon inaugurated a new collection, "Le Sens commun," which Bourdieu would direct.[46]

Bourdieu's ambitions are evident, even in the typically reserved prose of the Minuit catalog. According to the 1967 catalog, "Le Sens commun" presents, along with the "Arguments" series started in 1960, "works [. . .] that address, in the various fields of human sciences, the fundamental problems of today." Lindon's page-two text in 1967 presents Bourdieu's collection as one of Minuit's three primary areas of activity ("trois directions principales"): the first area consisted of the "Documents," the Algerian- and World War II-related non-fiction; the second referred to the New Novel. Cited as the third—and in a sense the most current—"Common Sense" comes across as Minuit's latest innovation, on a par with those ground-breaking collections. Lindon's promotional rhetoric reflects his investment in Bourdieu as an editor and standard-bearer of the Minuit label.

The "Common Sense" collection was initially rather small, and was limited to Bourdieu's publications and those of close collaborators. For instance, Raymonde Moulin's *Le Marché de la peinture en France* (1967) was her doctoral thesis, written under Bourdieu's direction. Luc Boltanski, co-author of *Un Art moyen*, contributed *Le Bonheur suisse* in 1970. In addition, editorial devices were used to make the collection look more varied in contributors and sources than it was. *Le Partage des bénéfices: Expansion et inégalités en France (1945-1965)* was attributed to "Darras," which stood for "the Arras Group"; the book consists of the proceedings of a conference led by Pierre Bourdieu. Titles by Jean Bollack, previously listed with the "Documents," were moved to "Common Sense." In comparison with Minuit's other series, Bourdieu's grew much more slowly; however, by the early 70s, additions of volumes by Edward Sapir, translations of Ernst Cassirer, Erwin Panofsky, Emile Benveniste, and William Labov had extended the thematic center of the series from cultural anthropology and sociology to linguistics and the history of philosophy.[47]

Texts on linguistics, sociolinquistics, and semiology joined Bourdieu's core anthropological and sociological publications, thus strengthening the links between the "Common Sense" collection and the aftermath of France's "structuralist moment."[48]

What oriented Bourdieu's writings and his collection in the first years, before the expansion of the collection in the late 60s, can be read broadly in his own first three Minuit publications. The two cited above on agriculture in Algeria and French education were followed in 1965 by the first foray into what would be another of his major realms of research, art and its market, with *Un Art moyen: essai sur les usages sociaux de la photographie*. This volume has more in common with *Les Héritiers* than with the Algerian research. Bourdieu undertakes for photography what he would achieve for literature years later in *The Rules of Art*, by examining the class and institutional identifications associated with the appreciation for and consumption of certain artistic forms. The interests expressed in *Un Art moyen* were also quite compatible with his concurrent investigations into Minuit's literary publishing and the social inscription of its publications. Discussed above, the 1965 catalog's "Sales Curves" presented Minuit's readers with a partial image of Minuit's and the New Novel's changing publishing fortunes through the prism of three texts, one by Beckett, one by Robbe-Grillet, and one by Butor. The apposition of "major events" with the sales graphs reveals the hand of the sociologist attempting to interpret the patterns of copies sold. At the same time, however, as it displays the work of the Minuit sociologist, it also satisfies the purposes of Minuit's promotional strategy, "documenting" in putatively neutral and objective fashion part of the publishing history of Beckett and the New Novel in France. In this respect, Bourdieu supplied the Minuit catalog with a French counterpart to its ample documentation of the New Novel's international dimension, asserting the steady success of certain titles. The sales chart remained—without changes—in the Minuit catalog for five years, a frozen image of Bourdieu's partial investigation and of a moment in Minuit's history, an unusual case of sociological research openly displayed as a promotional device.

The sales chart was one of several Bourdieu-signed contributions to a fragmentary sociology of Minuit publishing. A second appeared in the Minuit catalog beginning in 1967, and was made up of results from an inquiry distributed with the sale of *La Maison de Rendez-vous* by Robbe-Grillet beginning in 1965. Two years later, with 22,000 cards distributed—as many copies of the book sold—Bourdieu counted only 560 responses to his questionnaire; nonetheless, in line with his own stated notion of common sense—"you get what you can where you can"[49]—he published statistics from those questionnaire results. His inquiry asked readers their age, their career status, and for their judgment of Robbe-Grillet's novel. The published results correlated the three answers, to show that the average age of Robbe-Grillet's reader (who returned the response card) was thirty-four, and that readers who were favorable in their judgment were on average seven years younger than those who expressed mixed views (thirty-one and thirty-eight years of age, respectively), while those who thought negatively of the book averaged forty-four years of age. The largest percentage of positive reviews came from students, writers, and teachers, and the negative side was concentrated among members of the "management and liberal professions," though just as many members of that class gave the book a positive review.

While certainly published in the same spirit (that of a specialist's examination of the social scope of the New Novel, as well as an assertion of its circulation or diffusion), the questionnaire results are much less successful than the sales chart in performing that double duty. The small sample size and limited range of variables make it difficult to draw firm conclusions from the results or discern the purpose achieved by publishing them in the catalog. Little is revealed about Minuit's or the New Novel's readership, except perhaps that readers involved in education—whether students or teachers—were more inclined to appreciate the New Novel than not. Placement of the results in a diagram at the end of the Minuit catalog—whereas other such additional documentation accompanied the literature section of the catalog—suggests that they were considered to have only secondary importance and diminishes their power as promotional material. Perhaps they most prominently bear witness to the failure of Bourdieu's "survey": years later, in an exchange with Roger Chartier on reading, Bourdieu mentions the unwillingness of informants to give frank answers to questions regarding literary and high-cultural likes and dislikes, opting rather to give answers that reflect what they think they *should* like or dislike.[50] The question remains open as to whether readers of the New Novel felt more or less of an incentive to give an account of their readings than other readers.

There are other examples of similar initiatives Bourdieu undertook in the mid- to late-60s as the in-house sociologist for Editions de Minuit. Sylvie Patron, in her book on *Critique*, cites an "Enquête auprès des lecteurs de *Critique*" ["Survey for Readers of *Critique*"] that Bourdieu circulated in its December 1967 issue.[51] The five-page questionnaire sought to discern the broad social, economic, and political identifications of *Critique* readers. The results, drawn from 158 responses, can hardly claim to be any more representative of *Critique*'s readership than those in the Robbe-Grillet inquiry.[52] Regardless, the project provides another glimpse into Bourdieu at work measuring his publisher's position in the cultural field; at the same time, Bourdieu's own intellectual and editorial project was helping to shape that position. Before moving to an account of Lindon's other forays in the humanities and social sciences, I first discuss the nature of Bourdieu's project and why it was a suitable and valuable component of the Minuit of the mid-60s.

More so than either his anthropological work on Berber culture or his burgeoning work on the market for art, it was his critique of the French education system that was responsible for Bourdieu's notoriety in the late 60s.[53] He later protested that his purpose had not merely been to bring about educational reform; rather, his project had always been much larger: "[t]o start with, I had the intention of carrying out a social critique of culture."[54] *Les Héritiers* targeted the education system as the source of the categories and distinctions that compose the social sphere.[55] Theoretically, then, his intellectual purpose or activism was aimed at gatekeeping institutions, of which the education system would be his most well-known example. Looking back on the period, Bourdieu characterized his ambitions in ways that suggest why they were unquestionably congenial to and welcome at Editions de Minuit:

> The desire for a clean break [. . .] was in my case directed against institutional power, and especially against the institution of the university and all the violence, imposture and sanctified stupidity that it concealed—and, behind that institution, against the social order. [. . .] I think that the concern to *nicht mitmachen*, as Adorno put it—the refusal to compromise with institutions, beginning with intellectual institutions—has never left me.[56]

When the events of May '68 erupted, though Bourdieu himself was absent from the Paris streets, the news must have struck him and his publisher as a marvelous vindication of the editorial line of "Common Sense."[57] Although it was published six years after *Les Héritiers* and presented as its second part, *La Reproduction: éléments pour une théorie du système d'enseignement* was still cogent in the climate of post-'68 reform.[58] Regardless, however, of the consequences of May '68 on Bourdieu's prestige, as well as on that of various other members of France's new intellectual class, there were specific reasons why Bourdieu's anti-institutional stance already made sense for Minuit in 1964. Those reasons require that we turn once again to *Critique* and note the journal's rapidly expanding place in the Minuit catalog.

By 1967, the humanities and social sciences occupied twice as much space in the Minuit catalog as did its literary publishing. While, as I showed above, Lindon's literary publishing had become concentrated in the *œuvres* of his New Novel authors, some of his newer rubrics—namely, the "Arguments" and the "Critique" collections—had expanded tremendously. Conversely, in asserting the place of the "Documents" series—so critical for Minuit during the Algerian War—in a chapter of French history that had turned, Lindon took his focus off the series. Viewed in isolation, this shift in Lindon's publishing focus suggests that one of the capital rewards of Minuit's publishing strategy during the Algerian War (see Chapter III) had been the power to attract a new group of contributors from the humanities and social sciences. The example of Bourdieu himself is a more extraordinary one than most, since for many years he was, after Kostas Axelos in 1960, the last new contributor to receive his own collection to edit at Minuit. In contrast to Bourdieu's path, most new contributors came to Minuit via its journal *Critique*. It is the para-institutional orientation of

Critique that explains both the nature of its power as a pole of attraction for contributors in the early 60s and why Bourdieu, as a critic of the workings of institutions, was a logical addition to the Minuit constellation. Perhaps Bourdieu's most influential publication in the early 60s was his examination of the French education system in *Les Héritiers*.[59] In making the case for a link between the traditional, stratified system of pedagogy—stratified according to the differences among students as established by their literary training—and the social hierarchy implicit within it, Bourdieu participated in a broad challenge to the French system of education in general and to the university in particular. The timing of *Héritiers* was impeccable: it coincided with the first salvoes of another challenge to the French university, the Barthes-Picard quarrel.

No other single publishing event in 1960s French culture polarized the literary intellectual field more than the Barthes-Picard feud. As the exchange between Barthes and Sorbonne professor Raymond Picard played itself out over a roughly two-year period,[60] the spectrum of positions in the field was increasingly split between proponents and supporters of "Nouvelle Critique" and their detractors, who were most often allied with the traditional literary critical methods sanctioned by the Sorbonne. The expression "Nouvelle Critique" ["New Criticism"] came to represent the application of new theoretical trends in the social sciences—from Marxism to psychoanalysis and linguistics—to literary criticism. For the editor of *Critique*, Jean Piel, the quarrel was an event that begged to be weighed in on, and decidedly on the side of Barthes: in late 1965, he invited Barthes to use *Critique* to issue his response to Picard. Then, in early 1966, Piel began planning an issue on contemporary critical thought, intended to manifest the journal's "anti-picardism."[61] By Sylvie Patron's account, Piel later dropped the idea when Barthes recused himself from participation in the issue.[62] It was only in 1967 that the quarrel was mentioned in passing in the pages of *Critique*, by New Novelist and frequent *Critique* contributor Michel Butor.[63]

Though the journal never did weigh in on the affair directly, there were a number of reasons it never fundamentally needed to. First of all, as I showed when presenting *Critique* in Chapter II, from its very inception the journal had an anti-institutional stance. The editorial emphasis placed on research from abroad, for instance, reflected a desire to circumvent traditional French institutions of intellectual authority and introduce heterodox criticism and methodologies. Even in the absence of the direct ties between Barthes and the journal's editorship—indeed, Barthes's name figured on the editorial committee for many years—*Critique's* "difference" would explain its sympathies with Barthes's position as emblematic of critical discourses in opposition to institutional ones. In addition to its own editorial stance, in the course of its publishing in the late 50s and early 60s *Critique* had compiled contributors targeted by Picard no less than Barthes, but for whom Barthes had stood as scapegoat. Some of these figures would later become associated with French structuralism, taken in a broad and vague sense, when its "moment" came in 1966, but had in most cases already been contributing regularly for several years: Georges Poulet, Jean Starobinski, Paul de Man, Jean-Pierre Richard, Gérard Genette, and Michel Foucault.[64] Picard's label "Nouvelle Critique" overlapped, therefore, with Minuit's *Critique*.

Meanwhile, *Critique* the journal began to overlap with Minuit's book publishing. Once Minuit initiated the book series "Critique," the network of contributors to *Critique* started to become a rich resource for Minuit's humanities and social sciences publishing. It was in 1966 that Bourdieu's friend

Jacques Derrida began contributing to *Critique*; his essays were then published by *Critique* editor Jean Piel in the "Critique" series. Not long thereafter, Derrida's work was joined by Gilles Deleuze's first submissions.[65] In addition, Minuit's international reach helped keep a stream of foreign scholarship flowing into its humanities and social sciences publishing, in the "Arguments" series in particular. Translations of Hjelmslev and Jakobson in the early 60s provided key texts by structuralist linguists. "Arguments" also boasted another title that would become famous in the May '68 historiography: Herbert Marcuse's *L'Homme uni-dimensionnel*, an important essay of reference for leaders of the student revolt.[66]

These aspects of Minuit's publishing structure helped keep Minuit close to the intellectual trends of the mid-60s, as the watchword of the day changed from "Nouvelle Critique" to structuralism. What benefits did they represent for the New Novel in its ongoing battle for capital and prestige? In the next section of this chapter, I look at instances of how Minuit's key place with respect to those trends helped sustain the New Novel's claim to be the literary emblem of French cultural modernity. Representatives of "Nouvelle Critique" and French structuralism were destined to make the case for the New Novel's prestige, and in so doing forge a new "institution" in the place of the old.

4. Criticism and the Canonization of the New Novel

In the 1960s, two major patterns appear in the New Novel's critical reception: first, thanks to Minuit's active promotional strategy, the New Novel became a privileged object of first Nouvelle Critique and then structural analysis later on. The

New Novel's break with tradition, proclaimed by Robbe-Grillet throughout the late 50s (see Chapter III) and 60s, was appropriated by critics making their own break. Despite Bourdieu's inquiry results that showed the New Novel's strong appeal among participants in the educational system, the New Novel satisfied the needs and requirements of Minuit's critical publishing line. Second, as the critical reception of the New Novel moved through successive theoretical phases of increasing complexity, significant numbers of more rudimentary scholastic guides appeared on the market. Though perhaps ultimately coincidental, it was as if the headiness of New Novel criticism brought about efforts to vulgarize the New Novel for the broader readership; regardless, the end result was the same: a large quantity of New Novel-related criticism in the 60s, anticipating the New Novel's preponderance in the school manuals of the next decade.

Editions de Minuit were not idle in watching Nouvelle Critique build steam in the early 60s. We saw how *Critique* was a proponent of and attractor for this type of criticism; it was sufficient for Minuit to give some momentum to New Novel criticism. Morrissette's 1963 *Les Romans de Robbe-Grillet*, published in the "Arguments" series, was a first step; more significant was the 1964 publication of Ludovic Janvier's *Une Parole exigeante: Le nouveau roman*. Janvier's text was the first example of what would become a common type of New Novel study. Janvier performs a proto-structuralist analysis of a selection of Minuit authors, reiterating a New Novel group logic through the very categories of analysis he chooses. *Parole* stands out not only as one of the first lengthy monographs on the New Novel authors, but also by not appearing as part of the "Arguments" series edited by Kostas Axelos. It was edited by the publisher himself, and was furthermore expressly commissioned by Lindon.[67] The text's organization and presentation suggest that it was as much about timing—and capitalizing on intellectual trends—as about Janvier's theses on the New Novel.

The volume is additionally curious because of the definite article "Le" in the title; Robbe-Grillet's essays had been collected the previous year in *Pour un nouveau roman*. No longer a mere subject of speculation, here was *the* New Novel; Lindon had put his seal of approval on the highly significant turn from "a new novel" to "the new novel." While all later monographs from Minuit would concentrate on a single author, Janvier explores the Minuit œuvres of four different authors: Claude Simon, Michel Butor, Nathalie Sarraute, and Alain Robbe-Grillet. Is that the extent of the New Novel? The back cover competes with the grouping implied by Janvier's text, as it reproduces the more extensive list seen in other book flap copy and back covers, one that includes Beckett, Pinget, and Duras.[68]

Janvier's essays show a concerted effort to follow the methodology Roland Barthes set forth in various of his writings. I first use his 1963 essay "L'Activité structuraliste" to capture a sense of what structuralist critical practice meant in certain places at the time of Janvier's writing.[69] I will then discuss the correlation between Janvier's text and that practice. "L'Activité structuraliste" opens with a disclaimer: "What is structuralism? It is not a school or even a movement (at least not yet), for most of the authors who are ordinarily associated with this word do not feel at all linked to each other by a solidarity of doctrine or of struggle."[70] Barthes's disclaimer mirrors the New Novelesque gesture of creating an open classification to which anything bearing particular aspects can belong—"an *activity*," "a certain *exercise* of structure."[71] The definition this essay provides is a rather striking counterpart to the New Novel Robbe-Grillet defined throughout the essays collected in *Pour un nouveau roman*. Structuralism is part cultural trend, "we could speak of structuralist activity as we spoke of surrealist activity," and part object of critical detection, over and above any artist's awareness of belonging to a specific set of principles: "it is better [. . .] to seek [. . .] at another level than that of reflective language."[72] Barthes describes the nature of structuralist critique in this way:

> The goal of all structuralist activity, whether reflexive or poetic, is to reconstitute an "object," so as to manifest in this reconstitution the operating rules (the "functions") of this object. The structure is therefore in fact a simulacrum of the object, but a directed, interested simulacrum, since the imitated object reveals something that remained invisible.[73]

Structuralism in art is a *critical* mimesis, aware of its own status as reproduction, a revelatory de-composition of the structures that condition the object reproduced; in criticism, it represents the same reconstruction of the formal "rules of functioning" of the object of study. In looking to identify a "grammar" of narrative, Barthes calls these rules or functions units (unités), which must then be assigned rules of association or rules of combination. The rules of combination in turn determine the object's *form*: by having form, the object has been dissociated from that which it represents, which is why the rules of form are the center of focus, being that which defines the artist's intervention in nature. The antithesis of "structural man" is naïve realism, much like Balzac's bourgeois realism is Robbe-Grillet's foil. Formal technique is the privileged site of artistic distinction with respect to the outdated modes of artistic production and interpretation.

The particular kind of assertion behind both Robbe-Grillet's and Barthes's positions goes far in explaining the place and role of Janvier's *Parole*. It also shows why the book exemplifies

Lindon's brilliant timing as a publisher. Janvier's text performs the structuralist assignation of grammatical rules of selection and combination to a modern literature, using close reading to determine which categories to include into the commonality defining the New Novel, while simultaneously excluding other categories that render such ordering problematic. Indeed, Janvier struggles throughout the book with the varying results his version of structuralist procedure provides. The passage cited below exemplifies instances where—the constituents of a New Novel group having been named a priori, like Barthes's units—a common feature, privileged as a rule of functioning within the œuvres and made into a rule of association, stands in for or defines the New Novel. This procedure should not have displeased Robbe-Grillet, except that the rule of association chosen in this example, paradoxically, has nothing particularly new about it:

> Il est facile de lire les œuvres envisagées comme le produit d'expériences limitées, de les ramener à des résultats d'entreprises défectueuses.
>
> La démarche de Nathalie Sarraute s'éclairerait alors par le sentiment d'une séparation moi-autrui insupportable [. . .].
>
> Comme serait caduque la valeur libératrice contenue dans la vision du monde selon Robbe-Grillet, puisque ressortirait alors l'obsession du viol dont il ne peut échapper au lecteur attentif qu'elle est une des clefs des personnages.
>
> Le "héros" simonien, pris dans cette perspective, lui, va nous apparaître bousculé par l'Histoire et tentant de se rattraper dans sa chute, cependant que les essais de Butor, [. . .] sembleront animés par la volonté très optimiste de racheter par l'œcuménisme

> un univers qui s'écroule en miettes ou fuit dispersé.
>
> Ainsi, le Nouveau Roman se lirait à partir d'un échec, plus précisément il serait nourri d'un tragique sentiment de déperdition.[74]

~

> It is easy to read works in question as the product of limited experiments, to narrow them down to the results of flawed undertakings.
>
> Nathalie Sarraute's approach would then be clarified by the feeling of an unbearable separation between me and others [. . .].
>
> Just as the liberating value contained in Robbe-Grillet's vision of the world would be null and void, since the obsession with rape would then emerge, which the attentive reader cannot help but notice is one of the keys to the characters.
>
> Taken in this perspective, the Simonian "hero" appears to us to be jostled by history and trying to catch himself in his fall, while the efforts of Butor [. . .] seem animated by the very optimistic desire to redeem by ecumenism a universe that is falling to pieces or is dispersed into flight.
>
> Thus, the New Novel would be read as coming from failure, more precisely, it would be nourished by a tragic sense of wasting away.

The ordering of texts Janvier carries out here under the name of the New Novel cannot only be due to the common trope of tragedy identified in narrative terms and extended as a rule of form—although this is precisely Olga Bernal's thesis in her book on Robbe-Grillet's œuvre.[75] However, by starting with the principle that these four authors add up to the New Novel, Janvier's use of a "structuralist" formula creates a circular argument through which the New Novel becomes whatever these four works are deemed to have in common.

Other analyses published in 1964 demonstrate slightly different shades of the structuralist/Nouvelle Critique approach: Lucien Goldmann's *Pour une sociologie du roman* mixes structuralist criticism with a Marxist critique of ideology in looking at novels by Robbe-Grillet and Sarraute; Olga Bernal's work on Robbe-Grillet examines the theme of absence as both a thematic and formal condition of his writings.[76] In the same year, the New Novel's international dimension was reflected back to France in a collection of essays published by *La Revue des Lettres Modernes* that asked in its title: *Un Nouveau roman?* Edited by J.H. Mathews, the book introduced American, British, Italian, Belgian, and Swiss critics to their French counterparts, and revealed for the first time the enormous volume of academic publishing generated abroad by the New Novel.[77]

Janvier's book was an early structuralist attempt to define the New Novel, and appeared at a specific and significant conjuncture for literary criticism. In many ways, it is a fulfillment of the strategies Robbe-Grillet first presented to Jérôme Lindon in that letter from ten years before: do not say too much, let a critic make the connections.[78] The first of its kind, *Une Parole singulière* was followed by a flood of critical publications that bore the stamp of subsequent, and perhaps more sophisticated, structuralist critical thought and methodology. After a second critical publication for Editions de Minuit, Ludovic Janvier ceased to publish criticism for many years and never earned the same notoriety as a number of the later structuralist critics.[79]

The New Novel became a privileged object of structuralist criticism, though by no means its sole object. The use of the New Novel represented a means of appropriating its modern break to one's own field position. This precisely field-related operation corresponded to both the anti-institutional stance—the "outsider" positionality claimed by *Critique* or by Bourdieu, for example—and the generational revolt of the new, younger class of critics and intellectuals. One figure who illustrates the latter mode of appropriation also exemplifies the interaction between the intellectual trends of the 60s and Minuit's New Novel publishing: Jean Ricardou. Ricardou also points us to the last element of the critical institutionalization of the New Novel to be discussed: the development of a more rigorously theoretical tradition of New Novel criticism, coupled with a large para-literature of reader's guides, summaries, and other material meant to present the New Novel to the general public.

Jean Ricardou may always be the "forgotten" New Novelist: with two novels published at Minuit in the 60s (*L'Observatoire de Cannes*, 1961, *La Prise de Constantinople*, 1965) he certainly had as good a claim as any other new Minuit author to the title. By his own account of events, he was originally a welcomed equal of the New Novelists and then rudely cast out.[80] His contribution to New Novel history cannot be understood outside of the relationship between the New Novel and the Tel Quel group, whose emergence as an avant-gardist intellectual review—and movement—in the early 1960s hinged on the New Novel.[81] The words of Philippe Sollers apply generally to the experience of a number of the Tel Quellians, as well as to the identity of the group as a whole: "Have I changed since I started writing? Of course. The reasons that prompted me to write have not changed, but today the terrain around me has increased, my field has grown and I must say it of the 'New Novel' [. . .]. For me, they were like masters."[82] The Tel Quel "flirtation" in the early 60s provided the New Novelists with another forum for regular interviews, book reviews, and articles; in exchange, their theoretical stances helped position the Tel Quel group as another avatar of French literary modernity. In addition, both Ricardou and another member, Jean Thibaudeau, became published Minuit authors. Tel Quel, it appeared, was becoming a recruiting ground for Minuit, as well as a platform for structuralist critique.[83] In the pages of their journal, a Robbe-Grillet or Claude Simon text would appear next to an article by Sollers or Genette.

Perhaps inevitably, the union of the two groups was not to last, at least in a superficial sense. Ultimately, Tel Quel separated itself from the New Novel by charging that it was politically compromised.[84] That argument notwithstanding, the coherence or sense of identity of one group was likely to threaten that of the other. Implied in Sollers's comments was that his work, and that of Tel Quel, was moving beyond the New Novel; from the time he was quoted in the interview above, Sollers would come to emphasize more and more the differences between his writing and the New Novel. Minuit apparently saw disadvantages to their close relation, as well, since Lindon and Robbe-Grillet became disinclined to continue publishing new Tel Quel authors. Several of Thibaudeau's and Ricardou's manuscripts—including the latter's *Problèmes du Nouveau Roman*—were rejected by Minuit in the years 1963-66.[85]

Tel Quel's journal was a critical laboratory, occasioning a certain degree of dialog among critics, academics, and the New Novelists. Like *Critique*, early in its history *Tel Quel* welcomed structuralist and Nouvelle Critique approaches as hallmarks of its avant-gardist editorial direction. As those approaches gained notoriety and structuralism captured national and international attention, publishers produced books on or related to the subject in earnest. Publication in *Tel Quel*, for instance, led to publication by Editions du Seuil in numerous cases. Gérard Genette, author of the well-known *Figures* series, published essays in *Tel Quel* in the early 60s, including essays on the New Novel.[86] Though he sought to have it appear in the Minuit booklist, Jean Ricardou's *Problèmes du Nouveau Roman* followed the same trajectory, from the pages of *Tel Quel* to book form at Editions du Seuil. As the first of several large tomes on the New Novel—spanning a twelve-year period—Ricardou's *Problèmes* brings a new level of theoretical rigor to New Novel criticism.[87] His "construction principles" create a much more radical definition of the New Novel than Janvier's conclusions about a shared sense of "wasting away." By turning "the writing of an adventure" into "the adventure of writing," Ricardou argues, the New Novel explores the basic laws of fiction—of the signifier, of the referent, and of realism–and analyzes the modes of producing sense in writing.[88] His version of the New Novel blends this generative approach to writing with the Marxist goal of exposing the ideological underpinnings of literary practice.

From volume to volume Ricardou's critical writings moved the New Novel further and further into heady, theoretical discourse, marked by quasi-scientific—and often self-referential—neologisms, such as "the textolect."[89] Ricardou's activity in this regard continued well into the new millenium: in the summer of 2003, Ricardou hosted a ten-day conference in the remote Norman village of Cerisy-la-Salle on "Le Textique," a name coined by Ricardou for the specific brand of highly theoretically ambitious literary analysis he has developed and promoted in his teaching for many years.

Cerisy-la-Salle first welcomed the Tel Quellians in 1963, to deliberate on the subject "Une nouvelle littérature: Tel Quel." All of the New Novelists visited Cerisy in the early seventies, including Butor, Sarraute, Simon, and Robbe-Grillet. Ricardou's marked presence at each meeting appears in the published pages of the *Actes*.[90] The first of these Cerisy conferences was in 1971, when Ricardou organized a conference on the New Novel that brought together Barthes, the authors (Beckett and Duras declined to attend), and a group of critics—all academics—from around the world. Something of a high-water mark for the New Novel's dialog with criticism, the 1971 Cerisy conference was the culmination of the trends of the 60s that I have sought to identify in this chapter. With professors from abroad—by-products of the New Novel's international success—coming face to face with their French counterparts, themselves embodying the articulation of the New Novel and the intellectual trends of the 60s, the first Cerisy conference was the culmination of many of the themes I have discussed.

For the New Novel, the introduction of literature as a university discipline in the late 1960s and into the 1970s was a decisive factor in determining the cultural value of the authors and the publisher. First in the United States and other countries (from the early 60s on), and then later in France itself (after 1968), the works of Simon, Robbe-Grillet, Sarraute, and, to a lesser extent, Pinget were included in seminars for the university literature curriculum, and even appeared at the lower levels of the lycée in excerpted form. One of the more striking examples of this convergence is Robbe-Grillet's novel *Djinn*, which was originally designed as a French language-teaching tool for use in American high schools. The entrance of the New Novel into the university was both an honor and an obstacle for its authors. To be read in universities alongside or after Proust and Flaubert is the highest honor academia can bestow upon a contemporary French author; as recent discussions of canon formation have shown, this process puts France's highest literary works in the service of asserting a cultural identity and a certain underlying power structure.[91] On the other hand, after the Cerisy colloquia the New Novelists would go on to pursue efforts at evading conclusions that academia had drawn about their work. Nonetheless, by the time Claude Simon was awarded the Nobel Prize for Literature in 1985, the New Novel had come full circle: from the polemics in the literary press in the 50s over the state of the novel to the colloquia in the early 70s, the members of Minuit's first "family photograph" had vanquished much conservative university resistance and achieved canonical status in France. National theses on the New Novel authors would appear in droves, and references to and excerpts from the New Novel in the teaching of French and French literature would proliferate. In her work *Nouveau roman et discours critique*, Claudette Oriol-Boyer indexes the gradual, steady appearance of the New Novel authors in secondary and post-secondary educational manuals from the 1960s through the 1980s.[92] Meanwhile, Minuit would continue to publish Simon, Robbe-Grillet, Duras, Beckett, and Pinget during the 70s and 80s. In my final section, however, I examine the strategies—and difficulty—involved with Lindon's efforts to launch a new "school" of authors in the 80s and 90s, and in so doing reinvigorate the Minuit label.

CHAPTER V

Minuit, Succession, and the "Young Authors"

> [T]he existence of a group plays an important part in helping new kinds of writing penetrate the public awareness. If its constituents are recognized by the media as forming a significant whole, the group in its entirety often benefits—and fairly rapidly at that—from the success of only one of its members.
>
> Alain Robbe-Grillet, 1989

This chapter represents something of a "fast-forward" through the last decades of the twentieth century and into the new millennium. My aim is to give an account of Editions de Minuit's efforts to reinvent itself. Initially, those efforts would be unsuccessful, as the publisher seemed to grapple with the long shadow of the New Novel in his search new authors. By the early 1980s, however, Lindon would assemble the first authors of a new generation that would reaffirm Minuit's leading place in a dramatically reconfigured field of literary publishing. Taking its cue from comments made by Jérôme Lindon regarding the 1970s as a long pause in Minuit's publishing record, the first section of this chapter starts out by examining the variety of new publishing initiatives made by the publisher during that period. Namely, Lindon established the first and only in-house literary journal, titled *Minuit*, in 1972, and sustained it for ten years; the trace of these new initiatives can be found in its pages. As a testing ground for new creative prose, the *Minuit* journal was a means of vetting new talent, in search of the next generation of Editions de Minuit authors. In addition, *Minuit* evidences Lindon's flirtation with genres other than fiction, such as poetry and the graphic arts. Keeping in mind Robbe-Grillet's frank 1989 description of a group-based editorial strategy cited above, I argue that *Minuit* failed to accomplish its goal of finding a new generation of young authors to succeed the generation of the New Novel, and put forward some ideas about why. That generation would not materialize until the early 1980s, at roughly the moment Lindon would cease publication of *Minuit*. The second section represents something of a "fast-forward" overview of Minuit's publishing of this new generation from the 1980s to the 2000s. Much of Minuit's story remains to be told: indeed, another installment of its history begs to be written. The need to limit the scope of this book has created both advantages and disadvantages; the preceding chapters show, I think, the broad range of issues and questions to be explored in looking at the various moments in Minuit publishing that I have explored thus far, and which carry forward into the current period. A disadvantage of this focus is the inability to examine the contrasts between the earlier and latter periods; this final chapter points in some of the directions such a contrast might take.

With its newest publishing gambles Minuit sought to surpass its identification with the New Novel in order to adapt to the changes in the literary climate of the 80s and 90s. The New Novel authors themselves orchestrated a sort of dismantling of the New Novel image: New Novel autobiographies that began to appear in 1983 with the publication of Sarraute's *Enfance* were hailed as a "return" to convention and thus a renunciation of the challenging theoretical conceptions of literature discussed in the previous chapter. In hopes of again passing for the theorist of the group, Robbe-Grillet makes the bold assertion at the beginning of *Le Miroir qui revient* that the New Novel has become literary dogma—a questionable first assertion—and that for that reason he would now go "back to basics": "Now that the New Novel positively defines its values, enacts its laws, brings its bad students back to the straight and narrow [. . .] it becomes urgent to question everything, and, to put the pawns back to their starting points, writing to its origins, and the author to his first book."[1] As radical as he claimed his intentions to be, however, Robbe-Grillet pursued a much more elaborate agenda, one that had more to do with memorializing the New Novel—and self-promotion—than with embarking on any particularly innovative literary project. As did the autobiographical works of the other New Novelists, Robbe-Grillet's turn made literary news and captured the attention of critics and scholars.[2] My assessment of New Novelist publications from the 80s as a whole would be that the autobiographical New Novel greatly enriched its authors and Minuit. Shortly after his autobiographical work was published, Claude Simon was awarded the 1985 Nobel Prize for Literature—a resounding recognition of his *œuvre* that brought renewed worldwide attention and spawned a new wave of scholarly work. Though still peripheral to the New Novel, Duras accompanied her peers on their "return," publishing her autobiographical novel *L'Amant* at Minuit in 1984—the same year as *Le Miroir qui revient*. It was a major international bestseller and would become her biggest success ever.

The New Novel's latest turn coincided with the emergence of Lindon's newest series of authors, who have come to be referred to as the "young Minuit authors." The scale of Minuit's success in selling the New Novel autobiographies suggests that the gamble entailed in publishing the young authors was largely supported by these latest manifestations of the New Novel. Effecting the same transfer of capital from the New Novelists to the young authors—this time in symbolic rather than financial terms—was a more difficult and long-term proposition, and, ironically, faced resistance from readers trained by and in the New Novel. Consequently, Minuit came to depend on novel forms of approval and recognition, earning noteworthy successes in mainstream popular culture without initially garnering the intellectual credentials that had canonized the New Novel. Lending themselves to being viewed as a group—largely because Minuit promoted them as such—the young authors articulated their newness as a break with the New Novel, and signaled Minuit's departure from its line of difficult literary publishing. In this chapter, I discuss some of the ways in which Minuit's new literary production was variously cast as both continuous and discontinuous with the New Novel, as well as how Minuit's use of fresh associations earned the publisher a new place in literary culture, a literary culture that was by then itself radically transformed by the media revolution and the democratization of cultural institutions that followed the events of 1968.

For nearly thirty years, publishing the New Novel authors had been Lindon's claim to exceptional status and prestige among publishers of literature. Through the young authors, Lindon sought to maintain that status and prestige while embarking on a drastically different editorial line and production cycle. By publishing wittier, auto-referential, parodic fiction, Lindon reshaped Minuit's high literary capital into a more pop cultural image. In part, Minuit's new image likely reflects the material pressures faced by artisanal publishers in the contemporary cultural marketplace—namely, the fact that the kind of demanding, difficult literary publishing embodied by the New Novel was no longer possible, at least in anything other than small doses. At the same time, Lindon's decision implied that the New Novel was as historically contingent as any other putative benchmark of literary quality. As I show below, many quarters were eager to embrace the new concept of high literature at play in the promotion of Minuit's young authors. Still imbued with the New Novel, academic criticism was sluggish to follow Robbe-Grillet's lead and recognize the intellectual modernity of the young authors.[3] Here I can only raise the important question of how the new Minuit authors will fare in garnering of long-term capital.

1. Editions de Minuit's "Lost Generation" and the Search for an Avant-Garde

In proposing a sociology of literary culture, Pierre Bourdieu laid the foundation for critical inquiry into the material and historical dimensions of the production and dissemination of ideas. Bourdieu's legacy has led to numerous inquiries into French publishing history and culture, resulting in important scholarship on publishers and publishing firms, intellectual movements, and literary journals. Scholars working on French literary journals and cultural digests before and since Bourdieu have tended to concentrate on the most prestigious and enduring among them, such as *Les Temps Modernes* (Boschetti), *Tel Quel* (Kauppi, Forrest), *Critique* (Patron), and *La Nouvelle Revue Française* (Cerisier). The focus on the most prestigious journals makes sense: as scholars map different configurations of the literary field, it is important to consider the most influential positions shaping it. In their accounts, these scholars trace the accumulations and dispersions of power and prestige located with these journals—shifts that were often reflected in the fortunes of their authors and editors, as well as along familiar trajectories of rises and falls in prestige and symbolic capital. Such contributions to cultural historiography are vital, and have led to new understandings of the workings of the literary field at critical moments in its history: Boschetti's work on *Les Temps Modernes* in the immediate post-war period, for instance, and the avant-garde 1960s in the critical work on *Tel Quel*. Our focus in this section centers on a journal that in most respects—and for reasons I shall discuss—could be deemed a failure. This displacement raises the following pair of questions: what constitutes a failed literary journal, and what might it be able to reveal about the literary field at a particular juncture in that field's history? I argue that by examining the trajectory of French publisher Edition de Minuit's now-forgotten literary journal, *Minuit*, one can see a publisher in search of a new generation of the French literary avant-garde: a generation he would not find. In *Minuit* the journal, one can perceive a complex strategy to confer prestige and symbolic capital from one generation of Editions de Minuit authors onto another, vetted through the journal's pages. As a failure, the story of *Minuit* is a telling part of the literary history of 1970s France, of the literary avant-gardes after May '68, and of a publisher in search of a successor to the French New Novel.

Edition de Minuit's publisher Jérôme Lindon launched his first and only in-house literary review in 1972, and went on to publish four issues per year for the next decade. Lindon had published other journals previously—including *Critique* and *Médiations*—but *Minuit* was different, not least of all due to its bearing the firm's name, and thus the full weight of

Editions de Minuit's reputation, prestige, and symbolic capital. While *Critique* and *Médiations* focused on criticism and scholarship, *Minuit* was the first to feature original creative work. Also, unlike the other journals, which were linked to an editor other than Lindon and to an editorial committee, *Minuit* was entirely Lindon's own undertaking. If the journal ever had an editorial board beyond Jérôme Lindon's own involvement—and later, that of his son, Mathieu Lindon—such participation was never credited as such in the journal's masthead. For these reasons, the contents of *Minuit* were far more personal in nature to Lindon than Editions de Minuit's other journals and reflected his interests, tastes, and editorial strategies much more directly.

In my analysis of *Minuit*, I seek to highlight the following two points: first, *Minuit* provides insights into the moves made by Editions de Minuit as the firm sought to mark out new terrain in the literary field. The publisher's editorial strategies underscore the unusual position in which Editions de Minuit found itself in the wake of the New Novel's success in the late 50s and early 60s, and represent a very important—and ultimately, unsuccessful—gamble on a new generation of literary experimentation. As such, the misadventure of *Minuit* suggests that the field of French letters in the 1970s had little or no room for a new avant-garde. Furthermore, by rejecting certain forms of readability in preference for a New-Novelesque avant-garde, the review positioned itself to compete with the entrenched literary avant-garde, while at the same time apparently constricting its appeal to a readership and its ability to capture the interest of potential contributors. In assessing the strategies, stakes, and shortcomings of the *Minuit* enterprise, I view the journal as a productive failure, affording its publisher valuable lessons that paved the way for Editions de Minuit's resurgence in literary publishing in the next decade.

The publication of the review *Minuit* corresponds to a period in the publishing house's history that saw both considerable success and what must have been frustrating difficulty. In an interview published in 1994, Jérôme Lindon gives a rather stunning assessment of the aftermath of the success of the New Novel. His comments refer directly to the frustrations he faced as a literary publisher in the New Novel's wake. Addressing the span of years between 1957 and 1979, Lindon first states that for him, "nothing much was happening."[4] He continues: "the verdict on the generation that followed the New Novel is quite negative. At the time, I had the impression that the literary adventure of Editions de Minuit would be limited to the New Novel." In other words, Editions de Minuit was on the verge of becoming a victim of its own success: Lindon directly attributes the long literary " dry spell"—Lindon later refers to it as a "a hole, a void" "[*un trou, un vide*]"—to the reputation of the New Novel, seemingly hamstringing creativity and precluding Minuit's ability to discover new talent and sustain its important position in the literary field. In Lindon's judgment, potential authors who emulated the New Novel rarely created important work, while those who were against it were unlikely to send their manuscripts to Minuit, "which seemed like a publishing house under a bad sign [*terriblement marquée*]."[5]

Lindon's remarks simultaneously cut in two directions: first, the generation of writers after the New Novel fell short, and "nothing was happening." Second, the specter of the New Novel, a bad sign, was hovering over the publishing house. It is ironic that, as described below, Lindon made extensive use of his established and successful New Novel authors in the early years of the review as a means of lending *Minuit* capital and momentum. While difficult to prove or disprove, Lindon's observations are fascinating to consider against the context of his literary journal. Minuit consisted of fifty issues of original writing selected by Jérôme Lindon himself and later in collaboration with his son Mathieu (who is credited late in the journal's life as "literary director"—I return to this below). In the assessment he offers in the interview, Lindon chooses not to acknowledge the substantial body of writing he published over ten years in *Minuit.* In the same gesture, he jettisons the authors who made the move from the pages of *Minuit* to their own place in the Editions de Minuit booklist. Though few in number, these authors are the successes of *Minuit,* the authors who were vetted and recruited through the apparatus of the literary journal and its capacity as a network, and thus represent the "new generation" of the 70s—by Lindon's own account, a veritable "lost generation."[6]

The time period Jérôme Lindon summarily dismisses here coincides almost exactly with the duration of *Minuit,* and his words do more than discount *Minuit*'s literary and artistic production. He also keeps silent about a series of projects he invested in heavily and promoted vigorously in the journal. *Minuit* was the central part of a series of major undertakings by Lindon to capitalize on the success of the New Novel by expanding Editions de Minuit's reach into different realms and taking up a larger position in the literary field. As we have seen, the publisher's annual catalogs keep record of the significant number of new initiatives launched by the publishing house in the 70s, and puts the variety of material found in *Minuit* into broader context. Between 1972—when Lindon began publishing the review *Minuit*—and 1982, when he brought it to an end, Editions de Minuit would announce an impressive range of new collections, new journals, and other publishing series. For example, in 1974 the new rubric "Graphic Literature" appeared for the first time in the catalog, announcing Minuit's investment in works that mixed text and the graphic arts. The two authors appearing under the Graphic Literature rubric were some of *Minuit*'s most consistent contributors, together providing the largest share of the graphic art in the journal's pages. By 1982, the journal's final year, most of the collections, journals, and rubrics begun in the 70s were either moribund—meaning they were listed in the catalog, but had no new additions in years—or had been removed entirely from the catalog.

Despite Lindon's reductive view of the circumstances of literary production in France in the 1960s and 1970s, *Minuit* did not circulate in a vacuum, but instead in a literary field still marked by the theoretical and literary ferment of France's 1960s. A field in which avant-garde or experimental writing was still very much under the sway of *Tel Quel* and its authors, though that sway was beginning to weaken. In his analysis of the literary avant-garde leading up to and after May '68, Boris Gobille argues that the political battles waged on the left weakened *Tel Quel*'s power, and opened a space for competitors to articulate a literary avant-garde antithetical to *Tel Quel*'s theoretically elaborate, textualist vision of literary production. While Gobille is careful not to argue that either of *Tel Quel*'s competitors would in fact dethrone *Tel Quel* at any point in the following decade, his argument that they created room for maneuvering is compelling. Editions de Minuit's foray into the literary review hinged on the existence of such a space for maneuver, and Editions de Minuit positioned itself against the politically doctrinaire textuality of *Tel Quel* using its own novel brand of apolitical and unprogrammatic avant-garde writing.

The first issue of *Minuit* appeared in 1972. In 1982, a brief prefatory note by Jérôme Lindon in issue number 50 announced the journal's discontinuation. Browsing any one issue reveals the editorial pattern followed throughout most of the journal's existence, and conveys a sense of its aesthetic ambitions. *Minuit* was more than just a literary review, and sought to stand for something more important, more fundamental. It did so by highlighting its own eclecticism of genre, literary experimentation, and abstract graphic art. Every issue of *Minuit* combines writing and artwork with a number of critical essays. A hallmark of Lindon's style as a publisher and editor was his preference for a deceptive kind of simplicity: the texts and artwork are merely featured, with no presentation, commentary, or introduction. Original literary works appear back-to-back with critical essays. In the third issue, for instance, an excerpt of prose by New Novel author Claude Simon is followed by a critical essay on philosophers and sociology by Jean Lacoste, a student from the Ecole Normale Supérieure. Next comes an essay by Samir Amin—an economist whose work Editions de Minuit published frequently—on economics in the developing world. By mixing literary and critical work, *Minuit* is drawing from—and promoting—the twin strengths of the Editions de Minuit booklist and brand: literature and the humanities. In other words, the connection between the journal and the publisher catalog is, from the very inception of *Minuit*, a direct and deliberate one. As a platform for the publishing house, *Minuit* is to be the standard-bearer of the firm's offer to French letters. New Novel prose next to essays in sociology and economics, with artwork adding a layer of textual hybridity—such is the image of French thought promoted in the earliest issues of *Minuit*; such is, furthermore, the image of the journal's intended readership.

As substantial the amount of space given to artwork, poetry, and critical essays was, *Minuit*'s primary focus was new fiction. The critical essays and the artwork seem like accessories in support of the literary contributions. The essays were most often excerpts taken from Minuit's humanities titles, and the artwork was left in the hands of a small number of artists. The purpose of the editorial work at *Minuit* remained literary in nature throughout the journal's life. Lindon appears to have concentrated his efforts on literature by entrusting the bulk of the journal's graphics to a small number of contributors, suggesting that the artwork in *Minuit* was not the object of a search for new creative contributors. In its ten years, over 165 different writers were published in *Minuit*'s pages, while the number of artist contributors during that time is less than seven. Meanwhile, many of the critical essays come from titles that were forthcoming in the *Documents* or *Critique* series: the example of Samir Amin cited above is pertinent, as he would publish several volumes on economics in Editions de Minuit's "*Grands Documents*" collection. Portions of Deleuze and Guattari's *Capitalism and Schizophrenia* volumes were also published for the first time in *Minuit*'s pages. Publishing excerpts by established authors from Minuit's highly respected humanities list was one way of structuring *Minuit* as a literary testing ground in its quest to recruit the next generation of Minuit authors. With names in its tables of contents familiar to many readers, *Minuit* might reach a certain minimum of issue sales while developing a base of readership for its new authors. This strategy is very similar to what I identify below as a strategy of succession: by including a mixture of familiar names and new ones in the early issues, Lindon sought a reasonably safe—and marginally profitable—way of recruiting new authors for the Editions de Minuit booklist.

As mentioned above, *Minuit* stood out among Editions de Minuit's previous undertakings because of its artistic and literary eclecticism. *Minuit* published verse and prose poetry, fiction, art pieces mixing text and poetry or prose, photography, drawings, and other graphical arts. Prior to 1972, Lindon's publishing expertise had been essentially concentrated in publishing novels; indeed, the Editions de Minuit booklist from the late 1950s into the early 70s was almost entirely dominated by the work of the French New Novelists and writers associated with that group. *Minuit* represented an opening up to new literary genres as well as the visual arts.

Just as Editions de Minuit's critical and scholarly publishing was meant to bolster the symbolic capital behind the fledgling literary journal, so too would the publisher's booklist and its concentration of New Novel authors. Included in the pages of *Minuit* are texts by Robbe-Grillet, Pinget, Simon, and even Marguerite Duras—whose complicated relationship with Editions de Minuit and the New Novel we have discussed above. Consisting of excerpts taken from forthcoming Editions de Minuit titles, the frequent appearance of work by these authors in *Minuit* throughout the 1970s did lend valuable name recognition to the journal, but also set up certain expectations for the literary succession to occur in its pages. These were texts by New Novel authors *before* their "autobiographical turn" of the early 80s; how could *Minuit*'s readers not be led to draw comparisons between the new authors and the established members of Editions de Minuit's booklist?

Many of the themes discussed above can be read in publisher Jérôme Lindon's own introduction to the journal printed in the first issues. He underscores the journal's intended eclecticism, presenting it as a feature of its almost unplanned, non-programmatic nature, and articulates its purpose of transition or succession from old authors to new. The text, serving in lieu of an announcement of *Minuit*'s editorial direction, makes explicit Lindon's hope that *Minuit* will serve as ground for testing out new authors. He writes:

> We do not yet know what *Minuit*, a review to appear bimonthly, will be. In the beginning, it has brought together texts from our friends, fictional and theoretical texts, as well as drawings. Yet it is already

> *opening up* to a *new generation* of collaborators, a trend that will grow, we hope, in the course of the coming issues.[7]

Though unsigned, Lindon's authorship is highly likely for two reasons. First, in the early issues Jérôme Lindon is listed as the "Directeur de la publication," which he remains until issue 32 when Mathieu Lindon is listed as "Directeur littéraire"—the first time his name, and this title, appear. Second, for readers familiar with the modest traces of writing Jérôme Lindon left in his publisher's catalog, scant interviews, marketing material, and infrequent letters to readers, the stance here is recognizable. His note invites readers into a relation of complicity with the authorial "we" and asks them to witness the evolution of the journal, implying an equal footing between editor and reader who, it is hoped, will await with " us" the coming of a "new generation" of collaborators. There is no explicit editorial line or direction announced; instead, Lindon's characteristic modesty and simplicity. *Minuit* is an experiment, a literary journal in search of authors.[8]

Despite the impromptu tone in Lindon's note, much was riding on the success of the journal *Minuit*. Mirrored by the sharing of editorial control from Lindon *père* to Lindon *fils*, *Minuit* was about nothing less than a generational succession. The note alerts readers that the "friends" would, by design, no longer occupy the journal's pages, or so it was hoped. The first issue, from November 1972, demonstrates who the friends were. Its table of contents lists the following contributors: Tony Duvert, Samuel Beckett, Pierre Bourdieu, Robert Pinget, Alain Robbe-Grillet, Didier Coste, Sergio Fernandez, and Michel Longuet. These are all authors from the Editions de Minuit catalog—and many exclusively. Thus in the early issues of *Minuit*, Lindon regularly published work by his most established, most senior authors. In so doing, Lindon sought to accomplish several things: first, to solidify the identification between the publishing house and journal. As we have seen, Editions de Minuit had gone from the margins of the literary field—and the brink of financial collapse—to its center, to worldwide fame and success, through the canonization of Samuel Beckett—winner of the Nobel Prize, 1969—and the phenomenon of the New Novel. Editions de Minuit had become a brand, with a reputation as some of the most important contemporary writing in French. Second, publishing the authors from his booklist with the most symbolic value in *Minuit* conferred symbolic capital to the latter. By the frequency of appearance of Editions de Minuit's established authors in the journal, it is evident that Lindon felt they strengthened the journal's image and viability. However, that high frequency hints to a potential problem. The return of the established names throughout the journal's existence may help sell copies, but it may also have rendered achievement of a literary succession impossible.

Publishing young new authors alongside a Robbe-Grillet, Beckett, or Duras set up an expectation—whether intended or not—of quality, of aesthetic coherence. The *Minuit* journal is to present the same literary genius found in Minuit's publications, and will respect and extend that heritage through the work of the authors of a new generation. Readers who look for Beckett or Simon in an issue of *Minuit* will bring a certain set of aesthetic expectations to bear in reading the new authors who share the pages of *Minuit* and hence lay claim to what it represents. The "new generation" should have been the successors to the New Novel, and inasmuch as such a group failed to constitute itself through the journal, it is better termed as a "lost generation" and Lindon's ambitions as laid out in the introductory note would go unsatisfied.

At stake, then, was not merely the posterity of the French New Novel. The ability for Editions de Minuit to consolidate its gains in the literary field and stake out new terrain by recruiting a "new generation" was in question, as is made clear in Lindon's appositive cited above, "we hope." Before concluding this section with hypotheses as to why this did not work, I first review the handful of new authors who appear most frequently in *Minuit* over its ten-year run, and were thus top prospects to lead the renewal of Editions de Minuit's literary booklist.

By looking at overall publishing patterns among authors in *Minuit*, it is easy to see that the journal struggled to maintain a consistent authorship, as the most frequent contributors split out fairly evenly across several different time periods in the journal's history. In other words, the closest thing to a new generation is a very small number of authors spread out over the ten years of issues, making it difficult to really stand out as a coherent ensemble. To bring these patterns into focus, I divided the journal's issues evenly into three phases: the early phase refers to authors published in numbers 1 to 20, the middle phase is 21 to 35, and the late phase is 36 to 50. Of the over 165 authors published in *Minuit*, the great majority published just one or two texts—136 of them, to be exact. With so many new authors appearing in its pages, the journal loses out in terms of readability and recognition. This contrasts sharply with the role played by Sartre's reputation and symbolic capital in lending *Les Temps modernes* enduring prestige and readability; the journal's editorial direction was attached to the interests, tastes, and reputation of Sartre himself or those closest to him (including Merleau-Ponty).[9]

Of the twenty-nine writers who published more than twice in the journal, only thirteen can be considered regular contributors: these are authors who appeared between seven and fifteen times in *Minuit*'s pages. Two of the thirteen are easy to strike off the list; Beckett and Robbe-Grillet (with ten and eight contributions respectively) appear throughout the journal's existence. As argued above, their repeat appearances seem targeted to reinforce the journal's reputation, bringing their value to bear—again and again—in bolstering *Minuit*'s avant-garde claims. A third author in the top group is Mathieu Lindon, who published nine texts in the review. Lindon *fils* is a good candidate for the new generation, since his tastes and personal contacts were to become decisive in the journal's composition later in its existence. This leaves ten other candidates: Jean-Luc Parant, Eugène Savitskaya, Hervé Guibert, Pierre Alix, François Bouchard, Frédéric-Yves Jeannet, Christian Rullier, Olivier Dazat, Denis Jampen, and Philippe Jaworski. Initially striking is that these were all men, and young—in their twenties, with some even younger—when they were first published in *Minuit*. However, the timing of their publications works against their legibility as a group: Jaworski appeared only in the early phase, while Guibert and Dazat, for instance, appeared only in the late phase. Of these ten, just five writers span enough issues and time periods to stand out as members of a group that would have been identifiable to readers of *Minuit*: Parant, Bouchard, Jeannet, Savitskaya, and Alix. Individually, these writers represent a variety of literary destinies. Examining the careers of several of them during and since *Minuit* conveys a sense of how the new generation was "lost": not only because none of them went on to be published by Editions de Minuit—with one notable exception—but because none would achieve the level of prestige and renown of Minuit's New Novel authors.

Jean-Luc Parant developed a long career as a poet. The depth and breadth of his publishing since the 1970s make him one of the most prolific authors from the list above, and one of the most successful discoveries in *Minuit*. However, both before and after Parant's ten contributions to *Minuit* throughout each of the journal's phases, poetry had little place in the Editions de Minuit booklist. While his contributions helped *Minuit* expand across the literary genres as mentioned above, Parant never entered the Editions de Minuit catalog and the publisher never capitalized on Parant's success. It can be surmised that this was due to reticence on the part of the publisher to invest in publishing poetry.

Some or all of Frédéric-Yves Jeannet's eight contributions to *Minuit* were sent from Mexico, where he emigrated in the 1970s and became a professor of French ("Jeannet, Frédéric-Yves"). In 2008, Jeannet gained some notoriety for his attack on the awarding of the Nobel Prize to Le Clézio, published in *Le Monde*. Though they echo the travel narrative themes from his *Minuit* contributions, Jeannet's first novels were not published until the mid-1980s, by minor publisher Le Castor Astral.[10] His most recent work has been published by Argol, a small but ambitious independent imprint that has assembled an impressive catalog of work from parts of the French literary elite since the early 90s. Jeannet's *Minuit* contributions may have been important to his development as a writer; however, his literary productivity came much too late to suit the purposes of either the journal or its publisher.

François Bouchard was in high school in Caen when *Minuit* began publishing his stories. With nine contributions in all spanning the middle and late phases of the journal (1976-1982), Bouchard appears to have been a promising potential young author. Indeed, Bouchard's example is one of the most intriguing among the most frequent contributors to the journal, since no original literary work of his appears to have ever been published anywhere. Unlike the examples of authors mentioned above, who contributed regularly to *Minuit* but only published books with other editors and publishing firms,

Bouchard went from being a candidate to cross from *Minuit* to the publisher's booklist, to abandoning literature altogether. I present below an excerpt from one of Bouchard's contributions, for several purposes: first, as an example of writing by a leading potential member of Editions de Minuit's new generation it conveys a sense of the stylistic experimentation that one finds in much of the new fiction in *Minuit*. Second, it betrays the influence of French avant-garde writing in general—and the New Novel specifically—on the writing styles of *Minuit*'s new fiction, as much of the latter pays homage to that legacy. Finally, inasmuch as the excerpt does not take itself seriously, it represents a lighter, comedic tone that is also found throughout *Minuit*. The excerpt is taken from a short piece whose title places it squarely in the realm of auto-referentiality so familiar to readers of the New Novel, "Approche d'un genre: la detective-novel (en 7 points) [Approaching a Genre: the Detective Novel (in 7 Steps)]":

> Ils sont trois s'assoient dans les fauteuils de cuir dans le hall de l'hôtel semblent ne devoir jamais s'en aller. Feuillettent désinvoltes les revues abandonnées sur le guéridon prévu à cet effet, froissées défraîchies caduques que personne ne lit plus *réellement*. Ils ne se préoccupent pas, peu soucieux des nouvelles qu'elles sont censées leur apprendre qu'ils méprisent dont ils se moquent éperdument, il y a d'autres inquiétudes dans leurs yeux mais on ne parvient pas à y lire lesquelles. (Alors on s'arrête les scrute plus méticuleusement les examine dans les moindres détails de leur habillement dans les gestes qu'ils font et ne font pas dans les paroles anodines qu'ils s'échangent dans les silences plus nombreux qu'ils s'imposent, on compare le profil de leur visage on

> en évalue les proportions pour s'apercevoir qu'elles ne sont pas sans similitude avec celles de cristaux de quartz éclatés, avec celles des bas-reliefs qui s'émiettent dans les ruines de Khorsabad. On se refuse à y attacher de l'importance, on passe outre et cherche tel autre détail plus révélateur. On s'y attarderait en vain.)
>
> There are three sit in the leather chairs in the hall of the hotel seem to never have to leave. Browse nonchalant the magazines abandoned on the end table meant for this purpose, wrinkled faded worn out that no one *really* reads anymore. They pay no attention, little concern for the news they are supposed to relate to them that they scorn that they make fun of endlessly, there are other worries in their eyes but one cannot manage to read in them what they are. (So one stops inspects more meticulously examines them the least detail of their dress the gestures they make and do not make the banal words they exchange in the increasing number of silences they force on themselves, one compares the profiles of their faces one measures their proportions to discover that they are not without similarity to those of shattered quartz crystals, to those of the bas-reliefs crumbling in the ruins of Khorsabad. One refuses to give this any importance, one moves on and looks for some other more revealing detail. One would linger at this in vain.) (53)

The opening lines of Bouchard's text display certain syntactic characteristics of avant-garde writing, particularly in their dropped pronouns and missing punctuation and coordination. These characteristics result in verbs, adjectives, and clauses strung together improperly, with the overall effect of speeding up sentences. Absent coordination, sentence elements are juxtaposed, given an immediacy and simultaneity that disrupts the orderly presentation of events occurring over time.

Though very different in effect, Bouchard's use of the present tense here recalls Claude Simon's use of the gerund, as well as the frequent rhythmic use of juxtaposition throughout his writing. Simon's gerunds most often serve to slow narrative time, allowing for complex description of many different parts of a ramified visual field at once. This excerpt toys with stylistic acceleration in the first three sentences, which could be read as stream-of-consciousness from the point of view of an intra-diegetic narrator, perhaps a modernist spin on the hard-boiled detective. Spin, or genre pastiche there is—the characters' disdain for the magazines they browse a standard trope of the "tough guy" character—but it is most apparent in the second part of the excerpt, the lines introduced in parentheses. Begun with a "stop," the parenthetical indeed stops the entire scene presented quickly in the first three lines and stages a futile search for meaningful detail about the characters. The abrupt shift in pace brings attention away from the story elements and onto the narrative performance itself. With the use of the ambiguous pronoun "one"—which could refer to a single character or multiple, or could seek to involve the reader through its meaning "we"—the narrative perspective shifts to describe the act of inspection and observation itself. "One inspects," "one compares," "one measures [. . .] to discover," "one moves on": the second, and longer three lines introduced in parenthesis parody the narrative stance of description in the excerpt's first three lines, ending on a comic note with "one would linger on this in vain." The irony here plays on the fact that we have lingered, only to have readerly expectations of hefty symbolism somewhat served and then denied: the comparison of the characters' faces to broken quartz crystals and crumbling bas-reliefs of the ancient world alludes to jarring lines and angles, and hard jaws and cheeks from wear. These would be classic "tough guy" figures to be sure, but that are withdrawn in the next line ("[o]ne refuses to give this any importance"), and the reader is left with the spirit of the genre—the inscrutability of the bad guy—but none of the exotic details, dress, gesture, or words. Bouchard's text seeks to operate both within the detective genre and comment metanarratively on it, and to place the reader differently with respect to genre, trope, and expectations. By no means a mere copy of New Novel writing styles or practices, Bouchard's narrative pays homage to them in its syntactic and stylistic characteristics as well as its ironic and reflexive treatment of genre and narrative. Furthermore, Bouchard's witty treatment of the detective novel anticipates one of the dominant modes of writing among the "Young Minuit Authors" in the 1980s, when Editions de Minuit authors Christian Gailly, Jean-Philippe Toussaint, and Jean Echenoz would revisit the detective genre—among others—with a similarly tongue-in-cheek way, though more forthcoming with the kinds of narrative elements that Bouchard suspends.

Though we have looked at only a small sampling of Minuit's contributors, it underscores how very few of the top contributors to *Minuit* either held symbolic value at the time of their publication in the journal or went on to garner any later. There are counter-examples to these. In another note to readers, this time announcing the end of the *Minuit* adventure, Jérôme Lindon names *Minuit*'s successes. He cites the names of two authors, Eugène Savitskaya and Hervé Guibert, the former a contributor throughout *Minuit*'s existence and the latter a very prolific arrival in the last dozen issues. There are good reasons for him to name these authors: Savitskaya successfully went from being a regular contributor to *Minuit* to a valuable addition to the Editions de Minuit booklist, consistently earning critical acclaim for his sustained series of fiction publications. In many ways, Savitskaya was a model for how the journal should have worked for more authors, promoting them through regular appearances in its pages and then upshifting into regular novel publishing by Editions de Minuit. Editions de Minuit author Jean Echenoz, well-known member of the "Young Minuit Authors" in the 1980s, received a similar—albeit very brief—grooming in *Minuit*'s final issues.

Lindon's second name, Hervé Guibert, is more intriguing, since Lindon had only published one book by Guibert in 1981, an essay on photography. It would seem that Lindon cites Guibert at this point in early 1982 because he already has some sense of the investment he would soon make in this new author: later in 1982 he published three more titles by Guibert, and another three in the next two years. Though Guibert's arrival at *Minuit* comes late in its existence, his brief collaboration with the journal does indeed translate into a major and rapid addition to the publisher's booklist. Through their critical and commercial success, Savitskaya and Guibert would herald the new Editions de Minuit of the 80s and 90s. In ending *Minuit*'s run, Lindon must have reasoned that two successes were not enough to continue the experiment. Though not the new generation that Lindon had been looking for, they were the first of one that did come in the 80s—independently of the apparatus of a literary journal.

Started as a means of building on the success of the New Novel in the 60s and the consecration of Beckett in 1969, *Minuit* is a rare instance in which the difficult work of a book publisher appears to play itself out in the pages of a literary journal. Without the coherence of new rising literary figures with which the journal could be identified, and without the designation of a distinct group of authors or a literary movement, *Minuit* was unsuccessful at gaining and keeping a readership that could sustain it. As a reflection of Lindon's publishing strategies, *Minuit* reveals the difficulty he had in the aftermath of the New Novel phenomenon with finding new writers to invest in, witnessed by the scant number of new authors to make the crossover from the house journal to the publishing catalog. Ultimately, *Minuit* seems to have been the victim of the publishing house's success at imposing a certain notion of literary modernity with the New Novel, a legacy that continued to be present in the journal's pages. That these authors did not make it from the *Minuit* journal to the Minuit catalog attests to a failure with respect to literary value. In this light, Lindon's ending the journal can be interpreted as an abandonment of the search for successors to the New Novel and the creation of a break necessary to the re-crafting of the Minuit brand.

2. Retelling Minuit and the New Novel

As Lindon himself asserted, the series of new authors published in the 80s—beginning with Jean Echenoz in 1979—constituted a vital new beginning for Editions de Minuit. It was inevitable that a redefinition of the Minuit label would entail a recasting of its relationship to the New Novel. In various Robbe-Grillet essays as well as in rare published comments by Jérôme Lindon, a discrepancy over that relationship emerges for the first time. Their differences of opinion entail two very different visions of culture and cultural production. One of them is a critical interpretation that affirms a central role for the

New Novel in French intellectual history. Though much more influential, the second opinion was much less known, because it was strategically understated by its protagonist Lindon. Most striking are the differences in how each man speaks of the authors included in Lindon's 1980s publishing undertakings. Underlying their judgments is a tension over the New Novel that is as much about the memory of the New Novel as it is about the fate of Editions de Minuit.

Lindon's frankest discussion of Minuit's novel publishing history appeared in an interview granted in 1993. His recounting juggles the desire to assert a break with Minuit's New-Novel past and the wisdom of paying homage to its authors. Those authors—and the New Novel experience, as well—still constituted the lion's share of Minuit's capital: the ongoing scholarly sanctioning of the New Novel authors continued to provide an important symbolic credential, in addition to financial support for the Minuit imprint. For as long as the New Novel continued to signify literary excellence and seriousness—indeed, to embody all the qualities of high literature—Lindon would have incentive to assert his responsibility for and ownership of it. His remarks demonstrate an adept solution to his dilemma, at once firmly dissociating Editions de Minuit from the New Novel while revalorizing its authors. In this first quote, Lindon begins his summary of Minuit's publishing history: "I had the good fortune to get to know Alain Robbe-Grillet and what we now call the authors of the New Novel—a name which can give rise to endless discussions—during the 1950s [. . .]."[11] As we know, "what we now call the authors of the New Novel" came to be known as such in the late 50s and early 60s largely by Lindon's own efforts. By 1993, any "endless discussions" regarding the New Novel were updated appraisals of its authors—not, as there had been long before, debates over the meaning of the expression. So why does he make this lapse in historical precision, unless to dissociate himself from a movement declared to be over and done with?

At work in this first step in dissociating Minuit from the New Novel is the assertion of Lindon's editorial independence. Independence from Robbe-Grillet's editorial presence, which had perhaps gone too far in connecting Minuit with the New Novel, and whose memory threatened to obscure Lindon's present editorial activity. The New Novel had purchased Lindon's autonomy—in the 80s and 90s he showed he wanted to use it. By 1993, Lindon had published a considerable number of new novels by previously unknown authors: six titles by Jean Echenoz, five by Christian Gailly, six by François Bon, four by Eric Chevillard, as well as Jean-Philippe Toussaint's four best-known novels. The number of new authors and of titles published shows what was for Minuit a literary explosion, especially when compared to the period of the New Novel. As Lindon's summary of Minuit's history relates, between 1960 and Echenoz's first novel in 1979, he published virtually no novels by new authors. For better or for worse, Minuit published the New Novel only, with the exception of a handful of single novels by first-time authors issued and then quickly dropped from the booklist, as well as the works of Monique Wittig and Tony Duvert, which were—rightly or wrongly—readily associated with the New Novel.

In his comments about Minuit's "dry spell"—which, rather amusingly, he implies was also a dry spell for French culture generally—Lindon revealed how much of a burden on his position as editor and publisher the New Novel had become: his remarks seem almost to condemn the legacy of the New Novel experience. He characterizes it as having stifled younger writers and, by implication, constricted his activity as publisher. Still, he mutes his rebuke of the New Novel by naturalizing its effects:

> Et puis il s'est passé de nouveau quelque chose, mais dont je ne suis pas du tout responsable, car il s'agit sans doute d'un phénomène naturel. Il est en effet possible que, pendant un certain temps, une partie des jeunes écrivains aient été en quelque sorte stérilisés, non pas par les sciences humaines, mais par le Nouveau Roman qui était encore tout proche. [. . .] Il a donc fallu peut-être vingt ans pour que les écrivains puissent ne plus avoir à se situer à l'égard du Nouveau Roman. [. . .] Il faut peut-être, après les grandes périodes de création, un trou, un vide, une distance qui permet à une nouvelle génération de se reconstituer librement.[12]

> And then something happened again, but for which I am not at all responsible, because it is probably a natural phenomenon. It is indeed possible that, for a certain time, some of the young writers were in some way sterilized, not by the human sciences, but by the New Novel, which was still very close. [. . .] So it took perhaps twenty years for writers to stop having to relate to the New Novel. [. . .] It may be necessary, after the great periods of creation, a hole, a void, a distance which allows a new generation to reconstitute itself freely.

Se reconstituer librement—his expression is apt, and underscores the sense of constraint fueling Lindon's delicate break with Robbe-Grillet, the New Novel, and his own former editorial direction. That direction subscribed to a notion of literary value that, in the end, put unfortunate limitations on the Minuit imprint; in Lindon's words cited earlier: "[. . .] I had the impression that the literary adventure of Editions de Minuit would be limited to the New Novel."[13]

In 1989, Alain Robbe-Grillet wrote about Minuit's new literary production for the *Times Literary Supplement.* His article—based on a lecture given in Hungary that same year—sets out to "summarize the current literary situation in France." I mention the article's origins in order to suggest that Robbe-Grillet was attempting to reprise—even if in a smaller way—his former role as literary agent for Editions de Minuit. We saw how when the New Novel was developing into an international phenomenon, Robbe-Grillet put his duty as cultural ambassador for the Ministère des Affaires Etrangères to good use in promoting the authors he had assembled at Minuit. By championing Minuit's publications, Robbe-Grillet is not just promoting a publishing house he helped to build, but attempting to restore Minuit to the focus of critical attention, the situation Minuit had enjoyed for so long. Now, as then, "the current literary situation in France" revolved around the formation of a group of authors published by Editions de Minuit. Where Lindon asserts a discontinuity between the generations, Robbe-Grillet's argument is for the continuity both of French literary culture and the New Novel's role in it.

Robbe-Grillet describes the works of Jean Echenoz, Marie Redonnet, Jean-Philippe Toussaint, and Patrick Deville as reflective of similar overall traits, which in turn express a logical continuity with the development of literary modernism—modernism signified by the New Novel. He emphatically asserts that these authors do not constitute a group—they are a "non-group" that has been "lumped together by critics"[14]—and yet, he himself sets about identifying these authors as sharing common aesthetic principles and aims that, in his view, distinguish them as the voices of contemporary literary culture. There is nothing surprising or terribly novel about this dual strategy appreciable in what seems a contradiction: the same play on the notion of a group was central to the promotion of Minuit's New Novel authors. Instead of citing the existence of a group, this time Robbe-Grillet discredits the claims other critics have made to such effect, and in the same breath offers a theoretical framework for reading these authors as a group. He critically endorses the new Minuit authors while at the same time making their individualism just one of numerous traits that bind them together. In addition, he validates this new grouping mutually with and through the old group, the New Novel, and in so doing, articulates a paradoxically linear, unbroken narrative of French literary modernism, with Editions de Minuit at its core. As his article demonstrates, there is much at stake in the handling of this question of groups, including the question of how to assess the achievements of the New Novel with regard to literary culture in general and to Editions de Minuit specifically.

To judge by Robbe-Grillet's argument, other critics lack sensitivity toward Minuit's new authors' desire of to eschew signs of group-belonging. Yet, because of the implicit comparison with the New Novel that runs throughout his argument, he lays himself open to the same charge of insensitivity: "[t]he current reaction against community, the refusal to share anything with anybody, is, not surprisingly, accompanied and nourished by a common fear of advancing any theoretical reflection on evolving novelistic practices."[15] Robbe-Grillet's insensitivity stems from his belief in the deep continuity he identifies both in and through the punctual differences between the New Novel and the "young authors." It is the same kind of will for critical continuity that caused others to write about the "young authors" as a group, only Robbe-Grillet argues that the group of newcomers can only be understood in the context of a history of "subversive literature" that includes the New Novel.

> "[. . .] the subversive literature that has marked the twentieth century (from Kafka, Faulkner and Roussel to the *nouveau roman*) has been seen as "modernist" for its negative aspects alone, in other words for the erosion—beginning with the decorative details, then whole slabs of the façade, and finally the very foundations—of such ancient humanistic notions as chronology, causality, non-contradiction, stability of consciousness and of the equation of the relations that govern them with a well-defined network of reassuring meanings, and so on. The combined forces of modern philosophy, science, and art have thus rendered these notions obsolete."[16]

The "young authors" have chosen the better of two possible stances they might have taken against these past modernist achievements (the other being outright denial of them). The "young authors" are, in Robbe-Grillet's view, a logical posterity of the New Novel. The difference between Robbe-Grillet's triumphant vision of a modernist tradition and Lindon's pragmatic sense of contemporary literary culture (new authors were simply not able to produce, because they were "stérilisés" by the New Novel) is striking.

Their disagreement is reflected in their differing conceptions of Minuit's readership. Robbe-Grillet's typically New Novelesque marketing is supported by his credentials as both an author and something of a French literary intellectual, and is addressed primarily to an academic audience. Relying on assertion rather than analysis, Robbe-Grillet proceeds from substantial critical assumptions about twentieth-century literary cultural history and its recent course. One measure of his ability to stir critical debate is Fieke Schoots's *Passer en douce à la douane*, a dissertation developed out of reading Robbe-Grillet's piece that directly addresses his argument about continuity.[17] By contrast, we will see shortly how Lindon endorsed critics who rejected assertions like Robbe-Grillet's and expressed suspicion toward his "tradition," both in the sense of the tradition of continuity with "subversive literature" he suggests and the tradition of New Novel criticism he represents. Lindon's critics signal his choice to appeal to a different readership, vital to Minuit's repositioning.

3. Minuit Authors Young and Old

Various elements of Lindon's new handling of the New Novel appear in the Minuit catalogs from the late 80s into the 90s, show a continued predominance of the New Novel among Minuit's literary offerings, as well as showcase the young authors. The catalogs are the starkest representations of the transfer or succession of symbolic capital from the New Novel to the young authors.

Designed, first and foremost, to sell books, the catalog functions as a selling point for Minuit in subtler ways; that is, by signifying symbolic capital, as evidenced in the catalog's layout. The subsection of "*romans*" in the literature section is ordered alphabetically by author. Photographs, generally only two per page, stand in the margins, the results of meaningful selection. In the 1995 catalog, there are twenty-four photos in all, six of them related to the New Novel: Samuel Beckett, Marguerite Duras, Robert Pinget, Alain Robbe-Grillet, Nathalie Sarraute, and Claude Simon. Dispersed between these canonical figures are eighteen photos of younger authors, each published within the two years prior to the catalog's production. Other important figures, such as Georges Bataille, Maurice Blanchot, or Hervé Guibert, are not shown. Nor, for instance, is Tony Duvert, although he was the author of nine titles for Minuit between 1967 and 1982. As a counter-example, Patrick Deville, with fewer than half as many titles, is featured in a photograph. The catalog is not merely a showcase of Minuit's most prolific or well-known authors, then—only a handful of the eighteen younger authors had received any significant critical notice—but rather a careful admixture of authors who were clearly standing as the highest in prestige value (the six New Novel authors) with an array of entirely new authors. The early generation is deployed next to the new, to suggest similarity and continuity, as well as a kind of egalitarianism that relativizes the importance of the New Novel.

While highly suggestive, the photos do not hold the primary key to reading the Minuit catalog. Such a key is provided in the text on page two. As we have seen, in the past Lindon habitually used this space for a summary of Minuit's history and review of its publications. Throughout the 90s, however, Lindon opted to speak by proxy, including on page two an excerpt from *Le Monde* entitled "L'école Minuit,'" in which Pierre Lepape weighs in on Minuit's reconversion. It treats both the young authors and the New Novel, and, going against Robbe-Grillet's vision, emphasizes the differences among them:

> Il n'y a pas davantage d'"école de Minuit" aujourd'hui qu'il n'y eut hier d'école du "nouveau roman". Le "nouveau roman" est né du hasard d'une photographie, de l'opportunisme publicitaire de Robbe-Grillet et de l'amour universitaire des étiquettes. Comme il se trouvait que les écrivains de ladite "école" avaient du talent—du génie même,

pour certains d'entre eux—, l'illusion a pris consistance. Si l'on réunissait aujourd'hui sur le trottoir de la rue Bernard-Palissy Jean Echenoz, Marie Ndiaye, Jean-Philippe Toussaint, Jean Rouaud, Eric Laurrent, Eric Chevillard, Christian Gailly, quelques autres encore, il ne serait pas difficile de leur trouver assez de points de ressemblance pour donner l'image d'un groupe, à tout le moins d'un compagnonnage spirituel. Ils ont un air de famille.

On y trouverait d'abord le sentiment commun que la langue française est une vieille dame respectable qu'on ne fait danser sur des airs nouveaux qu'après lui avoir fait convenablement sa cour. Les écrivains de Minuit ne rêvent plus de briser la langue; ils savent qu'il n'y a rien à gagner à ce terrorisme, sinon à abandonner la place aux conservateurs et aux perroquets. Le français, ils préfèrent en connaître minutieusement, scrupuleusement toutes les règles, toutes les figures rhétoriques, toutes les subtilités étymologiques, toutes les contraintes séculaires pour mieux s'en jouer et en jouer: dans la parodie, dans les surprises de la métaphore, dans le raffinement des néologismes, dans l'incongruité des rapprochements. Ils n'inventent pas une langue: ils gonflent la nôtre jusqu'à la rendre aussi transparente et légère qu'une bulle de savon dont les irisations changeantes donnent leurs couleurs arbitraires au récit.

Leur second point commun doit aussi beaucoup à la leçon de Diderot, c'est le rire. Ils écrivent tous des livres drôles, chacun à sa manière: la farce, l'ironie, l'humour, la cocasserie, le sarcasme, la facétie, le persiflage, la dérision. Ils ne sont pas les seuls. (. . .) Après des années de dictature de la gravité—mais il y eut toujours d'indispensables pitres—, le rire est redevenu l'axe autour duquel tournent les perceptions de la comédie humaine, de la pantomime des gueux et du grand branle du monde. Les habitudes ne s'y sont pas encore faites: dire d'un roman qu'il est léger et drôle, dans un monde qui ne l'est guère, c'est l'envoyer dans l'enfer du divertissement, du superficiel, de l'éphémère. Nous avons encore un peu de mal à prendre le rire au sérieux.

~

There is no more a "Minuit school" today than there was a "New Novel" school yesterday. The "new novel" was born out of the fate of a photograph, Robbe-Grillet's advertising opportunism, and the academic love of labels. As the writers of the said "school" turned out to be talented—even genius, for some of them—the illusion took shape. If we gathered today on the sidewalk of rue Bernard-Palissy Jean Echenoz, Marie Ndiaye, Jean-Philippe Toussaint, Jean Rouaud, Eric Laurrent, Eric Chevillard, Christian Gailly, a few others, it would not be difficult to find in them enough points of resemblance to give the image of a group, at the very least of a spiritual companionship. They have a family resemblance.

One would find there first of all the common feeling that the French language is a respectable old lady who is not made to dance to new tunes until after having been properly courted. The writers of Minuit no longer dream of breaking the language; they know that there is nothing to be gained from this terrorism except by giving way to conservatives and parrots. French, they prefer to know

> meticulously, scrupulously all the rules, all the rhetorical figures, all the etymological subtleties, all the secular constraints to better play and play with it: in parody, in the surprises of metaphor, in the refinement of the neologisms, in the incongruity of the connections. They do not invent a language: they inflate ours to make it as transparent and light as a soap bubble whose changing iridescence gives the story their arbitrary colors.
>
> Their second common point also owes a lot to Diderot's lesson, and that is laughter. They all write funny books, each in their own way: farce, irony, humor, joke, sarcasm, joke, mockery, derision. They are not the only ones. [. . .] After years of the dictatorship of seriousness—but there were indispensable clowns all along—laughter has once again become the axis around which perceptions of human comedy revolve, of the pantomime of beggars and the great movement of the world. The habits have not yet taken hold: to say of a novel that it is light and funny, in a world which is hardly so, is to send it into the hell of entertainment, of the superficial, of the ephemeral. We still have a little trouble taking laughter seriously.

Lepape offers a broad interpretation of a new editorial line at Minuit. He argues emphatically that the experience of reading the young authors is a much different one from reading the New Novel. His veiled rejection of aspects of the latter—"[t]he writers of Minuit no longer dream of breaking the language; they know that there is nothing to be gained from this terrorism"—is at first a surprising posture for Lindon to sanction. But by reproducing the text of a critic writing in *Le Monde*,

Lindon afforded himself the various benefits of silence: citing a third-party authority allows Lindon to withdraw partially from the business of shaping interpretation. Quoting Lepape is a double borrowing, drawing from the symbolic capital of *Le Monde* and making Lepape's declarations serve Minuit's purposes.

Appropriated into the catalog, Lepape's text shares the unusual status of the press kits Minuit prepares for each novel it releases. A logical extension of the older practice of citing critics in flap copy, in recent times press kits have become an integral part of most publishers' marketing techniques. Newspaper and magazine reviews are reproduced in full as a packet—a literal appropriation of those reviews for the purposes of a publisher's argument in favor of a work's cultural significance. This use of otherwise heterogeneous texts and sources is a curious one, given that in the attempt to multiply the avenues of a novel's reach, the press kit participates in a leveling of cultural authority that reflects back on the publisher's imprint. While fully in line with Robbe-Grillet's acknowledgement of the importance of fomenting conversation about Minuit books—in the jargon of the most advanced cultural marketers, the Americans, this is now called "creating buzz"—the press kit blends very different degrees of literary prestige, mixing high and low, serious and popular sources, for the sake of selling books. This aspect of the press kit fits with Lindon's desire to "reconstitute itself freely," allowing the imprint to be reinvented in each review for its audience, or, for the most attentive readers, as a summation of the range of readings in the kit.

Sanctioning Lepape's interpretation, moreoever, reflects a desire to reset the critical value of the Minuit authors, both old and new. Lepape's declaration that "[t]here is no more a 'Minuit school' today than there was a 'New Novel' school yesterday" suits Lindon's eagerness to create some distance from the New

Novel well. Lindon's adoption of this piece for page two of the catalog hints at a pair of different strategies: first, a desire to change Minuit's reading audience in substantial ways by dissociating the imprint from the New Novel, and second, an attempt to form a second New Novel-like group that can then go on to be the focus of the cultural limelight. Like Robbe-Grillet's argument, Lepape's evaluation of the young authors grants them an overall coherence and unity in the same breath used to refute their putative group status. The emphasis on the question of grouping—again, similar to Robbe-Grillet's interpretation—powerfully recalls the promotion of the New Novelists and the spate of criticism and debate over if and how they constituted a group.

By separating the New Novelists—some of whom, he says, are great writers—from a vaguely mentioned radical project of "shattering" language associated with the New Novel, Lepape preserves them from his attacks and takes aim instead at the culture of the New Novel. That culture, marked by a love of labels and a "dictatorship of seriousness," belongs primarily to academics and many critics. His gesture is one of breaking free from critical categories, interpretation, and the expectations of readers of high literature. The young authors are no less serious in their literary and linguistic play than the New Novelists were serious: with roots in Diderot, they inhabit a realm of comic writing that plays a critical role in contemporary culture. Furthermore, it is one that is not devoid of political valences: their writing promises, by implication, to not "give way to conservatives and parrots."

Lepape's plea for the seriousness of levity constructs the terms in which the young authors may be seen as the vanguard writers of a new high literature. Those terms point up the enduring usefulness of reference to traditional notions of literary distinction in making claims on symbolic value for new authors and works. Seriousness and importance derive from their expansion of the French language's resources and from tested generic categories such as satire and farce. In constructing their importance against the culture of the New Novel, Lepape—and by extension Lindon—offered to redefine high literature for a new period of cultural production.

One cultural review was suited especially well to articulating the seriousness of Minuit's newfound levity. *Les Inrockuptibles*, a popular culture magazine begun in 1986, was one forum in which Minuit and the young authors enjoyed a leading presence. Initially a small monthly focused on music, the magazine gradually included cinema and literature, and when it became a weekly in 1995, boasted of a widely expanded table of contents and robust circulation. The magazine's success, as one scholar has pointed out, was unprecedented: "The magazine's trajectory [. . .] to culture weekly wielding considerable taste-making influence in the fields of literature and cinema is unparalleled in the recent history of French periodical publishing."[19] Andrews skillfully identifies the literary origins of the magazine's music criticism, arguing that the kinds of values the editors' criticism expresses stem from the fact that "they are engaged in the legitimisation of popular music, so they apply to it the aesthetic criteria by which they have been trained (largely through literary studies at school) to judge legitimate art."[20] Andrews cites its affinity for the artistic posture of decadent writers of the late nineteenth century among the magazine's ideals, whence its valorization of "the defective, the bad-mannered, the sick, and the melancholic."[21] Such "modernist exacerbations and decadent perversions" of "broadly Kantian values associated with legitimate high art" play themselves out as a preference in the magazine for works originating "from marginal positions analogous to [its] own."[22] Thus, in Andrews's view, the literary nature of the magazine's critical aesthetics is as much a mode of legitimization for pop music as for the magazine itself as cultural tastemaker.

The magazine's literary criticism bears out Andrews's intuitions about the editors' literary training. That it included the New Novel is suggested by their willingness to ally the magazine with the Editions de Minuit. Such an alliance entailed disproportionate space given to Minuit's young authors in the magazine's pages; in addition, Minuit made frequent use of the reviews and interviews of its authors that appeared in *Les Inrockuptibles*, reprinting them as marketing material and giving them wide distribution from its filial bookstore in Paris, Compagnie, to stores across France and abroad (including the chain operated by FNAC). The editors' training in the New Novel made them particularly apt to appreciate, and, more importantly, identify with the logic of succession that I argue frames the representations of the young Minuit authors. As, in Andrews's words, a growing "centre of cultural influence" *Les Inrockuptibles* was becoming an important forum for youth culture of the late 80s and 90s, the time period that coincides with the proliferation of new Minuit authors. Lindon's use of it as an outlet for his efforts to remake the Minuit label was brilliant. Identifying Lindon's new authors as "cool," the intelligent pop sensibilities of *Les Inrockuptibles* ushered them into the culture of the magazine's loyal reader base—a demographic group that no other single periodical could reach. In return, the new generation of Minuit authors lent *Les Inrockuptibles* their publisher's prestige in the literary field. The "young turks" of the New Novel's publisher brought the "seriousness" of their credentials and—with few exceptions—the accessibility of their levity—both aspects underscored in the magazine's reviews.

Examples of the young authors' softened rupture with the New Novel (Bourdieu's phrase) abound in *Les Inrockuptibles*'s Minuit criticism.[23] Jean Echenoz recounts how he never expected his first manuscript submission to Minuit to be accepted because of the house's reputation for difficult, erudite literary publishing—the very strain of French literature that had dissuaded him from writing anything at all.[24] Jean Rouaud tells how he received a very long and detailed letter from Claude Simon after the publication of his first novel at Minuit (*Les Champs d'honneur*). In it, Simon, whose novels Rouaud's have been compared to, advised him on the strengths and weaknesses of the text, cuts that would have improved it, and how to better his writing in general. Rouaud reports—with a grin—that he promptly threw the letter away without reading any further.[25] These stories denoted the determined irreverence of the young authors: a posture bound to suit the independent spirit of the magazine as well as appeal to its readers.

In addition to making for an interesting example of the Minuit-*Inrockuptibles* connection, one of the favorite Minuit authors among certain of the magazine's editors, Eric Laurrent, provides the basis for pushing my argument further. First published several years after the initial wave of young authors, Laurrent represented a further settling of Minuit's editorial line into a particular mold, by now clearly recognizable. Very much in the vein of Echenoz, Toussaint, and Deville, the novels of newcomer Laurrent combine a virtuoso writing style with an ironically genre-coded narrative. Even if Laurrent's novels were read separate from the context of their publication at Editions de Minuit, they would doubtlessly engender a discussion of parody: heavily ironic and exaggerated burlesque is Laurrent's means of articulating a "gentle" subversion of popular narrative forms. Style and linguistic virtuosity drive his sarcastic spectacle of generic conventions, and the reader is never allowed to forget that Laurrent's stories are vehicles for an arbitrary and anti-teleological play on genre. *Les Atomiques*, for instance, imitates spy thrillers, and *Liquider* mimics the plotlines of crime-of-passion, television-movie dramas. Laurrent subverts the novel of popular consumption from within, resulting in texts that are split between their absorption in popular culture and their parody of it. Like the official missives in television's "Mission Impossible" quoted in the epigraph of *Les Atomiques*, his performance of genre works a self-destruction—"This document will self-destruct in five seconds"—of the formal and logical constraints that define formulaic popular writing. Narrative continuity is undone since the "heroes" learn nothing from the clues that pile up, nor are they ever heroic in any way other than the fact that the narrative follows their movements. Everything merely *happens to happen* to them. The mostly flat and caricatured characters are simple set-pieces put into play in a narrative game of combinations.

It goes without saying that such détournements of genre fiction are not at all unique to Laurrent. Echenoz's series of novels from the 80s follows a progression through various popular genres; many of Jean-Philippe Toussaint's and Patrick Deville's novels also parody the conventional genres. By the time Laurrent's *Les Atomiques* was issued in 1996, Editions de Minuit had cultivated parody sufficiently for Laurrent to stand as confirmation of the editorial line begun with Echenoz in 1979. Laurrent typified the imprint's new image—one particularly compatible with the interests and sensibilities of *Les Inrockuptibles*. Their review of Laurrent's novel, which quickly made it into the Editions de Minuit catalog, makes all the right connections:

> *Les atomiques*, second roman d'Eric Laurrent après *Coup de foudre* (et d'essai) plutôt réussi, s'achève comme débutait *Jacques le Fataliste*: par le "ou bien" de toutes les fictions possibles, cet éventail qu'ouvrait

> la modernité sur l'arbitraire des histoires, leur infini. Des histoires, en effet, il y en a beaucoup dans ce récit furieusement véloce, terriblement Minuit: celle d'Atom Pexoto, d'abord, agent secret [. . .]. Si Eric Laurrent parvient à contenir le récit, c'est qu'il invente, en plus d'hallucinantes figures maniéristes, une réflexion proprement verbale sur le statut de la fiction. [. . .] Plutôt qu'un happy-end, l'auteur impose à ses pirouettes parodiques une morale de la représentation. Ce n'est pas la moindre surprise de ce roman décidément explosif.[26]
>
> ~
>
> *Les atomiques*, Eric Laurrent's second novel after *Coup de foudre* ([*Love at First Sight*]—and at first attempt) is quite successful, and ends as *Jacques le Fataliste* began: by the "or" of all possible fictions, the range opened up by modernity onto the arbitrariness of stories, their infinity. There are indeed many stories in this furiously swift, terribly Minuit story: that of Atom Pexoto, first of all, as a secret agent [. . .]. If Eric Laurrent manages to contain the narrative, it is because he invents, in addition to hallucinating mannerist figures, a properly verbal reflection on the status of fiction. [. . .] Rather than a happy-end, the author imposes a moral of representation on his parodic pirouettes. This is not the least surprise of this decidedly explosive novel.

As in Lepape's text, this review places emphasis on linguistic inventiveness, signaling its "hallucinating mannerist figures" and "parodic pirouettes." Like Lepape, the reviewer asserts the seriousness of Laurrent's levity; what is different in this review is its author's willingness to apply the standard formula of New

Novel criticism to the "young author." The flattering reference to canonical Diderot is a safely serious choice of reference, and evokes a notion of literary narrative that is at once sophisticated—"the 'or' of all possible fictions"—and sufficiently broad to pass smoothly. The real prior reference, however, is the line of New Novel criticism exemplified by, but by no means limited to, Jean Ricardou's writings. In concluding that *Les Atomiques* advances "a properly verbal reflection on the status of fiction," the reviewer asserts the properly New Novelesque credentials of the publisher's latest offering. His description of Laurrent's novel as a "moral of representation" recalls Ricardou's characterization of the New Novel as a "questioning of representation"—a definition of the New Novel oft-repeated in school textbooks throughout the 70s and 80s.[27] The reviewer's assimilation of New Novel criticism grounds his understanding of literary modernity, as well as his identification of the Minuit lineage, and unlike Lepape the reviewer is not at all concerned with asserting a break in that lineage and in that modernity.

The reviewer's approach is compatible with Robbe-Grillet's interpretation of the young authors in its emphasis on Laurrent's novel as metadiscourse. And while the New Novel had no particular monopoly on metadiscursivity, or on narrative experimentation more generally, it had, as I showed in Chapter IV, developed into the chief symbol of these aspects of French literary modernity. Reference to the New Novel exists only implicitly in the review of Laurrent's *Les Atomiques*—perhaps such a direct citation would have been too scholastic, too erudite? Nonetheless, that literary modernity and its second-degree take on consumer culture structure *Les Inrockuptibles*'s claim on cultural authority and the magazine's interest in promoting a book like *Les Atomiques*. Laurrent's critical sophistication marks his distance from commercialism and representational orthodoxy, and his position precisely mirrors that of the magazine. The cultural resonance of the stance signified by the rejection of the American-style "happy ending" is what makes Laurrent's "terribly Minuit" humor and irony so serious. The novel's explosiveness supports a prominent posture of rebellion useful to the system of taste the magazine is staging. At the same time, the adoption of Laurrent for such a purpose reflects the kinds of cultural spaces Editions de Minuit has come to inhabit in the new conjuncture, and the prevalent notions of literary value in play.

Though Laurrent's New Novel antecedents are elided in the review, Laurrent does not leave them out of his own thinking on fiction—a deliberation that, as its appropriation and recasting by *Les Inrockuptibles* has shown, is always and ever a staging of positionality. The very first paragraphs of the novel are an ironic rewriting of New Novel description, particularly in its most difficult phase (see Chapter IV). Laurrent reprises the New Novelists' problematization of the signifier in a way that both gently pokes fun at and reiterates it:

> Le ciel aura la pureté de son premier jour: il sera bleu, d'un bleu émanant directement des ténèbres, bleu tout juste séparé des eaux, vaporeux—s'il n'ignore pas encore la matière—, bleu pas tout à fait bleu donc, diaphane plutôt, en cours de bleuissement, bleu dans l'indécision de son bleu, bleu d'aucun bleu ou de la possibilité de tous les bleus, bleu épars, sans firmament, bleu inqualifiable bleu indicible en somme, bleu bleu, bleu. Atom Pexoto, à l'inverse, sera descriptible.[28]
>
> ~
>
> The sky will have the purity of its first day: it will be blue, of a blue emanating directly from the shadows, blue just separated from the waters, vaporous—if it

> does not ignore the matter yet—blue not quite blue therefore, diaphanous rather, the process of bluing, blue in the indecision of its blue, blue of no blue or of the possibility of all blues, scattered blue, without firmament, unqualifiable blue unspeakable blue in short, blue blue, blue. Atom Pexoto, on the other hand, will be describable.

The constant modifications ultimately push his blue well beyond the reader's grasp, resulting in a mocking exercise of description. Between the color of the sky and a new, unknown fictional character, the one the more conventionally describable turns out to be impossible to capture. The punchline at the beginning of the second paragraph is intended to make sure that the reader has understood that the play of modifications to the word *bleu* is precisely that, play. It is an acknowledgement that the description of the blue of the sky was a "failure," and a promise that the main character will be describable. This assurance to the reader that the genre conventions of realist narrative will be satisfied turns out to be as much a ruse as the blue paragraph, as no real description of Pexoto is ever supplied. The punchline turns out to be one of only two lines in the text that putatively describe the character; all we know is that he can be described. In these lines, a return to convention from New Novelesque description is set up but never completed.

Aside from their humor, the primary effect of these passages is to situate the narrative as discourse about narrative. A number of examples could be taken from New Novels as candidates for Laurrent's intertext, but it is less likely to be any single passage from a novel than the didactic spirit of the New Novel phenomenon whose "questioning of representation" incorporated a much-touted critique of traditional conventions of description. Nevertheless, juxtaposing the Laurrent text cited above with something from the New Novelists puts Laurrent's staging of positionality—and its attractiveness for a magazine like *Les Inrockuptibles*—into further relief.

One example from Claude Simon illustrates the use of repetition and accumulation in description—in this case of the word "black" [*noir*] and of a work of art as well. His descriptions of black in *La Chevelure de Bérénice* take on additional meaning from the fact that Simon was writing from and about black and white drawings by Mirò: ". . . and entered the water raising her skirt but not enough a higher wave reached her wetting an irregular wavy band blacker than black."[29] Simon captures the artist's line in the "irregular wavy band," a line whose nearly imperceptible gradations of black demarcate the woman's contact with water. With the hyperbolical phrase "blacker than black," Simon's text is as much a literary performance of Mirò's artistry as it is a depiction of the woman's entrance into the sea. Next to Simon's "blacker than black," Laurrent's "blue not quite blue therefore, [. . .] blue in the indecision of its blue, [. . .] blue, blue, blue" seems an irreverent mockery.

Laurrent's play continues, however, because Atom Pexoto turns out to be describable only insofar as he is perfectly nondescript. His description boils down to his being somehow like an anatomy study: "he will appear to be in the world as would an anatomy study."[30] For all the irony and sarcasm in his non-description of the color blue, Laurrent is no more inclined than were the New Novelists to offer a tangible or naturalistic description of the conventional sort. The denaturalized and often very witty names of his characters underscore the novel's winking, ironic playfulness: they include Pexoto's supervisor Caron-Pang and his "slow" assistant Max Larame. Aside from sporting a last name that is particularly unwieldy to pronounce in French, Atom Pexoto gives his first name to the title, which, like his description, further multiplies interpretive red herring.

In addition to referring to his eventual involvement in a plot over the illegal sale of nuclear waste, the character's name very likely derives from "anatomy" as the description of him hints. The title of Claude Simon's 1981 *Les Géorgiques* recalled Virgil's treatise on agriculture of the same name, as well as the figure of George Orwell whose experience of the Spanish Civil War is fictionalized in parts of the text. Ostensibly referring to the "atomized" character of the novel's plot, *Les Atomiques* puns on Atom's name the way *Les Géorgiques* does on that of Orwell. As in the case of the blue sky, the imitation is ironic and poking fun—not so much at "the status of fiction" per se as at a number of particularly New-Novelesque signs of literariness.

In what is perhaps the novel's consummate gesture of mocking rebellion, Laurrent extends his target to include his publisher. At one point, the character Caron-Pang—who is proffered as a kind of double for the author—handles a dossier with a certain unmistakable, tell-tale design: "he carried under his arm a white folder, edged in blue, embellished in the center of a small star—probably drawn during a moment of distraction."[31] Opening it, Caron-Pang becomes very upset to find it empty: "The backrest suddenly flew off, spun across the room, a kite spun out of control, twisting into its tail, and crashing into a wastebasket."[32] His gesture of trashing the Minuit novel seems a fitting metaphor for the "rupture" of the new Minuit authors and their publisher in the recent, "new" period. The staging of such a "rebellion" asserts their rearticulation of high literature. Their efforts to do so hinged on the help of old and new instances of cultural authority—such as, respectively, *Le Monde* and *Les Inrockuptibles*—to decode those efforts for their audiences. Otherwise incompatible interpretations of their relation to the New Novel—Lepape emphasizing discontinuity, *Les Inrockuptibles* implying a strong continuity—are brought together here to assert both the newness of Minuit's most recent avatar and its enduring literary modernity. Owing in part to these alliances, Lindon's Minuit achieved a highly successful transition from the New Novel. The literary honors given to the young authors were evidence of the literary field's readiness to embrace the new Minuit. What remains to be seen, however, is whether literary scholarship, universities, and schools can still play the traditional role of in conferring long-term capital and successfully canonize the young authors. While scholarly interest in these authors has long been substantial, it may be too early to tell.[33]

We have seen how, as the New Novelists were undergoing the final redefinition of their work as a group in the mid-1980s, Jérôme Lindon was undertaking the renewal of the Minuit imprint. He framed that renewal as a departure from the New Novel's legacy, despite the tendencies of various commentators—from Alain Robbe-Grillet to, in some respects, the editors of *Les Inrockuptibles*—to insist on the continuity between the New Novel and the new Minuit authors. The difficulty of Lindon's project lay in preserving Minuit's cultural capital—its reputation for literary quality—while asserting a break with the New Novel. Considerable help came in the form of support from a wide range of mainstream magazines and newspapers, including *Le Monde*, *Libération*, *L'Express*, and *Le Nouvel Observateur*. Much as Lepape does in the text Lindon included in the catalog, critics embraced Lindon's new authors as a new literary generation, indeed, even as a new literary group. A consistent theme in the articles on the Minuit authors appearing in the late 80s and 90s was a succinct version of Minuit's history, one that tended to stress Minuit's clandestine activity under the Occupation and the "revolution" signaled by the publication of Beckett. Mention of the New Novel was limited primarily to the audacity of its emergence in the late 1950s. There are recognizable traces of Lindon in this remembering of Minuit's past, especially in its effort to bring elements of that past to bear on promoting current publications. The support these journals gave to Minuit publications—in an era marked by the consolidation of France's cultural producers into large corporations (such as Hachette, Havas, and most recently Vivendi)—had something to do with the heroic value of Minuit's independent status, as if it had come, via its historical commitments, to incarnate one of the literary components of France's cultural exceptionalism. This same sentiment, I believe, motivates even the most erudite historical analyses, such as Simonin's *Le Devoir d'insoumission*, which underscores an image of Lindon as an unflagging champion of anti-commercial culture. It might be better, in my view, to see how Lindon's record of "heroic" publishing—taking a chance on Beckett, opposing the Algerian War, and so on—is not at all incompatible with the purposes of staying solvent.

There is every indication that Lindon's efforts at distancing Minuit from the New Novel were successful. In a survey Lindon conducted in the early 90s, readers of the young authors were asked if they saw any affiliation between those authors—the list included about a dozen names[34]—and the New Novel. Lindon's letter reporting the results indicated triumphantly that 89 percent of survey participants said there was none; and, he adds, "many welcome it!" The survey results pointed to other successes, as well. When readers were asked to indicate whom of the other "young Minuit novelists" they had read, the table of results shows that an impressive 52 percent of Jean Echenoz's readership had read Jean-Philippe Toussaint, 31percent had read Marie Redonnet, and an astonishing 66 percent had also read Jean Rouaud. This evidence suggests that, at least for Minuit's readership—Bourdieu's *lectorat*—Lindon had succeeded in renewing his imprint through the young author group.

In the 1970s and 1980s, Editions de Minuit continued to publish Beckett and the New Novelists and to oversee the dissemination of their work the world over, while simultaneously searching for the next generation to succeed them. Using the platform of its in-house literary journal *Minuit*, the firm vetted scores of young authors and explored new publishing initiatives in genres far flung from its signature prose novels. As Lindon was announcing to readers the end of Minuit in 1982, he already had the beginnings of a new set of authors in sight. And by 1999, when Jean Echenoz was awarded the Prix Goncourt, Lindon had accomplished yet another remarkable feat: once again, he had found ways to impose his authors in a newly reconfiguring literary field and assert Minuit's claim on literary value. As illustrated through the example of Eric Laurrent, in playing with themes of discontinuity and parody the writing of the young authors did not fail to address its predecessors. Sources of literary authority in the new era such as the pop cultural digest *Les Inrockuptibles* were receptive to such themes, conferring legitimacy and credibility to these authors and helping secure their prestige.

CONCLUSION

The history of Editions de Minuit is a remarkable lens through which to view twentieth-century French literary and cultural history. Tracing the development of Minuit's most significant contributions to the field of French literature has led to considering the structural conditions that made those contributions possible, and how they in turn effected new changes to that very field and its structure. Minuit's role as a clandestine publisher during the German Occupation of France illustrated the central, even national, importance of literature during wartime. Still, despite Minuit's singular claim to fame as the only outfit of its kind that continued to publish novels at that time, it was unable to translate its remarkable wartime accomplishments into a stable position in the postwar literary field. In the years immediately following the war, Minuit's fortunes fell while those of many publishers who had been powerful before the war rose. The contrast between Sartre's rise to prominence and Vercors's inability to promote Minuit's titles is striking, given that those titles were a good match for the Sartrean notion of literary value, which was defined as committed literature.

Minuit's story is arguably one of the most remarkable in publishing history: from watching its symbolic capital disintegrate in the immediate postwar to using an avant-gardist position a decade later to join the ranks of France's elite literary publishers. When the very young Jérôme Lindon took over the declining firm, a new direction and reinvention of the brand were a necessity, and while Lindon himself would often cite his encounter with the writings of Beckett as the first spark of his career as a publisher, we saw how other initiatives—like adopting George Bataille's *Critique*—were also vital to Minuit's transformation. The arrival of Robbe-Grillet as an in-house reader gave distinct shape to an editorial line that Minuit would follow in publishing the first titles of what would become known as the New Novel. In finding an echo among influential critics like Roland Barthes, Minuit managed to begin in the mid- and late-1950s to push a redefinition of literary value around a formalist and modernist aesthetic. That aesthetic can be read in both Robbe-Grillet's critical essays and the reports he prepared as a reader for Editions de Minuit, and is driven by a desire to articulate a break with both traditional literary genres and the contemporaries Sartre and Camus. By the early 1960s, Minuit could boast of an impressive catalog: one that provocatively put forward the New Novel alongside non-fiction collections addressing the Algerian crisis and the Holocaust. The notoriety of the *Documents* collections added new dimensions to Minuit's reputation.

The activities of Jérôme Lindon and Alain Robbe-Grillet garnered short-term success and capital for Minuit and its authors in the early 1960s; through Minuit's engagement with trends in intellectual culture broadly and literary criticism more specifically, the New Novel became a privileged object of study for the newly emerging structuralist critique. This, in turn, helped Minuit and its authors acquire long-term symbolic capital. Through its relation to structuralism, as well as its success in translation the world over, the New Novel achieved an unusually fast institutionalization and canonization—entering textbooks, university courses, serving as the subjects on the Baccalauréat exam, etc.—culminating in Claude Simon's Nobel Prize for Literature in 1985.

By 1985 the New Novel had become a prominent emblem of French intellectual and literary modernity, and incarnated a notion of literary value that held a dominant position in literary discourse for a very long time. For this reason, it is perhaps not surprising that Lindon's Minuit would labor so long to find new fiction authors to publish. Lindon himself suggested that perhaps some natural process had to unfold for authors to move beyond the New Novel's influence. Or perhaps instead, Minuit needed to catch up to changes in the literary field, particularly around ideas about literary value. With the publication of the young authors, Lindon sought to articulate a departure from the New Novel without sacrificing its investment in and reputation built on the New Novel. His success in doing so helped constitute yet another re-configuration of the literary field, one in which it was possible to propose a much less artistically demanding style of writing and still earn prestige and reputation from new forms of cultural authority.

What remains to be seen is the extent to which literature's place in French society, including the structures that control and organize its production and consumption, will transform in the era of the digital and internet-driven culture. Which parts of France's literary past and present will endure, and which will eventually be forgotten? Indeed, what is the future for the novel form itself, and will the structures that have regulated its selection and preparation—the traditional gatekeepers of legitimacy, the editors and publishers—still have a role in its production? Will some other form of cultural production take the novel's place? Finally, will the strategies Minuit used to carve out its place in the French literary field ultimately be seen as artifacts of a bygone era, or are they structurally homologous to the types of campaigns future cultural producers will still undertake as they jockey for position in the new paradigm of cultural production?

BIBLIOGRAPHY

A. Pierre Bourdieu

1. Primary Works

—. *Sociologie de l'Algérie*. Paris: PUF, 1958.

—. *Travail et travailleurs en Algérie*. Paris: Mouton, 1963.

—. *Les Héritiers: les étudiants et la culture*. Paris: Editions de Minuit, 1964.

—. *La Reproduction: éléments pour une théorie du système d'enseignement*. Paris: Editions de Minuit, 1970.

—. *La Distinction: critique sociale du jugement*. Paris: Editions de Minuit, 1979.

—. *Homo academicus*. Cambridge, UK: Polity Press, 1988.

—. *La Noblesse d'état, grandes écoles et esprit de corps*. Paris: Editions de Minuit, 1989.

—. *Photography: a Middle-brow Art*. Stanford, Calif.: Stanford University Press, 1990.

—. *In Other Words: Essays Towards a Reflexive Sociology*. Stanford: Stanford University Press, 1990.

—. *The Rules of Art: genèse et structure du champ littéraire*. Paris: Editions du Seuil, 1992.

—. *The Field of Cultural Production: Essays on Art and Literature*. New York: Columbia University Press, 1993.

—. *Acts of Resistance: Against the New Myths of our Time*. Cambridge,

UK: Polity Press, 1998.

—. *On Television.* New York: New Press, 1998.

—. "Une révolution dans l'édition," *Actes de la recherche en sciences sociales* 126-127, Mar. 1999, pp.18-36.

Bourdieu, Pierre and Roger Chartier. "La lecture: une pratique culturelle," in Roger Chartier, ed. *Pratiques de la lecture.* Marseille: Rivages, 1985.

2. Secondary Works

Martel, Frédéric. "Analyse d'un 'revirement' politique," *Magazine Littéraire* 369, 9 Jan. 1998, p.68.

Pinto, Louis. *Pierre Bourdieu et la théorie du monde social.* Paris: Albin Michel, 1998.

B. French Wartime and Resistance

Aveline, Claude, et. al. *L'Heure du choix.* Paris: Editions de Minuit, 1947

Boschetti, Anna. *Sartre et "les Temps modernes": une entreprise intellectuelle.* Paris: Editions de Minuit, 1985.

Carroll, David. *French Literary Fascism: Nationalism, Anti-semitism and the Ideology of Culture.* Princeton: Princeton University Press, 1995.

Debû-Bridel, Jacques. (Untitled), *Lettres Françaises* 7, 1943, p. 3.

Debû-Bridel, Jacques. (Untitled), *Lettres Françaises* 10, 1943, p.4.

Dictionnaire historique de la France sous l'Occupation. Paris: Tallandier, 2000.

Furet, François. *Le Passé d'une illusion.* Paris: Laffont, 1995.

Hewitt, Nicholas. *Literature and the Right in Postwar France.* Oxford: Berg, 1996.

Kaplan, Alice. *The Collaborator: the Trial and Execution of Robert Brasillach.* Chicago: University of Chicago Press, 2001.

Leclerc, Yvan. "Autour de minuit," *Dalhousie French Studies* 17,

1989, pp.63-74.

Mauriac, François. *Lettres d'une vie*. Paris: Grasset, 1981.

Mauriac, François. *Le Cahier* noir. Paris: Desclée de Brouwer, 1994.

Morgan, Claude. *Les Don Quichotte et les autres. . . .* Paris: Guy Roblot, 1979.

Ory, Pascal. *Les Collaborateurs: 1940-1945*. Paris: Editions du Seuil, 1976.

Paulhan Jean. "Réponse à l'enquête 'Approuvez-vous ou non cette forme de sanction qu'est l'interdiction de publier des écrits?'" *Le Figaro littéraire*, 9 Sept. 1944.

—. *Œuvres complètes de Jean Paulhan*. Paris: Cercle du Livre Précieux, 1970

—. *Choix de lettres*. Paris: Gallimard, 1986

—. *Choix de lettres* II. Paris: Gallimard, 1992

Rousso, Henry. *Le Syndrome de Vichy: de 1944 à nos jours*. Paris: Editions du Seuil, 1987.

Rousso, Henry. *Vichy: l'événement, la mémoire, l'histoire*. Paris: Gallimard, 2001.

Sapiro, Gisèle. *La Guerre des écrivains: 1940-1953*. Paris: Fayard, 1999.

Sartre, Jean-Paul. *Situations II*. Paris: Gallimard, 1948.

Sirinelli, Jean-François. *Intellectuels et passions françaises: manifestes et pétitions au XXème siècle*. Paris: Fayard, 1990.

Vercors. *La Marche à l'étoile*. Paris: Editions de Minuit, 1943.

Vercors. *Le Silence de la mer*. Paris: Editions de Minuit, 1942.

Yagil, Limor. *"L'Homme nouveau" et la révolution nationale de Vichy (1940-1944)*. Paris: Presses universitaires de Septentrion, 1997.

C. New Novels

1. Primary Works

Beckett, Samuel. *Murphy*. Paris: Editions de Minuit, 1947.

—. *Molloy*. Paris: Editions de Minuit, 1951.

—. *Malone meurt.* Paris: Editions de Minuit, 1952.

—. *L'Innommable.* Paris: Editions de Minuit, 1953.

—. *Nouvelles et textes pour rien.* Paris: Editions de Minuit, 1955.

—. *Comment c'est.* Paris: Editions de Minuit, 1961.

—. *Mercier et Camier.* Paris: Editions de Minuit, 1970.

Butor, Michel. *Passage de Milan.* Paris: Editions de Minuit, 1954.

—.*L'Emploi du temps.* Paris: Editions de Minuit, 1956.

—.*La Modification.* Paris: Editions de Minuit, 1957.

—. *Mobile.* Paris: Editions de Minuit, 1961.

Duras, Marguerite. *Moderato Cantabile.* Paris: Editions de Minuit, 1958.

—. *Détruire, dit-elle.* Paris: Editions de Minuit, 1969.

—. *La Maladie de la mort.* Paris: Editions de Minuit, 1982.

—. *L'Amant.* Paris: Editions de Minuit, 1984.

—. Marguerite Duras Archive, IMEC Archives, Paris.

Pinget, Robert. *Mahu ou le matériau.* Paris: Editions de Minuit, 1952.

—. *Baga.* Paris: Editions de Minuit, 1958.

—. *L'Inquisitoire.* Paris: Editions de Minuit, 1962.

—. *Quelqu'un.* Paris: Editions de Minuit, 1965.

—. *L'Apocryphe.* Paris: Editions de Minuit, 1980.

—. *Le Harnais.* Paris: Editions de Minuit, 1984.

Robbe-Grillet, Alain. "Jean Cau: *Le Coup de la Barre,*" *Critique* 49, Jun. 1951, p.559.

—. "Jean-Charles Pichon: *La Loutre,*" *Critique* 54, Nov. 1951, p.1002.

—. *Les Gommes.* Paris: Editions de Minuit, 1953.

—. *Le Voyeur.* Paris: Editions de Minuit, 1955.

—. "Littérature engagée, littérature réactionnaire," *L'Express*, 20 Dec. 1955.

—. *La Jalousie.* Paris: Editions de Minuit, 1957.

—. *Dans le labyrinthe*. Paris: Editions de Minuit, 1959.

—. *Instantanés*. Paris: Editions de Minuit, 1962.

—. *La Maison du rendez-vous*. Paris: Editions de Minuit, 1965.

—. *Topologie d'une cité fantôme*. Paris: Editions de Minuit, 1976.

—. Le *Miroir qui revient*. Paris: Editions de Minuit, 1985.

—. *Angélique ou l'enchantement*. Paris: Editions de Minuit, 1987.

—. *Les Derniers jours de Corinthe*. Paris: Editions de Minuit, 1994.

—. *Le Voyageur*. Paris: Christian Bourgeois, 2001.

Sarraute, Nathalie. *Portrait d'un inconnu*. Paris: Gallimard, 1956.

—. *Tropismes*. Paris: Editions de Minuit, 1957.

—. *Le Planétarium*. Paris: Gallimard, 1959.

—. *Les Fruits d'or*. Paris: Gallimard, 1963.

—. *Vous les entendez?*. Paris: Gallimard, 1972.

—. *Enfance*. Paris: Gallimard, 1983.

Simon, Claude. *L'Herbe*. Paris: Editions de Minuit, 1958.

—. *La Route de Flandres*. Paris: Editions de Minuit, 1960.

—. *Histoire*. Paris: Editions de Minuit, 1967.

—. *Les Corps conducteurs*. Paris: Editions de Minuit, 1971.

—. *Triptyque*. Paris: Editions de Minuit, 1973.

—. *Les Géorgiques*. Paris: Editions de Minuit, 1981.

—. *La Chevelure de Bérénice*. Paris: Editions de Minuit, 1984.

—. *L'Acacia*. Paris: Editions de Minuit, 1989.

—. *Le Jardin des plantes*. Paris: Editions de Minuit, 1997.

2. Secondary Works

Astier, Pierre. *La Crise du roman français et le nouveau réalisme: essai de synthèse sur les nouveaux romans*. Paris: Nouvelles Editions Debresse, 1968. (ponctutation)

Audry, Colette. "*Les Petits chevaux de Tarquinia de M. Duras*," *Temps Modernes*, Dec. 1953.

Bair, Deirdre. *Samuel Beckett: a Biography*. New York: Summit

Books, 1978.

Baque, Françoise. *Le Nouveau roman.* Paris: Bordas, 1972.

Bernal, Olga, Alain Robbe-Grillet. *Le Roman de l'absence.* Paris: Gallimard, 1964.

Bishop, Tom and Raymond Federman. *Samuel Beckett.* Paris: Editions de l'Herne, 1976.

Bloch, Béatrice. *Le Roman contemporain, liberté et plaisir du lecteur: Butor, des Forêts, Pinget, Sarraute.* Paris: L'Harmattan, 1998.

Bloch, Jean-Michel. *Le Présent de l'indicatif: essai sur le nouveau roman.* Paris: Gallimard, 1963.

Calle-Gruber, Mireille. *Les Partitions de Claude Ollier: une écriture de l'altérité.* Paris: L'Harmattan, 1996.

Combe, Dominique. *Poésie et récit: une rhétorique des genres.* Paris: J. Corti, 1989.

Contat, Michel, ed. L'auteur et le manuscrit. Paris: PUF, 1991.

de Boisdeffre, Pierre. *La Cafetière est sur la table: contre le nouveau roman.* Paris: La Table ronde, 1967.

de Magny, Olivier ed. Special issue on "Le nouveau roman," *Esprit*, Jul.-Aug. 1958.

de Magny, Olivier. "Panorama d'une nouvelle littérature romanesque: Voici dix romanciers," *Esprit*, Jul.-Aug. 1958.

Dort, Bernard. "Le Temps des choses", *Lettres Nouvelles*, Mar. 1955.

—. "Des Romans blancs," *Cahiers du Sud*, Apr. 1956.

—. "Sur les romans de Robbe-Grillet," *Les Temps Modernes*, Jun. 1957.

—. "Sur l'espace," *Esprit*, July-Aug. 1958.

—. "Des Romans innocents?" *Esprit*, Jul.-Aug. 1958.

Esslin, Martin. *The Theatre of the Absurd.* New York: Anchor Books, 1961.

Genette, Gérard. "Le Vertige fixé," *Tel Quel* 8, Winter 1962.

Goldmann, Lucien. *Pour une Sociologie du roman.* Paris: Gallimard, 1964.

Guers-Villate, Yvonne. *Continuité, discontinuité de l'œuvre durassienne.* Bruxelles: Editions de l'Université de Bruxelles, 1985.

Henriot, Emile. "Le Nouveau Roman: *La Jalousie*, d'Alain Robbe-Grillet, *Tropisme*, de Nathalie Sarraute," *Le Monde*, 22 May 1957, p. 13.

Higgins, Lynn. *New Novel, New Wave, New Politics: Fiction and the Representation of History in Postwar France.* Lincoln, Neb.: University of Nebraska Press, 1996.

Janvier, Ludovic. *Une Parole exigeante: le nouveau roman.* Paris: Editions de Minuit, 1964.

Janvier, Ludovic. *Pour Samuel Beckett.* Paris: Editions de Minuit 1965.

Luccioni, Gennie. "Marguerite Duras et le 'roman abstrait'," *Esprit*, July-Aug. 1958.

Mace, Marie-Anne. *Le Roman français des années 1970.* Rennes: Presses Universitaires de Rennes, 1995.

Mathews, J.H., ed. *Un Nouveau roman?* Paris: Minard, 1964.

Mauriac, Claude. "Alain Robbe-Grillet et le roman futur," *Preuves*, Oct. 1956.

—. "L'Alittérature," *Le Figaro*, 14 Nov. 1956.

—. *L'Alittérature contemporaine.* Paris: Albin Michel, 1958.

Minogue, Valérie and Sabine Raffy, eds. *Autour de Nathalie Sarraute: actes du colloque de Cerisy-la-Salle des 9 au 19 juillet 1989.* Paris: Diffusion des Belles Lettres.

Morrissette, Bruce. *Les Romans de Robbe-Grillet.* Paris: Editions de Minuit, 1964.

Nadeau, Maurice. "Samuel Beckett, ou le droit au silence," Temps Modernes 75 Jul. 1951, pp.1273-1282.

Oppenheim, Lois, ed. *Three Decades of the French New Novel.* Urbana: University of Illinois Press, 1986.

Oriol-Boyer, Claudette. *Nouveau Roman et discours critique.* Paris: Ellug, 1987.

Pingaud, Bernard. "Beckett le précurseur," republished in Samuel

Beckett. *Molloy*. Paris: Union Générale d'éditions, 1963.

Raillard, Georges, ed. *Butor: Colloque de Cerisy*. Paris: Union Générale d'éditions, 1974.

Ricardou, Jean. *Pour une Théorie du nouveau roman*. Paris: Editions du Seuil, 1971.

—, ed. *Nouveau roman: hier, aujourd'hui*. Paris: Union Générale d'éditions, 1972.

—. *Le Nouveau roman*. Paris: Editions du Seuil, 1973.

—, ed. *Claude Simon: analyse, théorie*. Paris: Union Générale d'éditions, 1975.

—, ed. *Robbe-Grillet: analyse, théorie*. Paris: Union Générale d'éditions, 1976.

Robbe-Grillet, Alain. *Pour un Nouveau roman*. Paris: Editions de Minuit, 1963.

Robbe-Grillet, Alain."The French Novel: from *Nouveau* to New," *Times Literary Supplement*, 13 Oct.1989, p.1122, p.1130.

Sebhan, Gilles. *Tony Duvert, l'enfant silencieux*. Denoël, 2010.

Sollers, Philippe. "Pour un Nouveau roman," *Tel Quel* 18, 1964.

Starobinski, Jean, et. al. *Sur Claude Simon*. Paris: Editions de Minuit, 1986.

Vircondelet, Alain. *Marguerite Duras*. Paris: Seghers, 1972.

Vircondelet, Alain, ed. *Marguerite Duras*. Paris: Ecriture, 1994.

Wolf, Nelly. *Une Littérature sans histoire: essai sur le nouveau roman*. Geneva: Droz, 1995.

D. The "Young Authors"

1. Primary Works

Bon, François. *Sortie d'usine*. Paris: Editions de Minuit, 1982.

—. *Limite*. Paris: Editions de Minuit, 1985.

—. *Le Crime de Buzon*. Paris: Editions de Minuit, 1986.

—. *Décor ciment*. Paris: Editions de Minuit, 1988.

—. *Calvaire des chiens*. Paris: Editions de Minuit, 1990.

—. *La Folie Rabelais*. Paris: Editions de Minuit, 1990.

—. *Un Fait divers*. Paris: Editions de Minuit, 1994.

—. *Parking*. Paris: Editions de Minuit, 1996.

Deville, Patrick. *Cordon-bleu*. Paris: Editions de Minuit, 1987.

—. *Longue vue*. Paris: Editions de Minuit, 1988.

—. *Feu d'artifice*. Paris: Editions de Minuit, 1992.

—. *La Femme parfaite*. Paris: Editions de Minuit, 1995.

Echenoz, Jean. *Le Méridien de Greenwich*. Paris: Editions de Minuit, 1979.

—. *Cherokee*. Paris: Editions de Minuit, 1983.

—. *L'Equipée malaise*. Paris: Editions de Minuit, 1986.

—. *Lac*. Paris: Editions de Minuit, 1989.

—. *Nous Trois*. Paris: Editions de Minuit, 1992.

—. *Les Grandes Blondes*. Paris: Editions de Minuit, 1995.

—. *Un An*. Paris: Editions de Minuit, 1997.

Laurrent, Eric. *Coup de foudre*. Paris: Editions de Minuit, 1995.

—. *Les Atomiques*. Paris: Editions de Minuit 1996.

—. *Liquider*. Paris: Editions de Minuit, 1997.

—. *Remue-ménage*. Paris: Editions de Minuit, 1999.

N'Diaye, Marie. *Un Temps de saison*. Paris: Editions de Minuit, 1994.

Oster, Christian. *Volley-ball*. Paris: Editions de Minuit, 1989.

—. *Paul au téléphone*. Paris: Editions de Minuit, 1996.

Redonnet, Marie. *Splendid hôtel*. Paris: Editions de Minuit, 1986.

—. *Forever Valley*. Paris: Editions de Minuit, 1987.

—. *Rose Mélie Rose*. Paris: Editions de Minuit, 1987.

Rouaud, Jean. *Les Champs d'honneur*. Paris: Editions de Minuit, 1990.

—. *Des Hommes illustres*. Paris: Editions de Minuit, 1993.

—. *Le Monde à peu près*. Paris: Editions de Minuit, 1996.

Serena, Jacques. *Basse ville*. Paris: Editions de Minuit, 1992.

—. *Lendemain de fête*. Paris: Editions de Minuit, 1993.

Toussaint, Jean-Philippe. *La Salle de bain.* Paris: Editions de Minuit, 1985.

—. *Monsieur.* Paris: Editions de Minuit, 1986.

—. *L'Appareil-photo.* Paris: Editions de Minuit, 1988.

—. *La Réticence.* Paris: Editions de Minuit, 1991.

—. *La Télévision.* Paris: Editions de Minuit, 1997.

Volodine, Antoine. *Alto Solo.* Paris: Editions de Minuit, 1991.

2. Secondary Works

Ammouche-Kremers, Michèle and Henk Hillenaar, eds. *Jeunes auteurs de Minuit.* Amsterdam: Rodopi, 1994.

Bessière, Jean, ed. *Passage du temps*: ordre de la transition. Paris: PUF, 1985.

Blanckeman, Bruno. *Les Récits indécidables: Jean Echenoz, Hervé Guibert, Pascal Quignard.* Villeneuve d'Ascq: Presses Universitaires du Septentrion, 2000.

Brami, Joseph and Madeleine Cottenet-Hage. Regards sur la France des années 1980: le roman. Saratoga, Calif.: Anma Libri, 1994.

Chossat, Michèle Aline. *Ernaux, Redonnet, Bâ, et Ben Jellou: le personnage féminin à l'aube du XXIème siècle.* New York: Lang, 2002.

Gillmann, Fabienne. "'Dire qui je suis:' *Rose Mélie Rose* de Marie Redonnet," masters thesis, Université Denis Diderot Paris 7, 1996-1997.

Lebrun, Jean-Claude. *Nouveaux territoires romanesques.* Paris: Messidor, 1990.

Leclerc, Yvan. "Autour de minuit," *Dalhousie French Studies* 17, 1989, pp.63-74.

Le Touze, Philippe. "Aspects de l'esthétique du temps chez quelques 'romanciers de Minuit,'" *Centre d'Etudes du Roman et du Romanesque*, 1996.

Récits de fin de siècle et Quête de mémoire, Echenoz, Ernaux, Modiano, Orsenna, Quignard, Rouaud, Proust. Université de Bretagne occidentale, 1994.

Schoots, Fieke. *'Passer en douce a la douane', L'Ecriture minimaliste de Minuit, Deville, Echenoz, Redonnet et Toussaint*. Amsterdam: Rodopi, 1997.

Tilby, Michael, ed. *Beyond the Nouveau Roman: Essays on the Contemporary French Novel.* New York: St. Martin's Press, 1990.

E. Publishers and Publishing

Anglès, Auguste. *André Gide et le premier groupe de La Nouvelle Revue Française*. Paris: Gallimard, 1978.

Assouline, Pierre. *Gaston Gallimard: a Half-century of French Publishing*. San Diego: Harcourt, Brace, Jovanovich, 1988.

Bordas, Pierre. *L'édition est une aventure*. Paris: Editions de Fallois, 1997.

Bothorel, Jean. *Bernard Grasset, vie et passions d'un éditeur*. Paris: Grasset, 1989.

Bouvaist, Jean-Marie. "Tendances d'évolution dans les structures de l'édition françaises," *Communication et Langages* 69, 3, 1986, pp.100-115.

Bouvaist, Jean-Marie. *Du Printemps des éditeurs à l'âge de raison, les nouveaux éditeurs en France, 1974-1988*. Paris: Editions du Cercle de la librairie, 1998.

Cabanis, José. *Le Diable à la NRF, 1911-1951*. Paris: Gallimard, 1996.

Cloonan, William J. and Jean-Philippe Postel. "Literary Agents and the Novel in 1996," *The French Review* 70, 1997, pp.796-806.

Cloonan, William J. and Jean-Philippe Postel. "Budgeting Culture, Buying Books and the Novel in 1998," *The French Review* 73, 1999, pp.48-58.

Flower, J. E. *Literature and the Left in France, Society, Politics, and the Novel since the Late Nineteenth-Century*. London: Macmillan, 1983.

Haymann, Emmanuel. *Albin Michel, le roman d'un éditeur.* Paris: A. Michel, 1993.

Judas. *Libre rapport sur le milieu, ce que tout le monde sait sur la République des lettres et quelque chose que tout le monde ne sait pas.*

Paris: Editions de la Nuit, 1981.

Kessel, Harlan. "Marketing in the 80s," *Scholarly Publishing, A Journal for Authors and Publishers* 13, no.2, 1982, pp.135-41.

Laffont, Robert. *Editeur.* Paris: R. Laffont, 1974.

Nadeau, Maurice. *Grâces leur soient rendues.* Paris: Albin Michel, 1990.

Poulain, Martine. "Marché de l'édition 1975-1989," *Bulletin des Bibliothèques de France* 36, no. 3, 1991, pp.237-8.

—. "Pratiques culturelles: Survey of leisure reading in France," *Bulletin des Bibliothèques de France* 36, no. 4, 1991, pp.342-3.

—. "Lecture étudiante: Ministry of Education survey," *Bulletin des Bibliothèques de France* 37, no. 6, 1992, pp.72-4.

Quignard, Marie-Françoise. *Le Mercure de France, cent un ans d'édition.* Paris: Bibliothèque nationale de France, 1995.

Santantonios, Laurence. *Auteur/Editeur: création sous influence.* Paris: Editions Loris Talmart, 2000.

Simonin, Anne. *Les Editions de Minuit, 1942-1955: le devoir d'insoumission.* Paris: Editions IMEC, 1994.

—. "La littérature saisie par l'histoire," *Actes de la recherche en science sociales* 111-112, 1996.

—. "La Mise à l'épreuve du Nouveau Roman: six cent cinquante fiches de lecture d'Alain Robbe-Grillet (1955-1959)," *Annales: Histoire, Science Sociales* 2, Mar. Apr. 2000, pp.415 437.

Surel, Yves. *L'Etat et le livre, les politiques publiques du livre en France (1957-1993).* Paris: L'Harmattan, 1997.

F. French Intellectual Culture

Cornick, Martyn. *Intellectuals in History: The Nouvelle Revue Française under Jean Paulhan, 1925-1940.* Amsterdam: Rodopi, 1995.

Ferguson, Patricia. *Literary France: the Making of a Culture.* Berkeley: University of California Press, 1987.

Ffrench, Patrick. T*he Time of Theory, a History of Tel Quel*

(1960-1983). New York: Oxford University Press, 1995.

Forest, Philippe. *Histoire de Tel Quel.* Paris: Editions du Seuil, 1995.

Hourmant, Francois. *Le Désenchantement des clercs, figures de l'intellectuel dans l'après-Mai 68.* Rennes: Presses universitaires de Rennes, 1997.

Kauppi, Niilo. *The Making of an Avant-garde, Tel Quel.* New York: Mouton de Gruyter, 1994.

Marx-Scouras, Danielle. *The Cultural Politics of Tel Quel: Literature and the Left in the Wake of Engagement.* University Park, Pa.: Pennsylvania State University Press, 1996.

Ory, Pascal. *L'Aventure culturelle française: 1945-1989.* Paris: Flammarion, 1989.

Pinto, Louis. *L'Intelligence en action, le Nouvel observateur.* Paris: Presses universitaires de France, 1984.

Rieffel, Rémy. *La Tribu des clercs, les intellectuels sous la Ve République, 1958-1990.* Paris: Calmann-Levy, CNRS Editions, 1993.

Ross, Kristin. *Fast Cars, Clean Bodies, Decolonization and the Reordering of French Culture.* Cambridge, Mass.: MIT Press, 1995.

Winock, Michel. *Le Siècle des intellectuels.* Paris: Editions du Seuil, 1997.

G. Miscellaneous

Andrews, Chris. "What's Cool in France: Categories and Values in the Music Reviewing of *Les Inrockuptibles*," *UTS Review* 2, vol. 5, Nov. 1999.

Atack, Margaret. *May 68 in French Fiction and Film.* Oxford: Oxford University Press, 1999.

Bair, Deirdre. *Simone de Beauvoir: a Biography.* New York: Summit Books, 1990.

Barthes, Roland. *Sur Racine.* Paris: Editions du Seuil, 1963.

—. *Essais critiques.* Paris: Editions du Seuil, 1964.

—. *Critique et vérité.* Paris: Editions du Seuil, 1966.

—. *Œuvres Complètes*. Paris: Editions du Seuil, 1993.

Beach, Sylvia. *Shakespeare and Company*. New York: Harcourt, Brace, 1959.

Blanc, Philippe, ed. Tours: Editions Farrago, 1998.

Campbell, James. *This is the Beat Generation: New York, San Francisco, Paris*. Berkeley: University of California Press, 1999.

Cayrol, Jean. *Je vivrai l'amour des autres*. Neuchâtel: La Baconnière, 1947-1950.

Calvet, Louis-Jean. *Roland Barthes*. Paris: Flammarion, 1990.

de Beauvoir, Simone. *Les Belles Images*. Paris: Gallimard, 1966.

de Boisdeffre, Pierre. *Où va le roman?* Paris: Del Duca, 1962.

Dosse, François. *Histoire du structuralisme*. Paris: Editions de la Découverte, 1992.

Emond, Paul. *La Mort dans le miroir: écriture et rePrésentation dans La Noire de Jean Cayrol.* Bruxelles: J. Antoine, 1974.

Fisson, Pierre."Pierre Fisson mène l'enquête," *Le Figaro littéraire*, Sept. 1962.

Gontarski, S. E., ed. *The Grove Press Reader: 1951-2001*. New York: Grove Press, 2001

Hemingway, Ernest. *A Moveable Feast*. New York: Scribner, 1964.

Marwick, Arthur. *The 60s: Cultural Revolution in Britain, France, Italy, and the United States, c.1958-c.1974*. Oxford: Oxford University Press, 1998.

Mollier, Jean-Yves and Patricia Sorel. "L'Histoire de l'édition, du livre et de la lecture en France aux XIXe et XXe siècles," *Actes de la recherche en sciences sociales* 126-127, March 1999, pp.39-59.

Nadeau, Maurice. "Les Lettres Nouvelles," *Les Lettres Nouvelles* 1, March 1953.

Oster, Daniel. *Jean Cayrol et son œuvre*. Paris: Editions du Seuil, 1968.

Patron, Sylvie. *Critique 1946-1996: une encyclopédie de l'esprit moderne*. Paris: Editions IMEC, 1999.

Perec, Georges. *Les Choses*. Paris: Julliard, 1965.

Picard, Raymond. "M. Barthes et la 'critique universitaire,'" *Le Monde*, 14 Mar. 1964.

Picard, Raymond. *Nouvelle Critique ou nouvelle imposture*. Paris: Pauvert, 1965.

NOTES

Introduction

[1] Paris: Raisons d'agir Editions.

[2] The essay is the transcript of a two-part video bearing the same name, made for television and broadcast on Paris Première in May 1996.

[3] The English translation of *Les Règles de l'art: genèse et structure du champ littéraire*, Paris: Editions du Seuil, 1992, [*The Rules of Art: Genesis and Structure of the Literary Field*, Stanford, CA: Stanford University Press, 1996] dates from the same year as *Sur la télévision*. The English introduction and other added materials were written close to the same time that the television essay and video were in production.

[4] Pierre Bourdieu, *Sur la Télévision*, p.44 and infra.

[5] Pierre Bourdieu, *Sur la Télévision*, p.46. The English translation is from *On Television*, New York: New Press, 1998, p.40. Translated by Priscilla Parkhurst Ferguson.

[6] Pierre Bourdieu, *Sur la Télévision*, p.45.

[7] The disciplinary difference I am asserting here in passing can be glimpsed within the breadth of Bourdieu's *œuvre*, between his more strictly anthropological, or ethnographic work and his analyses of mainstream culture. Their difference has more to do, I suggest, with audience—the latter of more interdisciplinary appeal than the other.

[8] Pierre Bourdieu, *Sur la Télévision*, p.44, and *On Television*, p.39; my italics.

[9] Cf. Pierre Bourdieu, *Les Règles de l'art*, prologue and pp.87-112.

[10] Cambridge: Harvard University Press, 1984 [originally published Paris: Les Editions de Minuit, 1979].

[11] Cf. Pierre Bourdieu, *Distinction*, part I.

[12] Cf. p.471 and infra.

[13] Pierre Bourdieu, *Les Règles de l'art*, p. 148, my italics.

[14] Pierre Bourdieu, *Les Règles de l'art*, p.168.

[15] Pierre Bourdieu, *Les Règles de l'art*, p.147.

[16] Pierre Bourdieu, *Les Règles de l'art*, 157.

[17] Pierre Bourdieu, *Les Règles de l'art*, 157.

Chapter I

[1] The Comité National des Ecrivains was the core organization of the literary Resistance. See Gisèle Sapiro. *La Guerre des écrivains: 1940-1953*. Paris: Fayard, 1999, pp.467-547.

[2] "Epuration" is a general term to refer to France's efforts to expose and punish those who collaborated with the Nazis. See Robert Aron. *Histoire de l'épuration*, vol.3, Paris: Fayard, 1967.

[3] Sapiro's tremendous historical analysis of the Académie Française is the only one of its kind that I have found. See *La Guerre des écrivains.* Paris: Fayard, 1999. For an analysis of the continuities between Vichy and the Third Republic, see David Carroll. *French Literary Fascism: Nationalism, Anti-semitism and the Ideology of Culture*. Princeton: Princeton University Press, 1995.

[4] See among others: Henry Rousso. *Vichy: l'événement, la mémoire, l'histoire*. Paris: Gallimard, 2001; *Dictionnaire historique de la France sous l'Occupation*. Paris: Tallandier, 2000; Limor Yagil. "*L'Homme nouveau" et la révolution nationale de Vichy (1940-1944)*. Paris: Presses universitaires de Septentrion, 1997.

[5] Sapiro p.505.

[6] Berkeley: University of California Press, 1987.

[7] *Le Silence de la mer*. Paris: Editions de Minuit, 1942, and *La Marche à l'étoile*. Paris: Editions de Minuit, 1943.

[8] Sapiro p.206, p.210 and infra. Drieu la Rochelle took over direction of *Nouvelle Revue Française* from Paulhan and also published articles regularly in *Le Figaro* and *Je Suis Partout* during the Occupation. While on trial for collaborating with the enemy Drieu la Rochelle committed suicide. See Pascal Ory. *Les Collaborateurs: 1940-1945*. Paris: Editions du Seuil, 1976; François Furet. *Le Passé d'une illusion*, Paris: Laffont, 1995.

[9] Sapiro pp.225-226. Unless otherwise marked all translations from the French are mine.

[10] Sapiro pp.225-226.

[11] Sapiro p.227.

[12] *Lettres d'une vie*. Paris: Grasset, 1981, p.270.

[13] Paris: Desclée de Brouwer, 1994, p.27, p.34.

[14] Mauriac, p.34; see "Réponse de François Mauriac," p.85. Perhaps Mauriac was concerned with alienating his reader.

[15] Jacques Debû-Bridel was one of the group of writers from *Nouvelle Revue Française* who in 1940 began to form alliances into what would be elements of the literary Resistance. With Pierre de Lescure and Vercors, he founded Editions de Minuit in 1942. He also contributed to *Lettres Françaises*. See Anne Simonin. *Les Editions de Minuit 1942-1955: Le devoir d'insoumission*. Paris: Editions de l'IMEC, 1994.

[16] 7, June 1943, p.3.

[17] Debû-Bridel p.3.

[18] Debû-Bridel p.3.

[19] 10, Oct. 1943, p.4.

[20] Sapiro p.582.

[21] The composition of the list changed over time; one of the earlier lists—dating from September 16, 1944—bore 94 names, including Robert

Brasillach, Céline, Alphonse de Chateaubriant, Chardonne, Drieu la Rochelle, Jean Giono, Charles Maurras, Paul Morand, Henri Bourdeaux, Alfred Fabre-Luce. The entire list can be found in Jean-François Sirinelli. *Intellectuels et passions françaises: manifestes et pétitions au XXème siècle*. Paris: Fayard, 1990, pp.145-147.

[22] Claude Roy. *Front National*, 5 May 1994; qtd. in Simonin. *Les Editions de Minuit 1942-1955: Le devoir d'insoumission*. Paris: Editions de l'IMEC, 1994, pp.204-205.

[23] Anne Simonin cites a 1961 edition of *Bulletin du livre*, (65, 15 Oct. 1961, p.33) which puts the total at 790,000 copies between its issue in 1942 and 1961 (qtd. in Simonin p.205, note 17).

[24] 29, 11 Nov. 1944, qtd. in Simonin p.231.

[25] "Le Pardon," *Les Lettres Françaises* 29, 11 Nov. 1944.

[26] Simonin p.231.

[27] Simonin p.280.

[28] Claude Aveline, Jean Cassou, Georges Friedmann, André Chamson, Louis Martin-Chauffier, and Vercors. Paris: Editions de Minuit, 1947, p.12 and infra.

[29] Aveline et al. p.14.

[30] Aveline et al. p.25.

[31] Aveline et al. pp.40-41.

[32] Aveline et al. p.48.

[33] Aveline et al. p.48.

[34] Aveline et al. p.141.

[35] Aveline et al. p.110.

[36] Martyn Cornick. *Intellectuals in History: The Nouvelle Revue Française under Jean Paulhan, 1925-1940*. Amsterdam: Rodopi, 1995.

[37] *Choix de lettres*, Vol. II. Paris: Gallimard, 1992, p.214-215.

[38] For Paulhan's correspondance, see *Choix de lettres*, and *Correspondance* (1941-1955); the unpublished collection is kept at the Archives IMEC (Paris).

[39] As recounted by Sapiro p.455-462.

[40] Simonin p.129.

[41] Sapiro pp.495-497.

[42] These assertions are from Claude Morgan himself; in *Les Don Quichotte et les autres* . . . Paris: Guy Roblot, 1979, pp.132-133.

[43] grid M-11489, available at the Bibliothèque Nationale (Paris).

[44] Morgan p.140.

[45] Paulhan, *Choix* p. 344. The editors explain that the essay in question is part of *L'Essai sur moi-même*, published in 1946.

[46] Paulhan, *Choix* p.344.

[47] Paulhan, *Choix* p.344.

[48] Paulhan, *Choix* p.345.

[49] Paulhan, *Choix* p.345.

[50] Sapiro p.391. Namely, Sapiro points out Paulhan's patriotic initiatives at the time of the Munich Accords and during the 'drôle de guerre'.

[51] "Les morts," *Bulletin de la Fédération du théâtre* 1, Jan. 1945, republished in *Œuvres complètes de Jean Paulhan*. Paris: Cercle du Livre Précieux, 1970, p.301.

[52] 9 Sept. 1944.

[53] Paulhan resigned from *Les Temps modernes* in 1948; see Anna Boschetti. *Sartre et "les Temps modernes": une entreprise intellectuelle.* Paris: Editions de Minuit, 1985.

[54] *Les Lettres françaises* 55, 12 May 1945, republished in *Œuvres complètes de Jean Paulhan*, p.306.

[55] "La Patrie présentée à des enfants," *Chroniques de Minuit*. Paris: Editions de Minuit, 1946, republished in *Œuvres complètes de Jean Paulhan*, p.308.

[56] Paris: Gallimard, 1948, republished in *Œuvres complètes de Jean Paulhan*, p.367.

[57] Paulhan, *De La Paille* p.343.

[58] Paulhan, *De la Paille* p.327.

[59] Paulhan, *De La Paille* p.329.

[60] How responsible were the intellectuals for their writings? The trial of Robert Brasillach was the occasion for many of the deep divisions among the intellectuals on this question to emerge. His trial prompted bitter debate, and when he was sentenced to death in January, 1945, a petition was circulated asking De Gaulle to commute his sentence. Mauriac and Camus were in favor, Sartre and Beauvoir did not sign. Brasillach was executed on February 6, 1945. See Alice Kaplan. *The Collaborator: the Trial and Execution of Robert Brasillach.* Chicago: University of Chicago Press, 2001.

[61] *Literary France: the Making of a Culture.* Berkeley: University of California Press, 1987.

[62] Ferguson p.5, my italics.

[63] Ferguson p.4.

[64] Ferguson p.6.

[65] On Sartre during the occupation, see Anna Boschetti. *Sartre et "les Temps modernes": une entreprise intellectuelle.* Paris: Editions de Minuit, 1985.

[66] These publications include first the volumes of *Les Chemins de la Liberté* written during the war, the two plays *Mort sans sépulture* and *La Putain respectueuse*, the essays *L'existentialisme est un humanisme*, *Baudelaire* and *Réflexions sur la question juive*, *Qu'est-ce que la littérature*, and *Situations.* Note that the last title is a collection of critical articles published from 1938 on.

[67] For Gallimard, see Pierre Assouline. *Gaston Gallimard: un demi-siècle d'édition française.* Paris: Balland, 1994. For *NRF*, see José Cabanis. *Le Diable à la NRF, 1911-1951.* Paris: Gallimard, 1996; Auguste Anglès. *André Gide et le premier groupe de La Nouvelle Revue Française.* Paris: Gallimard, 1978; Martyn Cornick. *Intellectuals in History.*

[68] Jean-Paul Sartre. *Situations II.* Paris: Gallimard, 1948, p.9. The English translations are from "Introducing *Les Temps modernes*," translated by Jeffrey Mehlman, in a collection of essays by Sartre titled *What is Literature? and Other Essays.* Cambridge, MA: Harvard University Press, 1988, 251-267. Here, p.249.

[69] Sartre, 1948, p.9, 1988, p.249.

[70] Sartre, 1948, p.10, 1988, p.249.

[71] Sartre, 1948, p.10, 1988, p.250.

[72] Sartre, 1948, p.10-11, 1988, p.250.

[73] Sartre, 1948, p.11, 1988, p.250.

[74] Sartre, 1948, p.19, 1988, p.257, his italics.

[75] Sartre, 1948, p.20, 1988, p.259 his italics.

[76] Sartre, 1948, p.13, 1988, p.252.

[77] Sartre, 1948, p.11, 1988, p.251.

[78] Sartre, 1948, p.11, 1988, p.251.

[79] Sartre, 1948, p.12, 1988, p.251.

[80] There are two assertions later in the piece that relate to the question of a sociological understanding of literature: "[. . .] we are of the opinion that a feeling always expresses a specific way of life and a specific conception of the world that are shared by an entire class or an entire era, and that its evolution is not the effect of some unspecified internal mechanims but of those historical and social factors" (Sartre, 1948, p.21, 1988, p.259); secondly, "every affect [. . .] *manifests* one's social situation" (Sartre, 1948, p.22, his italics; 1988, 260).

[81] Sartre, 1948, p.13, 1988, p.252.

[82] Sartre, 1948, p.25, 1988, p.262.

[83] Sartre, 1948, p.27, 1988, p.264.

[84] *Sartre et Les Temps modernes: une entreprise intellectuelle*. Paris: Editions de Minuit, 1985, pp.146-152. I will return to her point below.

[85] Sartre, 1948, p.27-28, 1988, p.265.

[86] Sartre, 1948, p.27, 1988, p.264.

[87] Sartre, 1948, p.24, 1988, p.262.

[88] Sartre, 1948, p.16, 1988, p.255.

[89] Sartre, 1948, p.29, 1988, p.266.

[90] Sartre, 1948, p.28, 1988, p.266.

[91] Sartre, 1948, p.30, 1988, p.267.

[92] Anna Boschetti's *Sartre et Les Temps modernes* offers an interesting discussion of the relationships among the editors of the journal over time. She suggests that after the departure of Merleau-Ponty in 1953 Sartre was more inclined to bring in younger, less-renowned editors likely to be more compliant with his desires.

[93] This is not to suggest that all literary schools and movements have followed an identical trajectory; rather, that the case of Sartre and *Les Temps modernes* shares with others the effects of the fame of one member on the others: as one figure rises in importance the others often either mark their difference through "rupture" or accept a subordinate standing within the group. Subordinates often remain overshadowed until they do articulate some form of departure from the figurehead.

[94] Paris: Editions du Seuil, 1987. The English translations are by Arthur Goldhammer. Cambridge, MA: Harvard University Press, 1994.

[95] Rousso p.30.

[96] Rousso p.32.

[97] Rousso p.89 and infra.

[98] Sapiro p.590, note 77.

[99] Simonin p.262.

Chapter II

[1] *Grâces leur soient rendues*. Paris: Albin Michel, 1990, pp.366-367.

[2] "Les Lettres Nouvelles," *Les Lettres Nouvelles* 1, Mar. 1953, p.1.

[3] Robbe-Grillet describes the offices of Gaston Gallimard and Jean Paulhan as where they 'held court'; *La NRF* and *La Nouvelle NRF* were extensions of that system. *Les Derniers jours de Corinthe*. Paris: Editions de Minuit, 1994, p.81.

[4] Jean-Jacques Servan-Schreiber and Françoise Giroud founded *L'Express* in 1953, and in little time the news magazine become both very successful and the object of scorn for its association with the new-bourgeois class of the 1950s. Among its most famous detractors were Simone de Beauvoir

(in *Les Belles Images*. Paris: Gallimard, 1966) and Georges Perec (in *Les Choses*. Paris: Julliard, 1965).

[5] Jean-Yves Mollier and Patricia Sorel provide an excellent summary of the issues involved and recent critical approaches to the role of the editor in "L'Histoire de l'édition, du livre et de la lecture en France aux XIXe et XXe siècles," *Actes de la recherche en sciences sociales* 126-127, Mar. 1999, pp.39-59.

[6] Paris: Editions Loris Talmart, 2000. Santantonios interviews published authors about their experiences with their editors, and then interviews editors about how they view their role in the publishing process. Little in her conversations reveals anything about the punctual exigencies that invariably weigh on a system which must keep a focused eye on the 'bottom line'—and this more now than ever, due to the absorption of most major publishing houses into a small number of multinational corporations.

[7] One such case is that of Marie Redonnet, one of comparatively few women authors published by Lindon in his fifty-three year career, who in an unpublished interview described him very negatively, verging on the charge of sexism. She had left Minuit definitively by her own choosing in 1994. Fabienne Gillmann. "'Dire qui je suis:' *Rose Mélie Rose* de Marie Redonnet," masters thesis, Université Denis Diderot Paris 7, 1996-1997.

[8] I had not hidden from him the fact that I was writing a *Diplôme d'Etudes Approfondies* thesis at the time, and that it was not destined for publication.

[9] These are of course translations of my questions.

[10] Lindon's moves here ran fully counter, as I discuss in chapter four, to the renewed strategy of grouping that occurred in the late eighties and nineties in the second moment of reconfiguring capital. By this time, the "jeunes auteurs de Minuit" title had become common currency, and Lindon clearly sought to spread the critical attention focused on the bestsellers to the less successful members of the new group.

[11] I recognize that such relationships are not uncommon in the literary world. The trials of literary researchers facing the virtual "dragon guarding the gates" have even been the stuff of absorbing narrative—witness A. S. Byatt's best-seller *Possession*—and incisive comedy—see Henry James' *The Aspern Papers*.

[12] I develop this point more fully in the section on Pierre Bourdieu in chapter 2.

[13] *Simone de Beauvoir: a Biography*. New York: Summit Books, 1990, p.346.

[14] "Suite," *Temps Modernes* 10, Jul. 1946.

[15] Beckett "Suite."

[16] See Deirdre Bair. *Samuel Beckett: a Biography*. New York: Summit Books, 1978, pp.352-353.

[17] Bair p.354.

[18] Paris: Editions de l'Herne, 1976, pp.34-36.

[19] Lindon p.35.

[20] The very notable exceptions include those who, even as contract authors for another publisher, can lend depth to a strategy of group-formation. I discuss some of these instances elsewhere, including the cases of Marguerite Duras and Nathalie Sarraute.

[21] Bernard Pingaud, "Beckett le précurseur," published in Samuel Beckett's *Molloy*. Paris: Union Générale d'éditions, 1963.

[22] Another novel, *Murphy*, had been published by Bordas in 1947 without attracting attention, and would later be integrated into the Minuit catalog. I am unable to find any indication of when this transfer took place; *Murphy* is in the Minuit booklist by 1954. In both the Minuit catalog and the title listings in the individual publications, *Murphy* is listed with the date of its first publication in English, 1938, and its first publication in French, 1947. Lindon asserts in *Murphy*'s catalog listing that the Bordas edition sold only "quelques dizaines d'exemplaires."

[23] Later existentialist interpretations of Beckett's œuvre tended to involve the plays more than the novels. Martin Esslin's 1961 *The Theatre of the Absurd* was a very successful and widespread gloss on the plays of Beckett, Ionesco, Adamov and Genet, and was heavily informed by Sartrean and Camusian existentialism. New York: Anchor Books.

[24] *Les Temps modernes* 75, Jan. 1952, p.153.

[25] Nadeau, "le droit au silence" p.157.

[26] Nadeau, "le droit au silence" p.160.

[27] Nadeau, "le droit au silence" p.160.

[28] Sept. 1953, p.863.

[29] Nadeau, "la dernière tentative" p.860.

[30] Nadeau, "la dernière tentative" p.861.

[31] See Philippe Blanc, ed. Tours: Editions Farrago, 1998. This reprint contains the issues plus a dossier of correspondence and interviews with Michel Fardoulis-Lagrange.

[32] See *Les Editions de Minuit* 1942-1955: *Le devoir d'insoumission*. Paris: Editions de l'IMEC, 1994, chap. 10, 424-450 and infra.

[33] Letter to Jean Paulhan, 31 September 1947, Gallimard Archives; qtd. in Simonin p.420.

[34] See *Les Règles de l'art: Genèse et structure du champ littéraire*. Paris: Editions du Seuil, p.206 and infra.

[35] The comparison of heroism implicit in her work seems jarring only if one does not take the literary value of Minuit's New Novel as a given.

[36] Sylvie Patron. *Critique 1946-1996: Une encyclopédie de l'esprit moderne*. Paris: Editions de l'IMEC, 1999, p.99.

[37] Listed in the June 1951 catalog brochure of the Editions de Minuit, available in the Bibliothèque Nationale (Paris), Q10 collection.

[38] Patron p.6, p.61.

[39] Although it is interesting to note that Blanchot—whose connection to the Minuit network I emphasize later in this chapter—published excerpts from his fiction in *Les Temps Modernes*.

[40] This is the version that appears in the 1956 catalog available in the Bibliothèque Nationale (Paris), Q10 collection.

[41] Patron chapter 5, pp.149-187.

[42] She became a member of Gallimard's comité de lecture in 1950 and served on the juries of several literary prizes. In 1953 she became Sécrétaire Générale of *la Nouvelle NRF*.

[43] Robbe-Grillet, *Corinthe* p.41.

[44] Robbe-Grillet, *Corinthe* p.44.

[45] Robbe-Grillet, *Corinthe* p.44.

[46] Robbe-Grillet, *Corinthe* p.45.

[47] Robbe-Grillet, *Corinthe* p.71.

[48] "Jean-Charles Pichon: *La Loutre,*" *Critique* 54, Nov. 1951, p.1002.

[49] Robbe-Grillet, "*La Loutre*" p.1002.

[50] "Jean Cau: *Le Coup de la Barre,*" *Critique* 49, Jun. 1951, p.559.

[51] Robbe-Grillet, "*Le Coup de la Barre*" p.559.

[52] Robbe-Grillet, "*La Loutre*" p.1002.

[53] Simonin pp.456-458.

[54] Simonin p.457.

[55] Simonin pp.458; my emphasis.

[56] Bernard Dort's article "Des romans 'innocents'?" includes one of the better criticisms of the violence in "Le Voyeur," *Esprit*, Jul.-Aug. 1958, pp.100-110.

[57] Robbe-Grillet, *Corinthe* p.80.

[58] Robbe-Grillet, *Corinthe* p.80.

[59] The quote is from Louis-Jean Calvet's *Roland Barthes* (Paris: Flammarion, 1990, p.133). Barthes received praise from a number of important sources, including *Carrefour* (8 Apr. 1953), *Le Monde* (3 Oct. 1953), *France-Observateur* (11 Jun. 1953), and *Les Temps modernes* (Nov. 1953).

[60] See Calvet pp.133-134.

[61] Calvet indicates that the essays in *Le Degré zéro de l'écriture* were composed in 1950.

[62] *Je vivrai l'amour des autres*. Neuchâtel: La Baconnière, 1947-1950.

[63] *Esprit*, Mar. 1952, republished in *Œuvres Complètes*. Paris: Editions du Seuil, 1993, pp.116.

[64] See Daniel Oster. *Jean Cayrol et son œuvre*. Paris: Editions du Seuil, 1968, and Paul Emond. *La Mort dans le miroir: écriture et rePrésentation dans La Noire de Jean Cayrol.* Bruxelles: J. Antoine, 1974.

[65] Barthes p.120.

[66] Barthes p.121.

[67] Barthes p.121.

[68] Barthes p.122.

[69] Barthes p.130.

[70] Barthes p.179. Also see part two of *Le Degré zéro de l'écriture*, "Triomphe et rupture de l'écriture bourgeoise," reprinted in *Œuvres Complètes*. Paris: Editions du Seuil, 1993, pp.169-178.

[71] Barthes p.416.

[72] Barthes p.416.

[73] Barthes p.417.

[74] Barthes p.417.

[75] *Le Miroir qui revient*. Paris: Editions de Minuit, 1983, p.68.

Chapter III

[1] *Fast Cars, Clean Bodies: decolonization and the reordering of French culture*. Cambridge, Mass.: MIT Press, 1995; *Une littérature sans histoire: essai sur le nouveau roman*. Genève: Droz, 1995. There is a third text that I do not discuss here: Dominique Combe's *Poésie et récit: une rhétorique des genres* (Paris: J. Corti, 1989). This work may be read alongside the former, adding a more traditional literary reevaluation of the New Novel that suggests that it is a moribund literary experiment. Combe situates the New Novelesque "exclusion du récit" within a Mallarmean rhetoric of negation that has come to a close with the return of plot, narrative and character (p.9, pp.190 192 and infra).

[2] Ross pp.183 185.

[3] The Hussards refers to a group of young right-wing authors associated predominantly with *La Table ronde* beginning in 1948; they got their name from the title of the novel *Le Hussard bleu* (Paris: Gallimard, 1950) by one of their members, Roger Nimier. The other members included Antoine Blondin and Jacques Laurent. See Nicholas Hewitt. *Literature and the Right in Postwar France*. Oxford: Berg, 1996.

[4] Wolf pp.194-195.

[5] "The French Novel: from *Nouveau* to New," *Times Literary Supplement*, 13 October 1989, p.1122, p.1130. The earliest mention of his role at Minuit seems to date from an article that appeared in Paris just after Claude Simon received the Nobel Prize for Literature. I discuss this article in Chapter V.

[6] "La Mise à l'épreuve du Nouveau Roman: six cent cinquante fiches de lecture d'Alain Robbe-Grillet (1955-1959)," *Annales: Histoire, Sciences Sociales* 2, Mar. Apr. 2000. Paris: Armand Colin, pp.415 437.

[7] Simonin, "La Mise à l'épreuve" p.421.

[8] I take this name for the unspoken category from the title of an article by Robbe Grillet dated from 1956: "Une Voie pour le roman futur," *La Nouvelle Nouvelle Revue Française* 43, Jul. 1946, pp.77-84.

[9] Robbe-Grillet qtd. in Anne Simonin, "La Mise à l'épreuve" p.421.

[10] Julliard began in the immediate postwar, with a similar editorial line to that of Vercors' Minuit. It struggled to survive as Minuit would; Françoise Sagan's 1954 international bestseller was no doubt instrumental in ensuring the publisher's continued existence.

[11] Simonin, "La Mise à l'épreuve" p.422.

[12] Simonin, "La Mise à l'épreuve" p.428.

[13] Simonin, "La Mise à l'épreuve" p.424.

[14] Simonin, "La Mise à l'épreuve" p.428.

[15] Simonin, "La Mise à l'épreuve" p.428.

[16] 20 Dec. 1955.

[17] Robbe-Grillet, "Littérature engagée" p.5.

[18] Robbe-Grillet, "Littérature engagée" p.5.

[19] Robbe-Grillet, "Littérature engagée" p.5.

[20] Robbe-Grillet, "Une Voie" p.77.

[21] Robbe-Grillet, "Une Voie" p.77.

[22] Robbe-Grillet, "Une Voie" p.78.

[23] Robbe-Grillet, "Une Voie" p.79.

[24] Robbe-Grillet, "Une Voie" p.79.

[25] Robbe-Grillet, "Une Voie" p.80.

[26] Robbe-Grillet, "Une Voie" p.80.

[27] Alain Robbe-Grillet, *Les Derniers jours de Corinthe*. Paris: Editions de Minuit, 1994, p.83.

[28] Robbe-Grillet, "Une Voie" p.80.

[29] Robbe-Grillet, "Une Voie" p.81.

[30] Robbe-Grillet, "Une Voie" p.84.

[31] *Critique* 100, Sept.-Oct. 1955, republished in *Essais critiques*. Paris: Editions du Seuil, 1964, pp.63-70.

[32] Barthes, "Littérature littérale" p.63.

[33] Barthes, "Littérature littérale" p.63.

[34] Barthes, "Littérature littérale" p.63.

[35] Barthes, "Littérature littérale" p.63, p.64.

[36] Barthes, "Littérature littérale" p.66.

[37] Barthes, "Littérature littérale" p.64.

[38] Barthes, "Littérature littérale" p.65-66.

[39] "Le Nouveau Roman: *La Jalousie*, d'Alain Robbe-Grillet, *Tropisme*, de Nathalie Sarraute," *Le Monde*, 22 May 1957, p. 13. Journalist and literary critic, Henriot also published poetry and novels. He was elected to the *Académie Française* in 1945, an election rich in political complexity. See Gisèle Sapiro. *La Guerre des écrivains*. Paris: Fayard, 1999, pp.616-617.

[40] Published, incidentally, by Gallimard with a preface by Jean Paul Sartre.

[41] Henriot p.13.

[42] Henriot p.13.

[43] Henriot p.13.

[44] Henriot p.13.

[45] Henriot p.13.

[46] Henriot p.13.

[47] Henriot p.13.

[48] Henriot p.13.

[49] Henriot p.13.

[50] That posture gained a little extra color in Henriot's hand, which only made his targets more likely to be considered controversial, as well as more easily identified. "Robbe Grillet," he decides, "n'aime pas la littérature (des autres);" as for Sarraute, "Mme Nathalie Sarraute ne croit pas non plus à la possibilité pour le roman moderne de créer des 'personnages'" (Henriot p.13).

[51] Henriot p.13.

[52] See "Alain Robbe-Grillet et le roman futur," *Preuves*, Oct. 1956; "L'Alittérature," *Le Figaro*, 14 Nov. 1956. Mauriac's essays in *Preuves* were collected in *L'Alittérature contemporaine*. Paris: Albin Michel, 1958.

[53] See "Des Romans blancs," *Cahiers du Sud*, Apr. 1956; "Sur les romans de Robbe-Grillet," *Les Temps Modernes*, Jun. 1957; "Sur l'espace," *Esprit*, Jul.-Aug. 1958; "Des Romans innocents," *Esprit*, Jul.-Aug. 1958.

[54] The former is from *Les Lettres françaises*, 18 Aug. 1960; the date for the latter is given in *Pour un nouveau roman*, the original publishing information is unavailable.

[55] Simonin, "La Mise à l'épreuve" p.423.

[56] Paris: Editions du Seuil, 1992, p.205 and infra.

[57] Bourdieu p.205.

[58] I discuss some of the underpinnings of Bourdieu's references to Minuit when I turn to Bourdieu and his role at Editions de Minuit in the next chapter.

[59] *Les derniers jours de Corinthe*. Paris: Editions de Minuit, 1994, p.95.

[60] *Catalogue de Minuit*. Paris: Editions de Minuit, p.2.

[61] In September 1960, 121 writers, academics and artists signed a manifesto asserting the "droit à l'insoumission dans la guerre d'Algérie." See Pascal Ory and Jean-François Sirinelli. *Les Intellectuels en France, de l'Affaire*

Dreyfus à nos jours. Paris: Armand Colin, 1986, p.202. Also see Anne Simonin, "La Littérature saisie par l'hitoire: Nouveau Roman et guerre d'Algérie aux Editions de Minuit," *Actes de la recherche en sciences sociales*, 1996, p.74.

[62] State censorship was exerted only after texts were published; texts deemed to be a "provocation" were the object of judicial inquiry and seizure.

[63] The contents of *La Question algérienne* include five parts, "Géographie algérienne, nationalisme et guerre coloniale, Colonisation et décolonisation, le Sous développement économique et le Régime de l'Algérie depuis 1834."

[64] Rousset's book was a reprint from 1945; Maurel's was published in 1957 and Wiesel's *La Nuit* is from 1958.

[65] *Catalogue de Minuit* p.2.

[66] Vian's book had long-term capital—an indication of which was the recent and still current "Collection Double," which consists of inexpensive livre de poche style editions of essential Minuit texts. The value of the Vian text did not come from Minuit's efforts with the New Novel, but from the capital accrued by his other novels published elsewhere.

[67] *Catalogue de Minuit* p.2.

[68] *Catalogue de Minuit* p.2.

[69] 1 November 1985, republished in Alain Robbe-Grillet. *Le Voyageur*. Paris: Christian Bourgeois, 2001, pp.209-213.

[70] Robbe-Grillet, "Le dragon" p.211.

[71] In her article "Françoise Giroud répond," the following question appears beneath photos of Marguerite Duras and Béatrice Beck: "Pourquoi, dans les études consacrées aux romancières ne trouve-t-on jamais leur nom?" (*L'Express*, 26 Mar. 1955, p.3).

[72] Anne Simonin. Personal interview, 24 Jul. 2000.

[73] "*Les Petits Chevaux de Tarquinia de M. Duras*," Dec. 1953, p.659.

[74] "Le temps des choses," *Lettres Nouvelles*, Mar. 1955.

[75] See Alain Vircondelet. *Marguerite Duras*. Paris: Seghers, 1972, and Yvonne Guers-Villate. *Continuité, discontinuité de l'œuvre durassienne*. Bruxelles: Editions de l'Université de Bruxelles, 1985.

[76] *Moderato Cantabile* manuscript, Marguerite Duras Archive, IMEC Archives, Paris, DRS2.A19-03.02, p.25.

[77] Marguerite Duras Archive, IMEC Archives, Paris. *Moderato Cantabile* manuscript, DRS2.A19-02.03, p.56. Her italics.

[78] *Moderato Cantabile* manuscript, DRS2.A19-02.03, p.64.

[79] *Moderato Cantabile* manuscript, DRS2.A19-02.03, p.83.

[80] Marguerite Duras Archive, IMEC Archives, Paris. *Moderato Cantabile* manuscript, DRS2.A19-02.02, p.37.

[81] *Moderato Cantabile* manuscript, DRS2.A19-02.02, p.40.

[82] *Moderato Cantabile* manuscript, DRS2.A19-02.02, p.54.

[83] Gennie Luccioni, "Marguerite Duras et le 'roman abstrait'," *Esprit*, Jul.-Aug. 1958, p.76.

[84] *Les Règles de l'art*. Paris: Editions du Seuil, 1992, pp.238-239.

[85] Marie Claire Ropars. Personal interview, 18 Jul. 2001.

[86] "Panorama d'une nouvelle littérature romanesque: Voici dix romanciers," *Esprit*, Jul.-Aug. 1958, p.19.

[87] *Esprit*, Jul.-Aug. 1958, p.103.

Chapter IV

[1] In addition to the high number of appearances of the New Novel authors in the French literary press, the New Novel spurred intense critical production abroad. It is significant that the first monologue on Robbe-Grillet's œuvre was written by an American academic and published by Minuit (see Bruce Morrissette below). I discuss the publication of the New Novel in translation later in this chapter.

[2] I am referring in the first case to Bruce Morrissette's *Les Romans de Robbe-Grillet* (Paris: Editions de Minuit, 1963). The next relevant critical essay Minuit published was Ludovic Janvier's *Une Parole exigeante* (Paris:

Editions de Minuit, 1964). I examine Janvier's text below.

[3] The subtitle is found in both the 1969 and the 1971 Minuit Catalogs.

[4] Cf. Chapter II p. 107 and note 43.

[5] Bruce Morrissette. *Les Romans de Robbe-Grillet*. Paris: Editions de Minuit, 1963. Anne Simonin indicated that Lindon and Robbe-Grillet commissioned *Une Parole Singulière* in the course of an interview with the author (personal interview, 24 July 2000).

[6] See note 4 in Chapter V.

[7] See Jean Thibaudeau. *Mes Années Tel Quel*. Paris: Ecriture, 1994; Mireille Calle-Gruber. *Les Partitions de Claude Ollier: une écriture de l'altérité*. Paris: L'Harmattan, 1996; Jean Ricardou. Le Nouveau Roman. Paris: Editions du Seuil, 1973.

[8] The first such photograph appears in the 1962 catalog and shows translations of titles by Beckett, Robbe-Grillet, Duras, Pinget, Butor, Sarraute and Simon.

[9] I have pursued this hypothesis in a case study of Minuit's entrance into the American literary marketplace; see my "Transatlantic *Translatio*: The Strange Case of the New Novel in America," *Variations*, 16, Fall 2008: 131-144.

[10] See Arthur Marwick. *The Sixties: Cultural Revolution in Britain, France, Italy, and the United States, c.1958-c.1974*. Oxford: Oxford University Press, 1998, especially chapter 4.

[11] Marwick pp.143-145. Also see James Campbell. *This is the Beat Generation: New York, San Francisco, Paris*. Berkeley: University of California Press, 1999, pp.184-186 and infra.

[12] A partial bibliography of Grove publishing is available online at https://jahsonic.com/GroveBibliography.html.

[13] S. E. Gontarski, ed. *The Grove Press Reader: 1951-2001*. New York: Grove Press, 2001, p.xix.

[14] Gontarski p.xxi.

[15] Pierre-Marcel Adéma. *Apollinaire*. New York: Grove Press, 1955.

[16] *Rimbaud's Illuminations: a Study in Angelism, with a New Translation*

and the French Text of the Poems. New York: Grove Press, 1953; *Mid-century French Poets: Selections, Translations and Critical Notices*. New York: Grove Press 1956.

17 Gontarski's introduction to *The Grove Press Reader* tells us that Rosset was a student of Fowlie's, but does not indicate if Fowlie himself introduced Rosset to Sylvia Beach.

18 See Sylvia Beach. *Shakespeare and Company*. New York: Harcourt, Brace, 1959, and Ernest Hemingway. *A Moveable Feast*. New York: Scribner, 1964.

19 Marwick p.145-147.

20 Erotic titles published by Grove Press ranged from Sade (such as *Justine* and *The 120 Days of Sodom*) to anonymous Victorian, gay and lesbian, and experimental erotica. Examples include: John Rechy. *City of Night*. New York, 1963; Pauline Réage. *The Story of O*. New York, 1965; *The Romance of Lust*. New York, 1968.

21 Marwick p.145.

22 *Tropic of Cancer* and *Tropic of Capricorn* were both published in 1961. Grove published *Black Spring* in 1963, as well as a number of ancillary titles thereafter (letters, criticism, biography).

23 Marwick goes into more detail regarding the legal actions surrounding *Lady Chatterley's Lover* and *Tropic of Cancer* in Britain (Penguin Press) and America (Grove). See Marwick p.147.

24 Gontarski p.xxi.

25 Gontarski p.xxii.

26 Richard Howard, translator of *Le Voyeur*, became Grove's primary French translator, and signed most of the translations of the New Novel. In an interview with the author in 2001, he asserted that at the time publishing Robbe-Grillet had seemed a "natural choice" to all involved.

27 In a number of respects an in-house marketing arm of Grove Press, *Evergreen Review* ran book excerpts and original essays by Grove authors, and criticism of their work. The second issue appeared in 1957 and showcased "The San Francisco Scene" to promote the Beats. In its first seven

years of existence virtually every issue of the journal included work relating to the Beats and to French authors (Minuit writers and others).

[28] Laurence Venuti, *The Translator's Invisibility*, New York: Routledge, 5 and infra.

[29] Venuti p. 8.

[30] Venuti p. 15.

[31] Marguerite Duras, *Moderato Cantabile*, Paris: Editions de Minuit, 1958, p. 123.

[32] Marguerite Duras, *Moderato Cantabile*, New York: Grove Press, 1960, p. 119.

[33] Duras, 1958 p. 13,

[34] Duras, 1960, p. 16.

[35] Duras, 1958, p. 55.

[36] Duras, 1960, p. 57.

[37] Duras, 1958, p. 70.

[38] Duras, 1960, p. 70.

[39] Duras, 1958, p. 16.

[40] Duras, 1960, p. 18.

[41] One consistent aspect of the New Novel would always be its detractors. See, for example, Pierre de Boisdeffre's *Où va le roman?* (Paris: Del Duca, 1962) and his *La Cafétière est sur la table: contre le Nouveau Roman* (Paris: La Table ronde, 1967).

[42] The second figure, Jean Piel, was the editor of *Critique* and the "Critique" series of publications; I discuss these elements of 60s Minuit publishing presently.

[43] The 1971 Minuit catalog is the last available in the Bibliothèque Nationale archive.

[44] In addition to two books, *Sociologie de l'Algérie* (Paris: Presse universitaire de France, 1958) and *Travail et travailleurs en Algérie* (Paris: Mouton, 1963), he had published nine articles dealing on the same topics in journals and edited volumes.

[45] Republished in *In Other Words: Essays Towards a Reflexive Sociology*. Stanford: Stanford University Press, 1990, p.4.

[46] The first editions of these titles do not bear the "Sens Commun" heading that they subsequently would—and still do. The 1967 Minuit catalog dates the collection from 1965.

[47] See Edward Sapir. *Linguistique*. Paris: Editions de Minuit, 1971; Cassirer, et. al. *Essais sur le langage*. Paris: Editions de Minuit, 1969; Erwin Panofsky. *Architecture Gothique et pensée scholastique*. Paris: Editions de Minuit, 1967; Alexandre Matheron. *Individu et communauté chez Spinoza*. Paris: Editions de Minuit, 1969; Emile Benvéniste. *Vocabulaire des institutions indo-européennes*. Paris: Editions de Minuit, 1969; William Labov. *Sociolinguistique*. Paris: Editions de Minuit, 1976.

[48] I am referring to the most common acceptation of this expression, as recounted in François Dosse's *Histoire du structuralisme* (vol. I and II, Paris: Editions de la Découverte 1, 1992, pp.368-372). The high watermark of structuralism in France is commonly dated to 1966, with the crest in popularity of the major figures associated with structuralism, Barthes, Foucault, Lacan and Lévi-Strauss. A moment commemorated, furthermore, by the famous cartoon depicting these four figures sitting cross-legged in loin cloths in the jungle.

[49] Pierre Bourdieu. *In Other Words*. Stanford: Stanford University Press, 1990, p.29.

[50] "La lecture: une pratique culturelle," in Roger Chartier, ed. *Pratiques de la lecture*. Marseille: Rivages, 1985, pp.275-276.

[51] Sylvie Patron. *Critique 1946-1996: une encyclopédie de l'esprit moderne*. Paris: Editions de l'IMEC, 1999, pp.130-135.

[52] Sylvie Patron summarizes major points of Bourdieu's results (Patron p.135).

[53] Dosse pp.92-93.

[54] Pierre Bourdieu p.24.

[55] Paris: Editions de Minuit, 1964.

[56] Pierre Bourdieu p.4.

[57] See Frédéric Martel. "Analyse d'un 'revirement' politique," *Magazine Littéraire* 369, 9 Jan. 1998, p.68.

[58] Paris: Editions de Minuit, 1970.

[59] Paris: Editions de Minuit, 1964.

[60] Picard's first attack against Barthes, titled "M. Barthes et la 'critique universitaire,'" was published in the March 14 1964 issue of *Le Monde*. In it Picard—a Racine specialist—took issue with Barthes' language and method in his *Sur Racine* (Paris: Editions du Seuil, 1963). Also see Roland Barthes. *Critique et vérité*. Paris: Editions du Seuil, 1966; and Raymond Picard. *Nouvelle Critique ou nouvelle imposture*. Paris: Pauvert, 1965.

[61] Sylvie Patron p.219.

[62] Sylvie Patron p.219.

[63] See "La Critique et l'invention," 247, Apr. 1967.

[64] See Dosse's *Histoire du structuralisme*, vol. I, especially chapter 33.

[65] Derrida, *De la Grammatologie*. Paris: Editions de Minuit, 1967; Deleuze, *Logique du Sens*, Paris: Editions de Minuit, 1969.

[66] See Margaret Atack. *May 68 in French Fiction and Film*. Oxford: Oxford University Press, 1999, p.6.

[67] See n.5 above.

[68] I have reproduced the back cover in Appendix B.

[69] Barthes pp.213-220.

[70] Barthes p.213.

[71] Barthes p.214.

[72] Barthes p.214.

[73] Barthes p.214.

[74] Ludovic Janvier. *Une Parole exigeante: le nouveau roman*. Paris: Editions de Minuit, 1964, p.175.

[75] Olga Bernal. *Alain Robbe-Grillet: Le Roman de l'absence*. Paris: Gallimard, 1964. I will return to this book presently.

[76] Lucien Goldmann. *Pour un sociologie du roman*. Paris: Gallimard, 1964;

Bernal *Alain Robbe-Grillet.*

[77] Paris: Minard. The critical bibliography is fifteen pages long.

[78] See chapter II.

[79] *Pour Samuel Beckett.* Paris: Editions de Minuit 1965.

[80] *Le Nouveau Roman.* Paris: Editions du Seuil, 1973, p.232 and infra.

[81] The group included Philippe Sollers, Marcelin Pleynet, Jean Ricardou, Jean-Edern Hallier, Denis Roche, Jean Thibaudeau, Jean-Louis Baudry. Julia Kristeva joined the group in 1966.

[82] "Pierre Fisson mène l'enquête," *Le Figaro littéraire*, Sept. 1962, p.12.

[83] For Thibaudeau's account of his relations to Robbe-Grillet and Lindon, see *Mes années Tel Quel.* Paris: Ecriture, 1994, pp.56-60, pp.105-106, and infra.

[84] Philippe Sollers, "Pour un nouveau roman," *Tel Quel* 18, 1964.

[85] Thibaudeau p.133.

[86] "Le Vertige fixé," Tel Quel 8, Winter 1962.

[87] See his *Problèmes du nouveau roman*, Paris: Editions du Seuil, 1967; *Pour une théorie du nouveau roman*, Paris: Editions du Seuil, 1971; *Le Nouveau roman*, Editions du Seuil, 1973; and *Nouveaux problèmes du roman*, Paris: Editions du Seuil, 1978.

[88] Ricardou. Paris: Editions du Seuil, 1967, p. 111 and infra.

[89] *Nouveaux Problèmes du roman*, 1978, p. 114. He invents the term to suggest that texts sometimes tend to construct their own vocabulary. His own texts certainly satisfy this requirement!

[90] Georges Raillard, ed. *Butor: Colloque de Cerisy*. Paris: Union Générale d'éditions, 1974; Jean Ricardou, ed. *Claude Simon: analyse, théorie*. Paris: Union Générale d'éditions, 1975; Jean Ricardou, ed. *Robbe-Grillet: analyse, théorie*. Paris: Union Générale d'éditions, 1976; Alain Vircondelet, ed. *Marguerite Duras*. Paris: Ecriture, 1994. Valérie Minogue and Sabine Raffy, eds. *Autour de Nathalie Sarraute: actes du colloque de Cerisy-la-Salle des 9 au 19 juillet 1989*. Paris: Diffusion des Belles lettres, 1995.

[91] See, for example, John Guillory, *Cultural Capital: the Problem of Literary*

Canon Formation, Chicago: University of Chicago Press, 1993, and Barbara Herrnstein Smith, *Contingencies of Value: Alternative Perspectives for Critical Theory*, Cambridge, MA: Harvard University Press, 1988.

[92] Claudette Oriol-Boyer. *Nouveau Roman et discours critique*. Paris: Ellug, 1987.

Chapter V

[1] Paris: Editions de Minuit, 1984, p.12.

[2] See Michel Contat. *L'Auteur et le manuscrit*. Paris: Presses universitaires de France, 1991, Chapters 1-4.

[3] Note, for example, Fieke Schoots's presentation and discussion of the critical reception that greeted the new Minuit authors in the 80s. Schoots devotes a chapter to arguing against the association of the *jeunes auteurs* and their predecessors at Minuit. *Passer en douce à la douane*, Amsterdam: Rodopi, 1996.

[4] Ammouche-Kremers and Hillenaar p. 2. All translations are my own.

[5] Ammouche-Kremers and Hillenaar p. 2. Lindon's adjective *marquée* is closely related to the term for brand, *marque*, lending an apt second meaning to his expression: Minuit had become a 'badly branded' publishing house.

[6] I borrow the term 'network' from post-Bourdieusian sociology of cultural production, which uses the term to emphasize the way in which structures like a literary review organize and shape the relations among actors in the literary field. Cf. Becker or Castells.

[7] My emphasis.

[8] In his 2010 book about Tony Duvert Gilles Sebhan asserts that Duvert was hired as part of the journal's staff as a way of providing him with a steady income; indeed, Lindon's investment in Duvert was a sustained one. It is difficult to discern the extent of Duvert's involvement in the journal's development, aesthetics, and direction or its impact.

[9] See Boschetti, op.cit.

[10] In recent decades, Jeannet's publishing record has dramatically expanded,

with titles at Flammarion and Galilée.

[11] Michèle Ammouche-Kremers and Henk Hillenaar, eds. *Jeunes auteurs de Minuit*. Amsterdam: Rodopi, 1994, p.2.

[12] Ammouche-Kremers and Hillenaar p.2.

[13] Ammouche-Kremers and Hillenaar p.2.

[14] *Times Literary Supplement*, 13-19 Oct. 1989, p.1122.

[15] *Times Literary Supplement*, Robbe-Grillet p.1122.

[16] *Times Literary Supplement*, Robbe-Grillet p.1122.

[17] Letter from the author, 10 Oct. 1996. Amsterdam: Rodopi, 1996. Her book remains the sole published critical work devoted singly to the young Minuit authors.

[18] *Catalogue de Minuit*. Paris: Editions de Minuit, 1997, p.2.

[19] Chris Andrews, "What's Cool in France: Categories and Values in the Music Reviewing of *Les Inrockuptibles*," *UTS Review* 2, vol. 5, Nov. 1999, pp.68-84.

[20] Andrews p.81.

[21] Andrews p.75.

[22] Andrews p.81.

[23] Pierre Bourdieu. "Une révolution dans l'édition," *Actes de la Recherche en sciences sociales* 126-127, Mar. 1999, p.18.

[24] Ammouche-Kremers and Hillenaar p.28.

[25] "Tu kiosquier, mi fili!" *Les Inrockuptibles* 144, 25-31 Mar. 1998, p.31.

[26] *Catalogue de Minuit*. Paris: Editions de Minuit, 1995, p.12.

[27] Jean Ricardou. *Le Nouveau Roman*. Paris: Seuil, 1973; Claudette Oriol-Boyer. *Nouveau roman et discours critique*. Grenoble: Université Stendhal Grenoble 3, Ellug, 1990.

[28] Paris: Editions de Minuit, 1996, p.9.

[29] Paris: Editions de Minuit, 1983, p.8.

[30] Laurrent p.9.

[31] Laurrent p.24.

[32] Laurrent p.24.

[33] Much substantive academic writing on the young authors began to appear in the 2000s. See Bruno Blanckeman. *Les Récits indécidables: Jean Echenoz, Hervé Guibert, Pascal Quignard.* Villeneuve d'Ascq: Presses Universitaires du Septentrion, 2000; Michèle Aline Chossat. *Ernaux, Redonnet, Bâ, et Ben Jellou: le personnage féminin à l'aube du XXIème siècle.* New York: Lang, 2002.

[34] Included were François Bon, Eric Chevillard, Patrick Deville, Jean Echenoz, Christian Gailly, Marie N'Diaye, Christian Oster, Yves Ravey, Marie Redonnet, Jean Rouaud, Eugène Savitkaya, Jacques Serena, and Jean-Phillipe Toussaint.

www.ingramcontent.com/pod-product-compliance
Lightning Source LLC
LaVergne TN
LVHW091731091026
849796LV00026B/314
* 9 7 8 1 6 2 8 9 7 3 9 9 0 *